Crucible of Beliefs

A volume in the series

CORNELL STUDIES IN SECURITY AFFAIRS

edited by

Robert J. Art, Robert Jervis, *and* Stephen M. Walt

A complete list of titles in the series appears at the end of this book.

Crucible of Beliefs

LEARNING, ALLIANCES, AND WORLD WARS

DAN REITER

Cornell University Press

ITHACA AND LONDON

First published 1996 by Cornell University Press.

Library of Congress Cataloging-in-Publication Data

Reiter, Dan.
  Crucible of beliefs: learning, alliances, and world wars / Dan Reiter.
      p.   cm.—(Cornell studies in security affairs)
  Includes bibliographical references and index.
   ISBN: 978-1-5017-7207-8
   1. International relations—Decision making.   2. International relations—
Philosophy.   I. Title.   II. Series.
JX1391.R45   1996
327.1′01—dc20   95-42350

This book is dedicated to my parents,
Aryeh and Chana Reiter, with love

Contents

Tables

Acknowledgments

This project has taught me that, to paraphrase Steve Walt, learning requires loyal allies. First, I thank my graduate school advisers. Each made a crucial contribution to my growth as a scholar; indeed, the years I spent as a graduate student at the University of Michigan served in many ways as my own crucible of beliefs. Paul Huth displayed incredible patience, offering insightful and welcome advice on all questions large and small. His work exemplified for me the importance of combining case study and quantitative methods of empirical analysis. I was also fortunate to benefit from the genius of Robert Axelrod, whose thinking about modeling and other issues spans the social sciences yet is sufficiently grounded in common sense to be elegantly self-evident. Bob's tenacious insistence on rigor both in the broad thinking and in the details improved the quality of my work immeasurably. Ted Hopf's boundless enthusiasm makes him, quite simply, one of the best teachers I have ever had. His curiosity about and fascination with political science puzzles served to motivate me. To these three teachers, I offer my greatest thanks.

For financial support, I thank the National Science Foundation for a Graduate Fellowship, the John D. and Catherine T. MacArthur Foundation, and the University of Michigan. Thanks also to the John M. Olin Institute for Strategic Studies at Harvard University for providing me with a postdoctoral fellowship to support the completion of the manuscript.

Several individuals provided me with much-welcomed feedback. Karl Mueller helped substantially in the case study work. Bear Braumoeller, Allan Castle, Kevin Clarke, Page Fortna, Scott Gartner, and Allan Stam were kind enough to read the manuscript at various stages and offer helpful advice. Christopher Achen, Nancy Burns, and Greg Markus all contributed to my understanding of quantitative methods of analysis. Thanks also to Scott Bennett, Lars-Erik Cederman, Michael Cohen, Christopher Gelpi, Theodore Gilman, Simon Hug, Ellen Lust-Okar, Craig O'Neill, David Rivera, Ricardo Rodriguiz, David Rousseau, Jennifer Shulman, Gerald Sorokin, Scott Tarry, and Joseph Underhill for feedback. Thanks to Bradford Perkins for improving this project's historical analysis. My research on Belgian history was facilitated greatly by the advice of Jonathan Helmreich and the assistance of Françoise Peemans, archivist at the Ministère des Affaires Étrangères in Brussels. Other individuals who provided helpful comments include Paul Diehl, Patrick James, Robert Jervis, Russell Leng, and Jack Levy. Thanks also to Roger Haydon and the staff at Cornell University Press for their assistance.

The Johns Hopkins University Press granted permission to reprint some text and tables from my article "Learning, Realism, and Alliances: The Weight of the Shadow of the Past," *World Politics* 46 (July 1994), copyright 1994 by The Johns Hopkins University Press, Baltimore, Maryland 21218. Overseas Publishers Association granted permission to reprint some text and tables from my article "Political Structure and Foreign Policy Learning: Are Democracies More Likely to Act on the Lessons of History?" *International Interactions* 21:1 (1995), copyright 1995 by Overseas Publishers Association, Amsterdam.

Perhaps I should recall one other memory, driving other, older beliefs. Before graduate school, I was privileged to become acquainted with individuals who helped kindle my interest in international relations and broaden my understanding of argument. A few in particular I mention by name: Ben Attias, Cori Dauber, Charles Kauffman, Scott Maberry, and Bruce Moon. I express my gratitude to them for their friendship and inspiration.

This book is dedicated to my parents, Aryeh and Chana Reiter. I can only marvel at their continued support and faith in me throughout my life.

D. R.

Atlanta, Georgia

Crucible of Beliefs

[1]

Introduction

History dominates both the actions and the rhetoric of international politics. Leaders and publics tend to think of current policy questions in terms of past experiences: Is a past failure about to be repeated? How can a previously successful policy be applied to a new problem? The twentieth century may come to be known as an era of syndromes, as international political discourse has been haunted by the ghosts of Sarajevo, Munich, and Vietnam. The Clinton administration was typically history-minded when it took office, as its careful study of the successes and failures of past Democratic administrations demonstrated. Elsewhere, the power of historical analogies motivated the president of Bosnia to cast the plight of local Muslims in the framework of what may be the most famous of more recent historical analogies: "Instead of Munich, it is Geneva. Instead of little Czechoslovakia, it is little Bosnia. Instead of negotiating for a real peace, they are negotiating for an imaginary one. And instead of [Czech president] Benes, it is me."[1]

The recent war in the Persian Gulf demonstrated powerfully the weight past experiences can have. Foreign policy on all sides seemed to be conducted straight out of history books, and many of the actors in the crisis drew lessons from past experiences to guide their decisions. Saddam Hussein drew the lesson from the Vietnam War that America would not take military action to liberate Kuwait, since the American public could not stomach high casualties. George Bush saw the Iraqi invasion of Kuwait as strikingly parallel to Nazi Germany's aggression

[1] Dan Balz, "Studying the Mistakes of Carter's Presidency," *Washington Post*, 29 November 1992, A1; John F. Burns, "A Plea to Clinton: Keep Bosnia United," *New York Times*, 3 February 1993, A6.

in Europe in the 1930s, arguing that the mistakes of appeasement must not be repeated. During the crisis, he read Martin Gilbert's history of World War II and, in the words of one aide, was "totally into World War II analogies." The Israelis were also predictably fearful of a new Hitler in the Middle East and echoed Bush's warning of the dangers of repeating the mistakes of appeasement. The Ethiopians were particularly impressed in Security Council debates when references were made to the failure of the West to stand up to Mussolini's aggression against Abyssinia in 1935. The Saudi leadership was initially wary of the American commitment to liberate Kuwait, for they had learned to doubt the commitment of an American president from Jimmy Carter's feeble gesture following the fall of the Shah of Iran: he dispatched one squadron of unarmed F-15 fighters to the Gulf. The American military, eager to escape the shadow of Vietnam, executed Desert Storm with an almost fanatical desire to avoid the mistakes of that conflict. On the British side, one commander was hesitant about the Marines' plan for direct assault on enemy fire, recalling his own "unpleasant" experiences from the Korean War. And later the Gulf War itself became an important historical referent for American foreign policy. When Iraq dispatched troops to the Kuwaiti border in October 1994, the Clinton administration made an immediate and firm response, believing that the Bush administration's softer policy in 1990 had encouraged the invasion of Kuwait. In the words of White House chief of staff Leon Panetta, "We are not going to allow the mistakes of the past to be repeated."[2]

The central proposition of this book is that decision makers look to past experiences for guidance when they make foreign policy. This is not a new argument: students of politics have observed the impact of history on the thinking of political leaders for centuries. So what is different or new in the approach taken here? This book makes two important advances toward understanding how the lessons of history affect the foreign policies of nations. First, it presents a theory of learning which predicts from what kinds of events lessons get drawn and what the content of the lessons will be. This theory, then, is an advance beyond the broad observation that decision makers learn from history and a step toward helping us understand and even predict what les-

---

[2] Lawrence Freedman and Efraim Karsh, *The Gulf Conflict, 1990–1991: Diplomacy and War in the New World Order* (Princeton: Princeton University Press, 1993); U.S. News & World Report, *Triumph without Victory* (New York: Times Books, 1992); Fred Barnes, "The Hawk Factor," *New Republic*, 28 January 1991, 8–9; Douglas Jehl, "Clinton's Line in the Sand," *New York Times*, 10 October 1994, A1, A10. See also Yuen Foong Khong, "Vietnam, the Gulf, and U.S. Choices: A Comparison," *Security Studies* 2 (Autumn 1992): 75–95.

sons get drawn and, ultimately, how policies are chosen. The theory is derived from ideas in social psychology and organization theory and makes essentially three propositions: lessons are drawn infrequently; they are most often taken from high-impact, politically significant events; and when drawn, lessons reflect the desire to repeat past successes and avoid past failures.

Second, this book uses learning theory to broaden our understanding of international relations. The mainstream theory of international relations, realism, is confronted by a peculiar puzzle about one of the most important areas of foreign policy, international alliances. Consider that realism sees alliances as a response to international threat; when a state is more threatened it should be more likely to ally, and when it is less threatened it should be less likely to ally. In the twentieth century, however, some states have chosen alliance when relatively unthreatened, and some have remained neutral even when facing serious international dangers. A good example is membership in the North Atlantic Treaty Organization (NATO), perhaps the most important military alliance of the century. After World War II, Western European nations felt seriously threatened by the Soviet Union. As realism would predict, several of these states, including Norway, Denmark, and Belgium, elected to join NATO. However, some of the neighbors of these NATO members, such as Sweden, Switzerland, and Ireland, elected to remain neutral in the face of the Soviet threat. There seems to be a gap between realist explanation and the historical record, for threat alone does not explain how a state makes the central foreign policy decision whether to join an alliance or remain neutral.

In this book I propose that states often decide between neutrality and alliance based on their historical experiences. They learn from past events whether neutrality or alliance best protects the national security, and then they act on these lessons. I test this learning proposition by examining the alliance choices of small powers in the twentieth century. My argument is that small powers learn lessons about alliance and neutrality from their experiences in world wars, and these lessons determine their alliance choices in the peacetime years that follow these wars. World wars, then, serve as crucibles within which beliefs about international relations are forged. This learning proposition is tested against a realist explanation which argues that the higher the level of international threat the more likely is a state to enter an alliance.

In the empirical portion of this book I use both quantitative and case study methods. Each of these approaches has an important contribution to make toward executing effective empirical tests: quantitative tests provide mathematical rigor and allow the simultaneous analysis of several cases, while the in-depth analysis of case studies permits a closer evaluation of causation. I will show that the two methods do not exclude, but rather complement each other.

Though the proposition that decision makers learn from history might seem to be common sense, realism largely neglects the influence of history on politics. Realism, perhaps the oldest theory of international relations, has throughout its evolution maintained an emphasis on the importance of power. Though its principles have fallen in and out of vogue, realism has seen a resurgence of popularity in recent decades as a result of the perceived failure of collective security arrangements to prevent the Second World War. The most recent, major, scholarly expression of realist principles, termed *neorealism*, was authored by Kenneth Waltz. Though realism is by no means a theoretical monolith, Waltz's work contains the basic theoretical core of all modern versions of realism.[3]

According to Waltz, three characteristics define a political system: the principle by which it is ordered, the specification of the functions of formally differentiated units, and the distribution of capabilities across units. For the modern, international system of nation-states, the ordering principle continues to be anarchy: thus far, a world government has not emerged to impose and enforce structure on international relations. States are the realist units of analysis, and they are assumed to have similar functions—seeking to provide for the security and welfare of their citizens—though different capabilities. Waltz sees the international system as analogous to a free market: no binding rules govern behavior, actors interact, and each actor seeks to maximize its utility, the primary component of which is military security. In other words, realism conceptualizes world politics similar to how microeconomists think about free markets, as in both cases players maximize their utilities, and agreements are unenforceable. Waltz uses microeconomic and oligopoly theory to predict that the world system is likely to be more

---

[3] The earliest statements of realism are Thucydides, *History of the Peloponnesian War*, trans. Rex Warner (Harmondsworth: Penguin, 1954); and Niccolo Machiavelli, *The Prince* (New York: Norton, 1977). For an argument that the traditional view of Thucydides in international relations scholarship is oversimplified, see Laurie M. Johnson Bagby, "The Use and Abuse of Thucydides in International Relations," *International Organization* 48 (Winter 1994): 131–153. For the leading, mid-twentieth-century realist critiques of idealism, see E. H. Carr, *The Twenty Years Crisis* (London: St. Martin's, 1962); Hans J. Morgenthau, *Politics among Nations* (New York: Alfred A. Knopf, 1949); and George F. Kennan, *American Diplomacy, 1900–1950* (Chicago: University of Chicago Press, 1951). Waltz's ideas are presented in *Theory of International Politics* (New York: Random House, 1979). For scholarly criticisms of neorealism, see Robert O. Keohane, ed., *Neorealism and Its Critics* (New York: Columbia University Press, 1986).

stable when the lion's share of global power is concentrated between two countries rather than among several.

An important aspect of the neorealist extension of economic rationality to international relations is the proposition that these assumptions are sufficient to understand an actor's utility function (that is, an actor's understanding of how his actions affect the attainment of his goals and what outcomes are preferred). Just as rationality in economics dictates that all firms will have similar ideas about how pricing and production strategies determine profit, neorealism assumes that all state leaders (or states, as realism assumes that states are unitary actors) will have similar assumptions about what effects various foreign policy actions will have. Realism predicts, then, that when faced with similar circumstances, states will react in the same way. There is no space in realist theory to permit states to have different beliefs about how international politics work.[4]

This assumption that leaders of states have uniform beliefs presents two problems. First, such a simplification of a tremendously complex decision environment like the international arena raises suspicions that parsimony may be coming at the price of a too simple and ultimately inaccurate view of the world. Even in economics, a model of rationality is not enough to predict behavior unless it includes some means of describing how firms make predictions about the future. Arthur Stinchcombe made this point effectively:

> Rationality necessarily involves an analysis of the future, because the consequences that give purpose to acts are necessarily in the future. Thus all rationality is based on predictions of one kind or another, not on knowledge. Assuming that actors are perfectly rational, of course, implies that they are certain what the future holds, that in all relevant respects our notions about the future constitute knowledge. . . . The assumption of neo-Keynesian economists (and apparently of Keynes himself) was that the idea that investment can operate with only financial and universally available knowledge assumes a kind of knowledge about the future that human actors do not and cannot have.[5]

Significantly, this dissatisfaction with the classical economic model of rationality, that is, a rationality model that does not provide a param-

---

[4] This point about realism is also made by William W. Jarosz with Joseph S. Nye Jr., "The Shadow of the Past: Learning from History in National Security Decision Making," in *Behavior, Society, and International Conflict*, vol. 3, ed. Philip E. Tetlock, Jo L. Husbands, Robert Jervis, Paul C. Stern, and Charles Tilly (New York: Oxford University Press, 1993), 137.

[5] Arthur L. Stinchcombe, *Information and Organizations* (Berkeley: University of California Press, 1990), 1.

eter for making predictions about the future, arises from its inability to explain a number of important empirical phenomena, as well as theoretical dissatisfaction with rationality's rather optimistic view of human decision-making capacities. One leading critic of this model of rationality, Herbert Simon, has pointed out that the universally recognized phenomenon of the business cycle cannot be explained within the tenets of classical rationality and that a complete explanation of this model must include understanding the process of the formation of predictions about the future.[6]

The insufficiency of classical rationality in predicting economic behavior casts dark clouds on the predictive power of realism. The international environment is qualitatively more uncertain and unpredictable than the economic marketplace: no laws of outcomes in world politics are comparable with the laws of supply and demand in the marketplace. For Waltz, uncertainty in the international system means that under anarchy, threats can arise from any corner, and preparations must be made to counter any possible future menace. A deeper and more problematic level of uncertainty exists, however: not only are the origins of future threats unknown, but there are also fundamental uncertainties about the consequences of foreign policy actions. Robert Jervis expressed the insufficiency of realism effectively: "Expected utilities are the valuation an actor places on a course of action or outcome; they involve both estimates of consequences and judgments about intrinsic worth. Contrary to the implications of many Realist writings, these estimates and judgments are not objective, and they should not be accepted without investigating their formations, as is done in most of the work on game theory and anarchy."[7]

The second problem with the realist assumption of uniform beliefs is that even if all states share the same beliefs about how international politics work, this leaves the question, Where did these beliefs come from? Decision makers must have beliefs about the effects of arms buildups, trade tariffs, and diplomatic appeasement in order to evaluate the merits of different policies and eventually to take actions. Waltz argues that system structure emerges from states' attempts to safeguard their own interests, but how do decision makers figure out how to protect their interests? For many areas of international politics, states

---

[6] Herbert Simon, "On the Behavioral and Rational Foundations of Economic Dynamics," *Journal of Economic Behavior and Organization* 3 (1984): 35–55. See also Simon, "Rationality in Psychology and Economics," *Journal of Business* 59, no. 2 (1986): S209–S224.

[7] Robert Jervis, "Realism, Game Theory, and Cooperation," *World Politics* 40 (April 1988): 340; Kenneth N. Waltz, "The Emerging Structure of International Politics," *International Security* 18 (Fall 1993): 60.

do not have the luxury of knowing with fair certainty what the result of taking certain actions will be. When faced with a direct threat, for example, rarely is appeasement or resistance indisputably superior as a response, yet decision makers must choose between the two. Jervis has made the point that taking a hard line is neither universally warranted nor counterproductive and that a choice is likely to emerge from one's belief in the spiral or the deterrence model of war.[8] Extreme realists might argue that states always make worst-case assumptions about the intentions and power of other states and then act in accordance with these fears. The empirical validity of this proposition aside, even if decision makers make worst-case assumptions about their adversaries' intentions and power, they still face uncertainty about the effects of their own actions. In other words, estimations of intentions and power are insufficient to determine optimal foreign policy behavior. For example, a prior assumption that an adversary is aggressive does not indicate whether other states are going to join the adversary if it makes a bid for empire or band together to fight against it. In short, realism does not provide a structure for understanding how decision makers act to advance their own interests under the condition that dominates international relations—uncertainty.

One way to understand how states behave under conditions of uncertainty is to assume that states act as if they have beliefs, or ideas, about international politics. This is a further specification of realism rather than a replacement of realist premises, for the realist assumptions that anarchy reigns and that states act to further their own interests are retained and a new assumption, that state behavior is guided by beliefs about the international system and what consequences are likely to follow particular actions, is added. This approach does not exclude the possibility that some states may retain beliefs that are in line with some of the classical realist propositions about state behavior, but it allows for the possibility that beliefs can vary among states, and it provides theoretical space for answering in a falsifiably empirical manner the question, Where do beliefs come from?[9] Judith Goldstein and Robert Keohane discussed the role of ideas in foreign policy, mak-

[8] Robert Jervis, *Perception and Misperception in International Politics* (Princeton: Princeton University Press, 1976), 58–113.

[9] Alexander Wendt has argued that anarchy itself is a socially constructed phenomenon and that it is defined by states' conceptions of their identities and interests. This view would imply that anarchy reigns only when states believe it does, so that a beliefs theory of international relations need not retain the realist assumption that anarchy reigns. In this book, I take as a given that all states make the anarchy assumption. Alexander Wendt, "Anarchy Is What States Make of it: The Social Construction of Power Politics," *International Organization* 46 (Spring 1992): 391–425.

ing a similar point to the beliefs argument made here by contending that realist structural factors are often insufficient to predict behavior and that ideas are often necessary to understand why certain choices are made.[10]

A number of international relations scholars have presented and tested theories that use this realism-plus-beliefs framework. In one early work, Nathan Leites argued that decision makers have belief paradigms that offer operational codes to guide and inform behavior. Specifically, he proposed that Bolshevik decision makers' views of the world were conditioned by the larger framework of Marxist-Leninist political and social ideology to which they ascribed. He described the Bolshevik worldview, laying out a sophisticated structure of beliefs about the driving forces of world politics and the enemies of the Soviet state, from which he derived more specific propositions for behavior. In a similar vein, a dominant explanation in the early 1990s of the new thinking in Soviet foreign policy which blossomed under Mikhail Gorbachev emphasized changes in Soviet beliefs about international relations, in opposition to the arguments that the USSR finally accepted the reality of its economic collapse and/or geostrategic defeat.[11]

---

[10] Within the Goldstein/Keohane ideas framework, in the argument in this book I look at ideas as causal decisions used as road maps. Judith Goldstein and Robert O. Keohane, "Ideas and Foreign Policy: An Analytical Framework," *Ideas and Foreign Policy: Beliefs, Institutions, and Political Change,* ed. Judith Goldstein and Robert O. Keohane (Ithaca: Cornell University Press, 1933), 3–30. For other works stressing the importance of beliefs, see D. Michael Shafer, *Deadly Paradigms* (Princeton: Princeton University Press, 1988); Robert Jervis and Jack Snyder, eds., *Dominoes and Bandwagons: Strategic Beliefs and Great Power Competition in the Eurasian Rimland* (New York: Columbia University Press, 1991); and Charles A. Kupchan, *The Vulnerability of Empire* (Ithaca: Cornell University Press, 1994). See also John Kurt Jacobsen, "Much Ado about Ideas: The Cognitive Factor in Economic Policy," *World Politics* 47 (January 1995): 283–310.

[11] Nathan Leites, *A Study of Bolshevism* (Glencoe: Free Press, 1953). See also Alexander George, "The 'Operational Code': A Neglected Approach to the Study of Political Leaders and Decision-Making," *International Studies Quarterly* 13 (June 1969). On new thinking in Soviet foreign policy in the late 1980s and early 1990s, see Jeff Checkel, "Ideas, Institutions, and the Gorbachev Foreign Policy Revolution," *World Politics* 45 (January 1993): 271–300; Sarah E. Mendelson, "Internal Battles and External Wars: Politics, Learning, and the Soviet Withdrawal from Afghanistan," *World Politics* 45 (April 1993): 327–360; Douglas W. Blum, "The Soviet Foreign Policy Belief System: Beliefs, Politics, and Foreign Policy Outcomes," *International Studies Quarterly* 37 (December 1993): 373–394; Janice Gross Stein, "Political Learning by Doing: Gorbachev as Uncommitted Thinker and Motivated Learner," *International Organization* 48 (Spring 1994): 155–183; Thomas Risse-Kappen, "Ideas Do Not Float Freely: Transnational Coalitions, Domestic Structures, and the End of the Cold War," *International Organization* 48 (Spring 1994): 185–214; Raymond L. Garthoff, *The Great Transition: American-Soviet Relations and the End of the Cold War* (Washington: Brookings Institution, 1994); and Matthew Evangelista, "The Paradox of State Strength: Transnational Relations, Domestic Structures, and Security Policy in Russia and the Soviet Union," *International Organization* 49 (Winter 1995): 1–38. For a review of the contending theories, see Matthew Evangelista, "Sources of Moderation in

A second theory emphasizing beliefs holds that perceptions of the dominance of the offense on the battlefield affect the probability of the outbreak of war. When the offense is believed to be more likely to win, the costs of attacking go down, which tempts aggression and encourages preventive wars in anticipation of a future attack. Significantly, the argument revolves around *beliefs* about the offense-defense balance, not the objective state of the balance itself; a number of these scholars have pointed out, for example, that the extreme belief in the offense before World War I both contributed to the outbreak of the war and turned out to be incorrect. Ted Hopf has expanded the offense-defense balance concept, arguing that beliefs about whether an enemy's resources can be captured and whether an aggressor's victories will lead to more countries joining its camp determine the character of war in the international system. Realism as laid out by Waltz does not include a variable of beliefs about offense dominance and certainly not one that permits the variation of beliefs from state to state.[12]

A third beliefs-oriented theory is the "democracies do not fight each other" hypothesis. This proposition states that the absence of wars between democracies emerges in part from the nature of democratic political structures and in part because democratic leaders have a different set of beliefs about the role of war in foreign policy and what causes are sufficient to justify war. More specifically, the liberal values of a democratic society percolate into its foreign policy, such that war is deemed to be an inappropriate means of resolving conflicts with other democracies. Realism does not allow for states to have different ideas about the moral acceptability of war; under realism, all states are willing to go to war to protect their own security, though states may have different conceptions of what their security requires. Adding the assumption that states act as if they have beliefs permits exploration of the possibility that differing propensities for war are explained by differing ideas about conflict resolution and the morality of war.[13]

Soviet Security Policy," in *Behavior, Society, and Nuclear War*, 2:254–354. On the importance of ideas throughout the cold war, see John Mueller, "The Impact of Ideas on Grand Strategy," *The Domestic Bases of Grand Strategy*, ed. Richard Rosecrance and Arthur A. Stein (Ithaca: Cornell University Press, 1993), 48–62.

[12] Robert Jervis, "Cooperation under the Security Dilemma," *World Politics* 30 (January 1978): 167–214; George Quester, *Offense and Defense in the International System* (New York: Wiley, 1977); Stephen Van Evera, "The Causes of War," Ph.D. diss., University of California at Berkeley, 1984; Thomas J. Christensen and Jack L. Snyder, "Chain Gangs and Passed Bucks: Predicting Alliance Patterns in Multipolarity," *International Organization* 44 (Spring 1990): 137–168; Ted Hopf, "Polarity, the Offense-Defense Balance, and War," *American Political Science Review* 85 (June 1991): 475–493.

[13] See Bruce M. Russett, *Grasping the Democratic Peace: Principles for a Post–Cold War World* (Princeton: Princeton University Press, 1993); James Lee Ray, *Democracy and*

Lastly, scholars of international economic policy have also built explanations of state behavior around the assumption that states act as if they have beliefs. A traditional realist explanation of trade policy is that when one country dominates the world order, it has an interest in maintaining a free trade system. An alternative, beliefs-oriented proposition is that state structures determine trade policy and the level of protectionism, and these structures are in turn determined by the beliefs of the decision makers who created them. Ideas have been identified as a main driving force behind the international monetary policy of the United States. Other research has pointed to ideas as important determinants of domestic economic policy in a wide variety of economic structures.[14]

A common critique realists make is that beliefs and lessons are essentially epiphenomenal, determined by structure and material interests rather than historical experiences or other factors. The implication of such an argument is that beliefs and lessons are not important concepts and that one need know only about structure to make accurate predictions about behavior. I deal with this critique by arguing that realism and learning make differing predictions about alliance behavior; specifically, realism predicts that alliance decisions are driven by current levels of threat a state faces, whereas learning predicts that states make alliance policy on the basis of past historical experiences. The empirical portion of the book tests the two theories, comparing cases in which lessons of history differ but structural conditions are the same and cases in which the structural conditions are the same but lessons of history differ. This will enable us to judge which theory better explains behavior. A realist might reply that such a test is rigged, using a straw

---

International Conflict (Columbia: University of South Carolina Press, 1995); T. Clifton Morgan, "Democracy and War: Reflections on the Literature," *International Interactions* 18 (1993): 197–203; and Randall Schweller, "Domestic Structure and Preventive War: Are Democracies More Pacific?" *World Politics* 44 (January 1992), 245–248.

[14] Stephen D. Krasner, "State Power and the Structure of International Trade," *World Politics* 28 (April 1976): 317–343; Judith Goldstein, "Ideas, Institutions, and American Trade Policy," *International Organization* 42 (Winter 1988): 179–217; Judith Goldstein, "The Impact of Ideas on Trade Policy: The Origins of U.S. Agricultural and Manufacturing Policies," *International Organization* 43 (Winter 1988): 31–71; and John S. Odell, *U.S. International Monetary Policy* (Princeton: Princeton University Press, 1982). On the importance of Keynesian ideas, see Peter A. Hall, ed., *The Political Power of Economic Ideas: Keynesianism across Nations* (Princeton: Princeton University Press, 1989). On how ideas about development guided the economic policies of Argentina and Brazil, see Kathryn Sikkink, *Ideas and Institutions: Developmentalism in Brazil and Argentina* (Ithaca: Cornell University Press, 1991). On the role played by Stalinist ideas in forming economic policy in China and Yugoslavia, see Nina P. Halpern, "Creating Socialist Economies: Stalinist Political Economy and the Impact of Ideas," in *Ideas and Foreign Policy*, ed. Goldstein and Keohane, 87–110.

man of realism, and that the lessons states learn are ultimately predictable by a structural model. To this, there are three rebuttals. First, the realist model used here is a leading realist model of alliance behavior: balance of threat theory. I have intentionally selected the most modern and popular realist theory of alliance behavior to strengthen the test of learning. Second, it is not enough to speculate that every decision is eventually explicable on the basis of *some* structural theory, perhaps as yet unconceived. Besides the problem that such a claim is to a degree unfalsifiable (as it is impossible to prove that one could not even conceive of a structural theory to explain some outcome), if such acrobatics are necessary to explain behavior and save realist theory, then this may be a good reason to discard (neo-)realism. One is reminded of a Ptolemaic astronomer who suggests adding more and more epicycles to improve the empirical fit of a celestial model when faced with Kepler's shockingly simple and more accurate formula for describing planetary orbits. Third, as an empirical matter there are many examples of states making decisions that turn out to be unwise because they are out of step with structural changes. This book will demonstrate that some states made alliance policies in accordance with lessons of the past which eventually brought disaster on the country because important structural factors were ignored. Such states demonstrate, then, that lessons do not merely reflect structure, for their leaders' disregard of structure eventually brought catastrophe.

In sum, an emerging view in international relations is that the barebones structure of realism is a good starting point for understanding international relations, but in many areas its parsimony either limits the accuracy of its predictions or displays an indeterminacy that prevents the construction of falsifiable hypotheses. Realism fails to address one of the most important concerns of world politics—how states cope with uncertainty. This indeterminacy applies to the issue area under examination here, the formation of alliance policy. Waltz proposed that one of two opposite alliance behaviors is possible in a multipolar world: chain-ganging (the tightening of alliance commitments) or buck-passing (the loosening of alliance commitments). As Thomas Christensen and Jack Snyder argued, traditional realism cannot predict when chain-ganging or buck-passing is more likely. They proposed that states' beliefs about the dominance of the offense on the battlefield determines which is more probable. Significantly, they specifically point to *beliefs* about offense dominance as the crucial independent variable, not the objective state of the balance.[15]

---

[15] Christensen and Snyder, "Chain Gangs and Passed Bucks."

[11]

Though these two scholars applied chain-ganging and buck-passing to great powers, the same basic logic can be applied to small powers, the class of states I examine in this book. In the face of a broad threat, small powers might either follow the logic of buck-passing and remain neutral or follow the logic of chain-ganging and ally. Neutrality offers the advantage of decreasing the risk of entanglement in other nations' wars at the cost of decreasing the chances of successful deterrence and defense should war come, whereas alliance offers the advantage of increasing the chances of successful deterrence and defense at the cost of increasing the risks of entanglement in other nations' wars. As do Christensen and Snyder, I posit that the *beliefs* of states about the desirability of neutrality or alliance determine their choice between the two. The central proposition is that states' beliefs about these two options emerge from their past experiences—in other words, they learn about alliance and neutrality from history.

This book presents a theory of behavior in world politics which assumes that states act as if they have beliefs. Understanding the role beliefs play requires we ask, Where do these beliefs come from, and how are they changed? I answer these questions by constructing a theory of learning in international politics, proposing that beliefs about international politics are often lessons drawn from past events. The strategy for the construction of this learning theory is to lay out a set of fundamental principles of decision making and then derive propositions that predict when and how learning occurs. Chapter 2 builds the learning theory, drawing primarily on principles in organization theory and social psychology.

The learning theory presented in Chapter 2 is tested on a specific empirical question: When do states choose alliance over neutrality in peacetime? As a theory of beliefs, learning is likely to be especially helpful in explaining alliance choices, as decision makers tend to rely on their beliefs when deciding crucial foreign policy issues such as alliance membership.[16] Alliances have long been considered central phenomena in international politics in general and in realism in particular, as alliances are the primary foreign policy means available to states to protect their security and increase their power. They are also the very machinery of that dynamic central to realist thinking about international political dynamics, the balance of power. No less a realist than Hans Morgenthau wrote, "The historically most important mani-

[16] Ole Holsti, "Foreign Policy Formation Viewed Cognitively," *Structure of Decision,* ed. Robert Axelrod (Princeton: Princeton University Press, 1976), 30.

festation of the balance of power, however, is to be found, not in the equilibrium of two isolated nations, but in the relations between one nation or alliance of nations and another alliance."[17] The area of alliances, therefore, is a crucial test for realism. If an alternative explanation can better explain alliance behavior, this would have to be considered a serious empirical blow to realism. The learning theory outlined in Chapter 2 presents a direct challenge to the realist explanation of alliance formation, proposing that a state makes alliance choices based on its beliefs about alliance and neutrality, rather than external, realist factors, such as levels of threat and the distribution of capabilities. Chapter 3 lays out the assumptions of realism and its treatment of the question of what causes states to join alliances.

My empirical strategy is to use quantitative and case study methods. Most previous studies of learning use case study methods; very few take a quantitative approach. Chapter 4 presents the argument for using both methods, in addition to discussing the data set and the quantitative model. The primary domain of analysis includes the peacetime alliance decisions of small powers after the two world wars of this century. The basic learning argument is as follows: a small power is either allied or neutral in a world war and has either a successful or a failed experience during the war. From this experience, the small power draws the lesson that alliance is best or that neutrality is best and chooses alliance or neutrality in the peacetime years following the war based on this lesson. The empirical analysis is limited to small powers, for the differences between the foreign policies of small and great powers preclude the simultaneous analysis of these two groups, and small powers are the more appropriate group for the empirical aims of this study (this issue is discussed in further detail in Chapter 4). Chapter 5 presents the results of quantitative tests of the data set, with a discussion of the statistical and substantive significance of the findings. These quantitative tests reveal strong empirical support for the learning hypothesis that individual national experiences determine the alliance preferences of small powers. They also indicate that the balance of threat explanation of why states enter alliances is not supported by the evidence. The robustness of these predictions is borne out by specification tests that indicate that these results are obtained even when the parameters of the model are altered.

By their nature, though, such tests can assess only correlations. To explore more deeply the proposed causal relationships, I present case

[17] Morgenthau, *Politics among Nations*, 137. Edward Vose Gulick commented, "The alliance, then, becomes one of the prominent means of putting balance theory to work."- *Europe's Classical Balance of Power* (New York: W. W. Norton, 1955), 61.

studies in Chapters 6 and 7. Chapter 6 examines examples in which the predictions of the learning hypotheses were accurate, including Belgium, Switzerland, the Netherlands, Norway, and Sweden. This analysis reveals that the kinds of decision-making processes envisioned by the learning theory accurately describe how alliance decisions were made in these cases. Chapter 7 looks at the cases that are not correctly predicted by the learning proposition, with the goal of understanding why learning may correctly predict alliance behavior for some cases but not for others. In Chapter 8 I explore in greater detail one explanation of why some states' foreign policies do not reflect the lessons of formative events, that the political structure of a state affects its propensity to act on these lessons. Analysis of the alliance data reveals that democracies are more likely to act in the manner predicted by the model of learning presented here, though this relationship was not found in other data sets for which alternative conceptions of learning were tested. In the final chapter I offer conclusions and directions for future theory building and empirical research.

[2]

Learning in
International Politics

Learning is a central concern of virtually all the social sciences: psychologists want to know how the human brain processes, stores, and recalls information; educators, how children grasp complex concepts; economists, how firms assess market conditions; sociologists, how group identities are diffused and inculcated; and anthropologists, how cultural norms are transmitted from generation to generation. In the study of international relations, scholars try to understand how past experiences exert influence over foreign policy decisions. Historians have often argued that policymakers use historical precedents as a guide for their actions. For example, Abraham Lowenthal hypothesized that it was the fear of the emergence of a second Cuba which led to American intervention in the Dominican Republic in 1965. Ernest May, a diplomatic historian, produced one of the first works treating the general question of the role of historical lessons in foreign policy decision making. He discussed in a mostly atheoretical fashion the historical lessons drawn by American decision makers and their application to a number of twentieth-century foreign policy decisions. His general conclusion was that decision makers tend to apply history poorly.[1]

[1] Abraham F. Lowenthal, *The Dominican Intervention* (Cambridge: Harvard University Press, 1972), 153–155; Ernest R. May, *"Lessons" of the Past: The Use and Misuse of History in American Foreign Policy* (London: Oxford University Press, 1973). Stanley Hoffmann agreed with May, contending that Americans use historical analogy poorly. *Gulliver's Troubles; or, The Setting of American Foreign Policy* (New York: McGraw-Hill, 1968), 109–114, 135–137. Gideon Rose argued that American war termination strategies in the twentieth century have been strongly driven by past experiences. "Victory and Its Substitutes: Foreign Policy Decisionmaking at the End of Wars," Ph.D. diss., Harvard University, 1994. For a more optimistic view of the use of history in the making of American

Since then, a growing body of scholarship has emerged which uses different theoretical tools to understand the role of learning in international politics. The most popular approach has been to base learning models on ideas from social and cognitive psychology. Robert Jervis's 1976 book, *Perception and Misperception in International Politics*, was one of the first works devoted to a systematic consideration of the application of social psychology to international relations. In it, he devoted an entire chapter to the question of how decision makers learn, drawing on findings in social psychology to propose that decision makers' beliefs tend to be determined by single, grand events, such as revolution or the last great war. Since then, others have followed in Jervis's footsteps, many of them applying ideas from social psychology to understand the question of how states and individual decision makers learn.[2]

Learning has also been addressed through other theoretical channels, though to a lesser extent. Formal decision models have occasionally been applied to questions of learning. One route that has been pursued in recent years is the application of information economics. An interesting effort is Robert Powell's work on nuclear crisis bargaining, in which he constructs models that relax assumptions of complete information and predict how states learn about each other's level of resolve in diplomatic crises. Unfortunately, the impressive sophistication of some

foreign policy, see Louis Morton, "The Cold War and American Scholarship," in *The Historian and the Diplomat: The Role of History and Historians in American Foreign Policy*, ed. Francis L. Loewenheim (New York: Harper & Row, 1967), 123–169. For a lucid discussion of the potential dangers of the study of history, see Herbert Butterfield, *History and Human Relations* (London: Collins, 1951), 158–181.

[2] Robert Jervis, *Perception and Misperception in International Politics* (Princeton: Princeton University Press, 1976), 217–287; Yaacov Y. I. Vertzberger, "Foreign Policy Decisionmakers as Practical-Intuitive Historians: Applied History and Its Shortcomings," *International Studies Quarterly* 30 (1986): 223–247; Jack Snyder, *Ideology of the Offensive* (Ithaca: Cornell University Press, 1984); Deborah Welch Larson, *Origins of Containment* (Princeton: Princeton University Press, 1985); Jack Snyder, *Myths of Empire: Domestic Politics and International Ambition* (Ithaca: Cornell University Press, 1991); George W. Breslauer and Philip E. Tetlock, eds., *Learning in U.S. and Soviet Foreign Policy* (Boulder, Colo.: Westview, 1991); Michael G. Fry, ed., *History, the White House, and the Kremlin: Statesmen as Historians* (London: Pinter, 1991); Yuen Foong Khong, *Analogies at War* (Princeton: Princeton University Press, 1992); John R. Raser, "Learning and Affect in International Politics," in *International Politics and Foreign Policy*, ed. James N. Rosenau (New York: Free Press, 1969), 432–441; James M. Goldgeier, *Leadership Style and Soviet Foreign Policy: Stalin, Khrushchev, Brezhnev, Gorbachev* (Baltimore: Johns Hopkins University Press, 1994); Ted Hopf, *Peripheral Visions: Deterrence Theory and American Foreign Policy in the Third World, 1965–1990* (Ann Arbor: University of Michigan Press, 1994). For reviews of the literature on learning in international relations, see Jack S. Levy, "Learning and Foreign Policy: Sweeping a Conceptual Minefield," *International Organization* 48 (Spring 1994): 279–312; and William W. Jarosz with Joseph S. Nye Jr., "The Shadow of the Past: Learning from History in National Security Decision Making," in *Behavior, Society, and International Conflict*, vol. 3, ed. Philip E. Tetlock, Jo L. Husbands, Robert Jervis, Paul C. Stern, and Charles Tilly (New York: Oxford University Press, 1993), 126–189.

of these modeling techniques has ironically limited the degree to which they can be subjected to empirical tests; tellingly, the classic maxim of statistical inference, Bayes's Theorem, has rarely been built into models of international politics.[3]

Still other scholars have used organization theory to get at the question of learning in world politics. A few works have attempted to present a theoretical framework for application of organization theory to political questions, and others have offered tests of organization theory propositions.[4] Of course, not all scholarship on learning in international politics draws directly on formal theory, social psychology, or organization theory. Some works discuss learning in the context of certain policy or historical issues without a real focus on decision-making theory,[5] whereas others are prescriptive, striving to answer the question of how decision makers *should* learn, rather than how they *do* learn.[6]

BUILDING A THEORY OF LEARNING IN INTERNATIONAL POLITICS

Learning in academic scholarship, then, suffers from a bit of theoretical schizophrenia. No real political theory of learning has been discov-

[3] Robert Powell, "Crisis Bargaining, Escalation, and MAD," *American Political Science Review* 81 (September 1987): 717–735; Robert Powell, "Nuclear Brinksmanship with Two-Sided Incomplete Information," *American Political Science Review* 82 (March 1988): 155–178. For other formal models of learning see R. Harrison Wagner, "Uncertainty, Rational Learning, and Bargaining in the Cuban Missile Crisis," in *Models of Strategic Choice in Politics*, ed. Peter C. Ordeshook (Ann Arbor: University of Michigan Press, 1989), 177–205; and James D. Morrow, "Bargaining in Repeated Crises: A Limited Information Model," in *Models of Strategic Choice*, ed. Ordeshook, 207–228. One application of Bayes's theorem is Nicholas Schweitzer, "Bayesian Analysis for Intelligence: Some Focus on the Middle East," *International Interactions* 4 (1978): 247–263.

[4] Scott Sagan, *The Limits of Safety* (Princeton: Princeton University Press, 1993); Matthew Evangelista, *Innovation and the Arms Race* (Ithaca: Cornell University Press, 1988); John P. Lovell, "Lessons of U.S. Military Involvement: Preliminary Conceptualization," in *Foreign Policy Decision Making*, ed. Donald A. Sylvan and Steve Chan (New York: Praeger, 1984), 129–157; John D. Steinbruner, *The Cybernetic Theory of Decision* (Princeton: Princeton University Press, 1974); Barry Posen, *Sources of Military Doctrine* (Ithaca: Cornell University Press, 1984); Snyder, *Ideology of the Offensive*; Edward Rhodes, "Do Bureaucratic Politics Matter? Some Disconfirming Findings from the Case of the U.S. Navy," *World Politics* 47 (October 1994): 1–41.

[5] See, for example, Joseph S. Nye Jr., "Nuclear Learning and U.S.-Soviet Security Regimes," *International Organization* 41 (Summer 1987): 371–402; and Stephen Peter Rosen, *Winning the Next War* (Ithaca: Cornell University Press, 1991). For a discussion of learning with a public policy focus, see Richard Rose, "What is Lesson-Drawing?" *Journal of Public Policy* 11 (January–March 1991): 31–54.

[6] Michael Howard, "The Use and Abuse of Military History," *Parameters* 11 (March 1981): 9–14; Earl Ravenal, *Never Again* (Philadelphia: Temple University Press, 1978); Richard E. Neustadt and Ernest R. May, *Thinking in Time: The Use and Misuse of History in American Foreign Policy* (Oxford: Oxford University Press, 1986); Lloyd S. Etheredge, *Can Governments Learn?* (New York: Pergamon, 1985).

ered: instead, other areas of decision analysis have been mined to provide insights into the peculiar problem of learning in international relations. This book will, for the most part, continue in this theoretical tradition, using ideas from other fields of decision analysis, mainly social psychology and organization theory, to build a theory of learning in international relations.[7] Of course, the conceptual building blocks used by these fields differ fundamentally from those of international politics: formal decision theory uses abstract, mathematical concepts and structures; social psychology formulates ideas about how people deal with information and form beliefs; and organization theory examines the behavior of groups of individuals. Addressing questions in international politics, however, means thinking about events in the global arena and actions taken by governments. There is, then, a gap between the theory—couched in terms of individuals and organizations—and application to the behavior of nations.

One solution to this problem would be to keep the levels of analysis at individuals and organizations, the same as that of the basic theories. Propositions would be made about the learning of political leaders and governmental institutions rather than whole states.[8] The primary dependent variables used in this study, however, will be behavior at the state level. In general, the most powerful level of analysis, in the sense of explaining most directly the phenomena of greatest interest in world politics, uses nations as primary actors. Individuals and substate organizations usually have an impact on world events only in terms of how their actions are reflected by the nation in which they reside or the government of which they are a part. This motivates the theoretical tack of conceptualizing the state as an individual or an organization, rather than testing theories on individuals or organizations. Anthropomorphizing the state has become virtually a theoretical tenet of international relations: realism visualizes the state as if it were a single decision maker reacting to threats and amassing power, and works using microeconomic rationality theory view the state as if it were a

---

[7] Another model of foreign policy learning which integrates ideas from social psychology and organization theory is presented by Andrew Owen Bennett, "Theories of Individual, Organizational, and Governmental Learning and the Rise and Fall of Soviet Military Interventionism, 1973–1983," Ph.D. diss., Harvard University, 1990. A model of learning which accounts for some basic political and structural variables is presented in Chapter 8 of this book.

[8] Of course, the idea that international relations scholarship can proceed at different levels of analysis is not a new one. See Kenneth N. Waltz, *Man, the State, and War: A Theoretical Analysis* (New York: Columbia University Press, 1959); J. David Singer, "The Level of Analysis Problem," *World Politics* 14 (October 1961); and Graham T. Allison, *Essence of Decision: Explaining the Cuban Missile Crisis* (Glenview, Ill: Scott, Foresman, 1971).

single, rational utility maximizer. Similarly, some analysts have applied organization theory to questions of world politics by considering the entire state as an organization, making the behavior of the state the primary dependent variable, rather than (or in addition to) analyzing individual substate organizations.[9] An additional consideration is that using the state as a level of analysis facilitates the execution of empirical tests on larger groups, increasing confidence in the validity and generalizability of the results. Lastly, using state behavior as the level of analysis permits the comparison of predictions made by learning and those of classical, state-oriented realist theory.

Although we may prefer predictions of state behavior (as opposed to individual or organizational behavior) because they are more interesting, this leaves the problem of building bridges between the theoretical levels of analysis, individuals and organizations, and the empirical level of analysis, state behavior. For organization theory, the state can itself be conceptualized as an organization, which facilitates the application of ideas from this area to questions of international relations. For theories of individual decision making, the learning theory proposed here predicts that everyone in a society ought to be affected by a national event, further predicting what lesson ought to be learned by the typical citizen. If foreign policy reflects the preferences of some individuals in society, whether the public at large or the leadership elite, then theories of individual decision making can be applied toward understanding foreign policy. One might argue that if a state's political structure affects whose preferences steer policy, then one ought to see different learning patterns in different regimes; I take up this issue more extensively in Chapter 8. It is worth noting, finally, that the depth of examination in the case study chapters will permit the level of analysis to shift down to the substate organizational and individual levels, so that it can be determined whether individuals and organizations are really behaving in the manner predicted by the theories.

BASIC DECISION THEORIES

The term *learning* has virtually as many meanings as applications.[10] For this study, *learning* means the application of information derived

---

[9] See Stephen Van Evera, "The Causes of War," Ph.D. diss., University of California at Berkeley, 1984; Evangelista, *Innovation and the Arms Race*; and Posen, *Sources of Military Doctrine*.

[10] For a discussion of various definitions of *learning* used in international relations scholarship, see Philip E. Tetlock, "Learning in U.S. and Soviet Foreign Policy: In Search

from past experiences to facilitate understanding of a particular policy question. It is not assumed that the "correct" lesson is learned, in the sense that following the lesson necessarily ensures a better outcome for the learner than does not following the lesson. I take a behavioral approach to the question of learning, seeking to understand what kinds of lessons get drawn given certain experiences. Though this presents an easier methodological task than trying to assess the objective validity of a lesson for policy, it is not a trivial task. Three theoretical areas are examined to explore learning in this form: formal models of decision analysis, social psychology, and organization theory.[11]

The first area, formal decision theory, addresses questions of decision making in rigorous, mathematical terms. Actors are conceptualized as being unitary, having utility functions, and knowing possible strategies for action. For the decision problem under consideration here, it is also necessary to assume that uncertainty exists about what outcomes will occur after strategy selection. This means that actors have beliefs as to what outcomes are likely to follow different strategies as well as ordered preferences for different outcomes.[12]

Formal theory does provide theoretical space for exploring how a decision maker will use new information to make better choices. This approach assumes that the decision maker sees the received information as being related to objective reality, so that the information can be used to inform the current decision problem in some useful way. Formal theory would permit the precise prediction of action if the decision maker's belief about the mathematical relationship between the information and reality is known. The most famous such inference is Bayes's Theorem, which makes predictions based on a decision maker's beliefs about the mathematical probability of receiving the information given the occurrence of an event.

The fundamental problem with this formal approach is that it is

---

of an Elusive Concept," in *Learning in U.S. and Soviet Foreign Policy*, ed. Breslauer and Tetlock, 20–61; and Levy, "Learning and Foreign Policy." Closely related to the question of defining learning is the methodological issue of determining when learning has occurred, which I address in Chapter 4.

[11] This trio parallels Steinbruner's analytic, cognitive, and cybernetic paradigms. Steinbruner, *Cybernetic Theory of Decision.*

[12] One of the earlier discussions of this idea is Leonard J. Savage, *The Foundations of Statistics*, 2d rev. ed. (New York: Dover, 1972). This idea that actors have tastes and beliefs was called Bayesian rationality by Ken Binmore, *Fun and Games* (Lexington, Mass.: D.C. Heath, 1992), 117–120. It has also been used as a method of refining the idea of Nash equilibria, in which preferences and beliefs are used to find what are called sequential equilibria. See, for example, David M. Kreps, *A Course in Microeconomic Theory* (Princeton: Princeton University Press, 1990), 425–432.

ultimately insufficient. No prior, reliable means exists for assigning the kinds of probabilities demanded by formal theory. For example, if a nation's adversary builds a nuclear weapon, there is no formal way of assessing mathematically either the probability that the adversary has aggressive intentions or what the nation's leadership thinks is the probability that the adversary has aggressive intentions. Without knowing such mathematical relationships, the (laudable) goal of formal theory to make precise predictions about behavior cannot be met. Put another way, though the framework of a formal approach to learning may be logically sound, its requirements are too demanding; formal decision theory provides a general framework for thinking about the problem of choice in an uncertain environment, but in the end it raises more questions than it answers. What is needed is a theory that more usefully and directly answers the question, How do decision makers draw inferences from new information to help guide their decisions? Bayes's Theorem relies on the establishment of mathematical relationships in order to update beliefs, but these mathematical relationships are themselves assumed beliefs, leaving us back at square one in trying to analyze the origin of beliefs.[13]

Social psychology studies the individual and how he or she relates to the environment. A dominant model of social psychology views the individual as a cognitive miser, that is, someone who evaluates incoming information and the environment with the tools of human intuition.[14] An important insight of this model is that these tools favor cognitive economy but tend to incur certain systematic biases. One such technique is the tendency of individuals to organize information into ordered knowledge structures, sometimes called schemata. The important benefit of schemata is that they lend order to an otherwise incomprehensible confusion of information and experience. Schemata serve several functions: they lend structure to experience, determine what information will be encoded or retrieved from memory, affect the speed of cognition, and facilitate problem solving. There are different kinds of schemata; for example, a script schema describes a sequence of

---

[13] On the severe limitations of the applicability of Bayes's Theorem, see Ken Binmore, "DeBayesing Game Theory," Center for Research on Economics and Social Theory Working Paper, no. 16 (Ann Arbor: University of Michigan, September 1991); and Detlof von Winterfeldt and Ward Edwards, *Decision Analysis and Behavioral Research* (Cambridge: Cambridge University Press, 1986), 163.

[14] On the cognitive miser model, see Richard Nisbett and Lee Ross, *Human Inference: Strategies and Shortcomings of Social Judgment* (Englewood Cliffs, N.J.: Prentice Hall, 1980). For a discussion of some of the shortcomings of this model, see Susan T. Fiske and Shelley E. Taylor, *Social Cognition*, 2d ed. (New York: McGraw-Hill, 1991), esp. 554–558.

events (like going to a restaurant), whereas a persona schema describes an idea of a type of individual (such as a garage mechanic). Schemata are used for the attribution of causation: to analyze a phenomenon, an individual extracts a schematic cue from the environment and then recalls the appropriate schema from memory to offer an explanation of the phenomenon in question. For example, if a student sees his professor searching her office for her wallet and he has a previously established knowledge structure that professors are absentminded, then he is likely to arrive at the explanation that she has misplaced her wallet (as opposed to alternative explanations, such as that her wallet has been stolen).[15]

An important implication of the schema insight is that individuals tend to rely on analogies, special types of schemata. In brief, an analogy is a comparison of some past experience with a current decision problem, so that some important aspect of the past experience can be used as an insight into the current problem. For example, the 1990 Iraqi invasion of Kuwait is compared with Nazi German threats against Czechoslovakia in the late 1930s because both involved a stronger aggressor threatening a weaker neighbor, from which it is inferred that appeasement of Saddam Hussein would lead to further Iraqi aggression since the appeasement of Hitler led to further Nazi aggression. This idea fits in well with the basic principles of knowledge structures laid out above; individuals reason on the basis of drawing on schemata/analogies to facilitate data storage and retrieval.[16] One experi-

---

[15] Nisbett and Ross, *Human Inference*; Shelley E. Taylor and Jennifer Crocker, "Schematic Bases of Social Information Processing," in *Social Cognition: The Ontario Symposium*, vol. 1, ed. E. Tory Higgins, C. Peter Herman, and Mark P. Zanna (Hillsdale, N.J.: Lawrence Erlbaum Associates, 1981), 89–134; Roger Schank and Robert Abelson, *Scripts, Plans, Goals, and Understanding* (Hillsdale, N.J.: Lawrence Erlbaum Associates, 1977); Robert P. Abelson, "Script Processing in Attitude Formation and Decision Making," in *Cognition and Social Behavior*, ed. John S. Carroll and John W. Payne (Hillsdale, N.J.: Lawrence Erlbaum Associates, 1976), 33–45; Robert P. Abelson and Mansur Lalljee, "Knowledge Structures and Causal Explanation," in *Contemporary Science and Natural Explanation*, ed. Denis J. Hilton (New York: New York University Press, 1988), 175–203. For a comparison of schema theory with other approaches, see Robert P. Abelson and John B. Black, "Introduction," in *Knowledge Structures*, ed. James A. Galambos, Abelson, and Black (Hillsdale: Lawrence Erlbaum Associates, 1986), 1–20. For a discussion of the uses of schema theory for understanding how foreign policy gets made, see Deborah Welch Larson, "The Role of Belief Systems and Schemas in Foreign Policy Decision-Making," *Political Psychology* 15 (March 1994): 17–33.

[16] An excellent example of the application of analogical reasoning principles to questions of political science is Yuen Foong Khong's Analogical Explanations model. He argues that decision makers often rely on analogical reasoning to inform their decisions. His model does not, however, make any predictions as to which analogies will be used by individuals. Khong, *Analogies at War*. For an application of analogical reasoning to the resolution of security dilemmas, see Hayward R. Alker Jr., James Bennett, and Dwain

mental study found subjects prone to reasoning on the basis of a single instance, especially when facing a complex causal relationship, confirming the basic logic of schema theory: schemata are used to cope with situations requiring great cognitive effort.[17]

It is worth noting that analogies are generally kept simple to facilitate generalization; the more complex the analogy, the more difficult is its application to a different context.[18] For example, if the lesson from the Western appeasement of Nazi Germany in 1938 was "when faced with a German threat to annex an ethnically similar piece of territory from a neighbor, the British and French should not give in," it would have been more difficult for American decision makers to apply the analogy to the contextually different decision to defend South Korea in 1950. Instead, the lesson taken from Munich was kept broad and simple— "aggressors must be opposed to prevent future aggression"—so that it could be applied to other circumstances. It requires less cognitive effort to construct lessons that are simple and to apply lessons that are simple, in the latter case because fewer historical idiosyncrasies have to be matched between the past event and the current context. One experiment found that subjects tended to apply consistent analogies and avoid complicated analogies when comparing World War II to the Gulf War.[19] Of course, relying on overly simple lessons and neglecting important historical details can lead to inappropriate analogizing and misguided choices.[20]

An important charateristic of schemata is that they tend to acquire inertia, that is, once established they are not easily changed, even with the appearance of discrepant information. Quite considerable experi-

---

Mefford, "Generalized Precedent Logics for Resolving Security Dilemmas," *International Interactions* 7 (1980): 165–206. For a discussion of the place of metaphors, similes, and analogies in political discourse, see Elliot Zashin and Phillip C. Chapman, "The Uses of Metaphor and Analogy: Toward a Renewal of Political Language," *Journal of Politics* 36 (May 1974): 291–326; and Keith L. Shimko, "Metaphors and Foreign Policy Decision Making," *Political Psychology* 15 (December 1994): 655–671. For a more general discussion, see David Hackett Fischer, *Historians' Fallacies: Toward a Logic of Historical Thought* (New York: Harper & Row, 1970), 243. For a variety of psychological and computer models of analogy, see Stella Vosniadou and Andrew Ortony, eds., *Similarity and Analogical Reasoning* (Cambridge: Cambridge University Press, 1989).

[17] Stephen J. Read, "Once is Enough: Causal Reasoning from a Single Instance," *Journal of Personality and Social Psychology* 45 (1983): 323–334.

[18] This point is made by D. Michael Shafer, *Deadly Paradigms* (Princeton: Princeton University Press, 1988), 35.

[19] Barbara A. Spellman and Keith J. Holyoak, "If Saddam Is Hitler Then Who Is George Bush? Analogical Mapping between Systems of Social Roles," *Journal of Personality and Social Psychology* 62 (1992): 913–933.

[20] May, *"Lessons" of the Past*; Neustadt and May, *Thinking in Time*; Khong, *Analogies at War*; Howard, "Use and Abuse of Military History."

mental evidence supports the idea that beliefs tend to persevere even when the original information that led to the formation of the belief has been completely discredited.[21] An example of perseverance of beliefs is the reaction of the American media to reports of the Holocaust in World War II. In World War I, the British had exaggerated the extent of war crimes committed by Germany in Belgium. When these deceptions were uncovered after the war, this created the belief among many in the press that reports of wartime atrocities need to be treated with extreme skepticism, given the incentives of the belligerents to demonize their adversaries. This belief lasted into World War II, when a steady stream of information about Nazi genocidal policies against Jews and other groups during the war were largely dismissed by the American media as propaganda. The reporters became convinced of the veracity of the reports only when the Nazi death camps were opened in 1945 and firsthand observation presented the reporters with incontrovertible evidence of the Holocaust.[22]

In addition to highlighting the importance of schemata, the cognitive miser model proposes that individuals use certain cognitive shortcuts, called judgmental heuristics, to facilitate comprehension. Although these heuristics improve cognitive economy, they do so at the expense of introducing certain systematic biases.[23] One important heuristic is called the representativeness heuristic. This strategy guides individuals to associate an event and a model based on how well one character-

[21] Lee Ross, Mark R. Lepper, and Michael Hubbard, "Perseverance in Self-Perception and Social Perception: Biased Attributional Processes in the Debriefing Paradigm," *Journal of Personality and Social Psychology* 32 (1975): 880–892; Craig A. Anderson, Mark R. Lepper, and Lee Ross, "Perseverance of Social Theories: The Role of Explanation in the Persistence of Discredited Information," *Journal of Personality and Social Psychology* 39 (1979): 1037–1949; Berndt Brehmer, "In One Word: Not from Experience," *Acta Psychologica* 45 (1980): 223–241. One study found that if the same set of mixed, objective evidence on capital punishment was presented to individuals with differing views, the polarization of views among the individuals increased, as each individual took out of the body of evidence those bits that supported his or her view. Charles G. Lord, Lee Ross, and Mark R. Lepper, "Biased Assimilation and Attitude Polarization: The Effects of Prior Theories on Subsequently Considered Evidence," *Journal of Personality and Social Psychology* 37 (1979): 2098–2109. Though some have attributed these effects to the greater ease of remembering schema-consistent information, a comprehensive analysis of experimental studies on memory found support for the more complex associative networks model, which takes into account a number of mediating factors determining memory of schema-relevant information. Krystyna Rojahn and Thomas F. Pettigrew, "Memory for Schema-Relevant Information: A Meta-Analytic Resolution," *British Journal of Social Psychology* (1992): 81–109. For a discussion of the role of schemata in belief change, see Jennifer Crocker, Susan T. Fiske, and Shelley E. Taylor, "Schematic Bases of Belief Change," in *Attitudinal Judgment*, ed. J. Richard Eiser (New York: Springer-Verlag, 1984), 197–226.

[22] Deborah E. Lipstadt, *Beyond Belief* (New York: Free Press, 1986).

[23] Daniel Kahneman, Paul Slovic, and Amos Tversky, eds., *Judgment under Uncertainty: Heuristics and Biases* (Cambridge: Cambridge University Press, 1982).

izes the other. The degree of representation can emerge from physical, personal, or other types of similarities. The representativeness heuristic can work in a consistent fashion with the scientific method if the representation is along a dimension that may be genuinely connected to the posited relationship. But the representativeness heuristic can lead to certain systematic biases in the estimations of causality and probability, if the dimension of representativeness is logically unrelated to the causal process. Biases in human judgment which are related to the representativeness heuristic, such as insensitivity to prior probability of outcomes, insensitivity to sample size, misconceptions of chance, insensitivity to predictability, the illusion of validity, and misconceptions of regression, have been observed in experimental research.[24]

An important implication of the representativeness heuristic is that individuals will tend to focus on individual, representative events more than they "should," that is, more than might be dictated by laws of scientific inference. Often, the representativeness heuristic will impel an individual to assess probability improperly, such that a single event will affect his estimation of probability too much and lead him to give insufficient weight to the base rate estimate of probability held before observation of the event. The significant implication is that individuals might rely on a single, representative event—often an analogy from past experience—to guide their decisions. Additionally, the representativeness heuristic can also cause individuals to draw connections between events based on surface similarities, characteristics that are essentially unsubstantive but are representative and give an event persuasive force as an analogy.[25] In one study, subjects who read descriptions that included substantively irrelevant items intended to cue certain analogies made judgments in accordance with the cued analogies more frequently than subjects who read descriptions without such cues.[26]

---

[24] See Mark Schaller, "Sample Size, Aggregation, and Statistical Reasoning in Social Inference," *Journal of Experimental Social Psychology* 28 (1992): 65–85; and chapters 1–6 in Kahneman, Slovic, and Tversky, *Judgment under Uncertainty*. Robert Jervis has argued that contrary to experimental results on representativeness, makers of foreign policy are not slanted toward crediting too highly a specific event at the expense of giving sufficient credit to base rates. "Representativeness in Foreign Policy Judgments," *Political Psychology* 7 (September 1986): 483–505. Jervis does believe that formative events have an exaggerated effect on determining lessons. Letter to author, October 5, 1994.

[25] See Kahneman, Slovic, and Tversky, *Judgment under Uncertainty*; and Mark Schaller, "Sample Size, Aggregation, and Statistical Reasoning in Social Inference," *Journal of Experimental Social Psychology* 28 (1992): 65–85.

[26] Thomas Gilovich, "Seeing the Past in the Present: The Effect of Associations to Familiar Events on Judgments and Decisions," *Journal of Personality and Social Psychology* 40 (1981): 797–808.

Foreign policy–makers often exhibit such behavior. For example, when Ghanaian leader Kwame Nkrumah made a number of anti-American statements in 1961, President Kennedy chose not to withdraw American aid for a massive hydroelectric dam project in Ghana for fear of creating another Nasser, the Egyptian leader who had become pro-Soviet after the United States withdrew support for the Aswan Dam in 1956.[27] Here, the surface similarities of the cues proved to be cognitively powerful for Kennedy: both Nkrumah and Nasser were radical African leaders not firmly in the Western camp, and the issue for both was American support for a hydroelectric project.

Sometimes the connection between past case and current environment is more tenuous than the Nkrumah-Nasser comparison, however. Saddam Hussein, for example, used religious symbols and myth to motivate his military commanders on the eve of conflict with the United States. "[Saddam] declared that, as the symbol of the Republican Party was the elephant, the Qur'anic story of the defeat of the forces equipped with elephants which had attacked Mecca was a portent of the Iraqi victory to come. He was moved to cite the appropriate verses: 'See you not how the Lord dealt with the companions of the elephant? Did He not make their treacherous plan go astray?' A tape recording of the meeting reveals that cries could be heard from the audience, 'Yes, Mr. President, how history repeats itself!'"[28] The Western reader should not take comfort in the thought that only Third World leaders engage in such haphazard analogizing. In the early months of World War I, for example, President Wilson looked to the experience of President Madison during the War of 1812 for guidance, noting that they were the only two Princeton men to have become president.[29]

Another important analytic shortcut discussed by the cognitive miser model is that events which are especially vivid are more likely to be persuasive. Information has been described by social psychologists as vivid "to the extent that it is (a) emotionally interesting, (b) concrete and imagery-provoking, and (c) proximate in a sensory, temporal, or spatial way." These sorts of ideas are easily applied to international politics, as one can distinguish between events that have more or less emotional or physical impact (such as wars with greater or lesser casualties) and events that are directly experienced, and therefore vivid,

---

[27] Richard J. Walton, *Cold War and Counterrevolution: The Foreign Policy of John F. Kennedy* (New York: Viking Press, 1972), 206.

[28] James Piscatori, "Religion and Realpolitik: Islamic Responses to the Gulf War," in *Islamic Fundamentalisms and the Gulf Crisis*, ed. Piscatori (Chicago: Fundamentalism Project, American Academy of Arts and Sciences, 1991), 2. See also *The Guardian* (Manchester), 11 June 1991.

[29] May, *"Lessons" of the Past*, ix.

versus those which happen to another state and are therefore experienced only vicariously. Vivid information is theorized to be easier to recall not only because of emotional affect and the greater amount of sensorily interesting detail associated with vivid information but also because a vivid experience can mean the recruitment of entirely new schemata.[30] Additionally, vivid information is almost by definition more salient perceptually, and salient information is hypothesized to be more available for memory recall and therefore more persuasive.[31]

Despite the strong theoretical support for the vividness effect, however, the experimental evidence is mixed. In 1982, Shelley Taylor and Suzanne Thompson conducted a comprehensive review of the vividness literature, finding the empirical evidence generally unsupportive of the proposition that vivid information has a disproportionately high impact on judgment in a number of different operationalizations of vividness, including concrete and specific language, use of videotapes as opposed to pictures, direct experience versus secondhand experience, and case history versus base rate or other statistical information.[32] They found this to be an extraordinarily odd experimental finding given the extremely strong theoretical support and common sense of the proposition.[33] Soon after, Taylor and Joanne Wood explored a number of explanations as to why experimental studies have failed to find support for the vividness effect, postulating two explanations. First, vivid information may be more persuasive only when it is in direct competition with pallid information for attention. The vividness studies do not put vivid information directly in competition for atten-

[30] The definition is from Nisbett and Ross, *Human Inference*, 45. For an extensive theoretical discussion of the vividness effect and its implications for judgment and inference, see ibid., 43–62.

[31] On the availability heuristic, see Kahneman, Slovic, and Tversky, *Judgment under Uncertainty*. The salience effect has attracted empirical support in a wide variety of conditions. Shelley E. Taylor, Jennifer Crocker, Susan T. Fiske, Merle Sprinze, and Joachim D. Winkler, "The Generalizability of Salience Effects," *Journal of Personality and Social Psychology* 37 (1979): 357–368. Chaim D. Kaufmann found empirical support for the salience effect in foreign policy decision making. "Out of the Lab and into the Archives: A Method for Testing Psychological Explanations of Political Decision Making," *International Studies Quarterly* 38 (1994): 557–586.

[32] Shelley E. Taylor and Suzanne C. Thompson, "Stalking the Elusive 'Vividness' Effect," *Psychological Review* 89 (1982): 155–181. A decade later, experimental evidence in support of the proposition that vivid information is more persuasive remains elusive: "So far, we have seen no clear evidence for the effects of vivid information on persuasion and judgments, when information is held constant in other ways," state Fiske and Taylor, *Social Cognition*, 256. One recent study found that under some conditions, vividness can make a message less persuasive by distracting attention away from the argument itself. Kurt P. Frey and Alice H. Eagly, "Vividness Can Undermine the Persuasiveness of Messages," *Journal of Personality and Social Psychology* 65 (July 1993): 32–44.

[33] Taylor and Thompson, " 'Vividness' Effect."

tion with pallid information, so the postulated effect was not found. The second explanation is what they refer to as the "Carl Sagan Effect" (so named for the colorful style of the popular astronomer): when an individual encounters vivid information, he believes that it is persuasive and others would have been persuaded by it, though he is not "actually" persuaded.[34] A few years later, Taylor and Wood, along with Thompson and Rebecca Collins, discovered support for the Carl Sagan Effect in their own laboratory test for vividness, finding that vivid information was generally not more persuasive but that the subjects believed that other people would be subject to the vividness effect.[35] There is evidence, however, that behavior is more likely to be affected by attitudes based on direct experience than by those based on indirect experience, because such attitudes are more specific, held more confidently, more stable, and more resistant to counterargument.[36]

Though the general findings regarding the vividness effect are mixed, the more sophisticated interpretations of the experimental findings indicate that some form of the vividness effect ought to play an important role in the making of foreign policy. The Carl Sagan Effect of people believing vividness effects to be persuasive *of others* is quite relevant to politics. Political leaders need to maintain the support of their constituencies, and this may motivate them to undertake policies that they believe their constituencies subscribe to, which may mean that the decision makers will act as if they were persuaded by vivid events so as to please their constituencies. This implies that the Carl Sagan Effect is less likely to affect policy in nations in which decision makers are less dependent on constituency support, a proposition that I examine and test in Chapter 8. Additionally, experiments support the idea that if a belief (or schema) is acquired from a vivid event, it is more likely to spur behavior than if it is acquired from a pallid event. Either way, support is garnered from social psychological findings that vivid events are more likely to be formative and guide behavior than are nonvivid events.

Finally, though only limited experimental support exists for the vividness proposition from social psychology, some evidence from inter-

[34] Shelley E. Taylor and Joanne V. Wood, "The Vividness Effect: Making a Mountain out of a Molehill?" in *Advances in Consumer Research*, vol. 10, ed. Richard P. Bogozzi and Alice M. Tybout (Ann Arbor: Association for Consumer Research, 1983), 540–542.

[35] Rebecca L. Collins, Shelley E. Taylor, Joanne V. Wood, and Suzanne C. Thompson, "The Vividness Effect: Elusive or Illusory?" *Journal of Experimental Social Psychology* 24 (1988): 1–18.

[36] Fiske and Taylor, *Social Cognition*, 520–521. See also Sanford L. Braver and Van Rohrer, "Superiority of Vicarious over Direct Experience in Interpersonal Conflict Resolution," *Journal of Conflict Resolution* 22 (March 1979): 143–155.

national relations research indicates that vivid events are more likely to guide decision makers' beliefs than other events. One example of such work is Yuen Foong Khong's examination of the 1965 American decision to escalate the Vietnam War. He found that the individuals involved in making the decision analogized from events that were personally experienced, one example of vividness. Both Dean Rusk and Lyndon Johnson were heavily and personally involved with the Korean War and, as would be expected, compared the situation in South Vietnam with that in South Korea, whereas George Ball, who had worked closely with the French in Southeast Asia in the 1950s, found the French experience at Dien Bien Phu to be analogous to the American situation in Vietnam.[37]

The third theoretical area presents an alternative approach to anthropomorphizing the state, instead viewing the state as an organization or as a collection of organizations. In the last several years, political scientist's have increasingly come to realize that organizations have an impact on politics which extends beyond merely being fora for the interaction of political interests.[38] How organizations learn and adapt to changing environmental circumstances is a central topic of concern for organization theorists, since the organization (like the individual) has limited resources with which to meet its goals, and the strategies for optimal attainment of these goals are often uncertain and affected by environmental changes.

Though the literature on organizational behavior is vast and in some respects not well integrated, it can be safely said that at least three central principles of organizational behavior relevant to organizational learning have emerged from the last several decades of research.[39] The first principle is that organizations are oriented toward targets. The achievement of a set of goals is an organization's raison d'être; organizations are created to accomplish tasks. This idea is at the heart of thinking about organizations, going back to earlier works on organizational behavior by Herbert Simon, Richard Cyert, and James March. Organizational tasks include victory for an army, profit maximization

[37] For examples of international relations research that finds that vivid events guide policy choices, see Jervis, *Perception and Misperception*; Manus I. Midlarsky, "Polarity, the Learning of Cooperation, and the Stability of International Systems," *From Rivalry to Cooperation: Russian and American Perspectives on the Post–Cold War Era*, ed. Manus I. Midlarsky, John A. Vasquez, and Peter V. Gladkov (New York: HarperCollins, 1994), 26–39; and Khong, *Analogies at War*, esp. 104–105. See also the sources listed in n. 63 in this chapter.

[38] James G. March and Johan P. Olsen, "The New Institutionalism: Organizational Factors in Political Life," *American Political Science Review* 78 (September 1984): 734–749.

[39] Barbara Levitt and James G. March, "Organizational Learning," *Annual Review of Sociology* 14 (1988): 320.

for a business firm, or finding good jobs for graduates for a university placement office. The environment and structure of an organization produce a heavy emphasis on success at meeting organizational goals. Failure to meet goals is often the primary motivator for organizational learning, encouraging searches for new ways to meet institutional goals.[40]

The second principle is that organizational behavior is determined by routines, also known as standard operating procedures. An organization maintains preset responses to changes in the external environment to meet its needs. The idea of a routine is a broad one, including a wide range of formally and informally codified prescriptions for behavior. The focus of this study is on the broader rather than narrower routines of nations' foreign policy apparatus, specifically on larger questions of foreign policy, such as whether neutrality best protects national security, as opposed to more specific, operational questions, such as what the best procedure is for implementation of a naval blockade. These broader routines are, then, beliefs about the dynamics of the international environment, which, in turn, determine behavior. The organization theory literature has found strong evidence that organizational beliefs have important effects on organizational behavior.[41]

The third main principle of organizations is that their behavior is history-dependent. An organization is formed and behaves in accordance with what its founders understand about the organization's environment and the mission of the organization; it does not begin tabula rasa. Routines and beliefs are then developed from the interpretation of experience, and the continuing stream of experience provides feedback that is used to understand why changes in organizational structure are necessary. This is one of the central tenets of adaptive rationality.[42]

[40] Richard M. Cyert and James G. March, *A Behavioral Theory of the Firm* (Englewood Cliffs, N.J.: Prentice Hall, 1963); Herbert A. Simon, *Administrative Behavior*, 3d ed. (New York: Free Press, 1976); Philip Mirvis and David Berg, "Failures in Organization Development and Change," in *Failures in Organization Development and Change*, ed. Mirvis and Berg (New York: John Wiley, 1977), 1–18; Bo Hedberg, "How Organizations Learn and Unlearn," in *Handbook of Organizational Design*, vol. 1, ed. Paul C. Nystrom and William H. Starbuck (London: Oxford University Press, 1981); James G. March and Herbert A. Simon, *Organizations* (New York: John Wiley, 1958); James G. March, *Decisions and Organizations* (Oxford: Basil Blackwell, 1988).

[41] Paul C. Nystrom and William H. Starbuck, "Managing Beliefs in Organizations," *Journal of Applied Behavioral Science* 20 (1984): 277–287; Hedberg, "How Organizations Learn and Unlearn," 6. The idea of an organizational belief is similar to Morton Halperin's "shared images." See Halperin, *Bureaucratic Politics and Foreign Policy* (Washington: Brookings Institution, 1974), 150–155.

[42] George P. Huber, "Organizational Learning: The Contributing Processes and the Literatures," *Organization Science* 2 (February 1991): 91; Cyert and March, *Behavioral*

Together with the first two principles, a vision of organizational learning emerges in which "experiential lessons of history are captured by routines in a way that makes the lessons, but not the history, accessible to organizations and organizational members who have not themselves experienced the history. Routines are transmitted through socialization, education, imitation, professionalization, personnel movement, mergers, and acquisitions."[43]

The relationship between historical experiences and standard operating procedures, however, is not one of simple, one-way cause and effect. Though historical experiences can be instrumental in creating such procedures, these organizational routines often have a rigidifying effect, such that they impede the assimilation of new experiences that may be at odds with current organizational beliefs and procedures. The collective interpretation of history is often an explicit goal of organizations; events are invested with meaning and then developed into organizational stories or paradigms. The tendency in organizations is to sustain conventional interpretation of these myths, such that they are resistant to change even in the face of disconfirming evidence.[44] Sometimes only a crisis can encourage an organization to draw new lessons or create new procedures. This idea of crises driving myths or beliefs that in turn determine behavior is very similar to the model proposed in a study of Swedish investment firms, which posited that myths operate in cycles, such that one myth holds sway until a crisis emerges, at which point a new myth emerges to replace the old one.[45] In international relations, a good example is the tendency of militaries to fight the last war—each major war establishes a set of beliefs about the dynamics of combat and strategy, and it usually takes a new war to establish new beliefs. This perseverance of organizational beliefs is partly due to the use of organizational routines and standard operating procedures, which tend to resist change, as organizational memory.[46] When there is an event that by external judgment would be viewed as a failure, incentives exist for potentially responsible subgroups within the or-

Theory of the Firm, 99; Levitt and March, "Organizational Learning," 320; Mirvis and Berg, "Failures in Organization Development," 4.

[43] Levitt and March, "Organizational Learning," 320.

[44] Ibid., 324; Nystrom and Starbuck, "Managing Beliefs in Organizations." The idea that organizational inertia is a counterforce to adaptation and innovation is the central assumption of ecological views of "learning." Michael T. Hannan and John Freeman, *Organizational Ecology* (Cambridge: Harvard University Press, 1989).

[45] Sten A. Jönsson and Rolf A. Lundin, "Myths and Wishful Thinking as Management Tools," in *Prescriptive Models of Organizations*, ed. Paul C. Nystrom and William H. Starbuck (Amsterdam: North-Holland Publishing, 1977), 157–170.

[46] Cyert and March, *Behavioral Theory of the Firm*, esp. 102.

ganization not to portray the experience as a failure to avoid recrimina-tions.[47] As a result, only high-impact failures will be recognized as indisputable failures and attract the examination necessary to extract lessons.

Some scholars have taken this point of organizational inertia further, arguing that organizations are not very adaptive and learn very rarely, if ever. Therefore, if the environment changes to be less rewarding to some strategies, the organizations holding those strategies will die off rather than learn and adapt. It is, in other words, a Darwinian view of organizational evolution, as opposed to adaptive rationality's Lamarckian view.[48] This view, however, is difficult to apply to an ecology of nations, given the low death rate of states.[49] One might conceptualize there to be an ecology of proponents of ideas *within* a society, such that the individuals or institutions that promote these ideas cannot change their views as the environment changes and cer-tain ideas (and their proponents) are selected (that is, gain prominence) while others die off (the ideas fall out of favor and their proponents lose power). However, this leaves unknown the actual mechanism for the prosperity and fall of the proponents of ideas. And if we accept that proponents remain in power (or are listened to) when an idea is suc-cessful and fall from grace when their ideas do poorly, this constitutes, essentially, adaptive rationality at the level of the society or state.

The literature on organizational learning has outlined a number of different means by which organizations can learn. I will focus on learn-ing from experience because it is more appropriate for learning in international politics. For example, grafting, the process of increasing an organization's store of knowledge by acquiring new members pos-sessing desired knowledge, does not apply here because the focus in this study is not on technical, task-oriented learning but on broader, more general beliefs. Hence, the problem is not a lack of information for which the recruitment of new personnel is a solution. Further, the individuals who are recruited into the top circles of foreign policy decision making are often selected because their beliefs match those of the selecting individuals, such as Nixon's appointment of Kissinger as secretary of state. A second category, searching, can be folded into the category of learning from the experience of others.[50]

[47] Mirvis and Berg, "Failures in Organization Development," 8; Charles Perrow, *Normal Accidents* (New York: Basic Books, 1984); Sagan, *Limits of Safety*.

[48] Hannan and Freeman, *Organizational Ecology*.

[49] Kenneth N. Waltz, *Theory of International Politics* (New York: Random House, 1979), 139.

[50] For a summary of the literature on these different forms of organizational learning, see Huber, "Organizational Learning: The Contributing Processes."

Lessons can be drawn from events experienced either directly or vicariously. If experience is direct, learning occurs primarily through two mechanisms: trial-and-error experimentation, and organizational search through alternatives based on failure and success.[51] Alternatively, organizations can learn from the experiences of other organizations, as information is diffused throughout the population of organizations.[52] Some organization analysts contend that organizations most frequently adopt new beliefs after experiencing failure, as it both spurs action and provides a rich source of information for determining how to improve operations. Successes provide information and often the resources necessary to conduct searches for improvements in strategy, but they also tend to produce complacency and stifle the drive to innovate.[53] Conversely, success can be a myopia-inducing intoxicant inhibiting the drawing of new lessons, as "organizations which have been poisoned by their own success are often unable to unlearn obsolete knowledge in spite of strong disconfirmations."[54]

For organizations, learning from direct experience needs to be differentiated from learning vicariously (often referred to as learning through diffusion), as each involves different mechanisms for learning. The latter tends to be more complicated: it involves a number of additional factors, such as the degree of secrecy embraced by other organizations in sharing their experiences and the existence of institutions to facilitate this sharing.[55] Direct experience, on the other hand, can uniquely facilitate learning, especially if the experience is one of failure, as failure provides a target for corrective action and its impact can serve to unfreeze old beliefs and provide impetus for new thinking.[56] Therefore, organization theory offers the strong hypothesis that learning from direct experience ought to be distinguished from vicarious learning. It also offers the weaker hypothesis that learning from direct expe-

---

[51] Levitt and March, "Organizational Learning," 321. The trial-and-error mechanism is similar to Steinbruner's cybernetic theory; see *Cybernetic Theory of Decision*.

[52] The literature on diffusion is itself diffuse, spanning a number of social scientific disciplines in addition to a variety of industries. For reviews of the literature, see Levitt and March, "Organizational Learning"; Huber, "Organizational Learning: The Contributing Processes." See also Wesley M. Cohen and Daniel A. Levinthal, "Absorptive Capacity: A New Perspective on Learning and Innovation," *Administrative Science Quarterly* 35 (1990): 128–152.

[53] Sim B. Sitkin, "Learning through Failure: The Strategy of Small Losses," in *Research in Organizational Behavior*, vol. 14, ed. Barry M. Staw and L. L. Cummings (Greenwich, Conn: JAI Press, 1992), 231–266; Mirvis and Berg, *Failures in Organization Development*; Hedberg, "How Organizations Learn and Unlearn," 17–18. Failure-driven learning is similar to Hedberg's idea of unlearning old ideas (9).

[54] Hedberg, "How Organizations Learn and Unlearn," 19.

[55] Levitt and March, "Organizational Learning," 329–331.

[56] Sitkin, "Learning through Failure," 238.

rience ought to be easier and more frequent than learning from vicarious experience. Research indicates that direct failure is the best and perhaps only motivator for organizations to innovate, for they tend not to learn from the experiences of other organizations. One empirical study of a particular type of organizational innovation, the M-form or multidivisional structure, could not find empirical support for the hypothesis that the reputedly superior M-form organizational structure was adopted by competing firms.[57]

General Learning Propositions

Now that some basic ideas about learning have been laid out, the next task is to draw out a few general propositions about learning in international relations. This means considering more carefully the specific propositions implied by each of the basic theories, paying special attention to their similarities and differences. To begin with, two important similarities between social psychology and organization theory are worth highlighting.[58] First, both social psychology and organization theory predict that the drawing of new lessons is likely to be generally infrequent and to occur after a certain class of events. Social psychology argues that individual beliefs are difficult to change and that often a highly vivid experience is necessary to encourage the reconsideration of old ideas. At the level of society, it has been argued that sometimes single events are powerful enough to shape the thinking and ideas of an entire generation.[59] Similarly, organizational inertia means that organizations are most likely to draw new lessons from crises rather than from the steady stream of operational experience. Additionally, international alliances are often organizations, and as organizations they possess a considerable institutional ability to perpetuate themselves. Therefore, an alliance may continue to exist out of bureaucratic inertia absent a massive formative event that demonstrates its obsolescence. This point was made by Gunther Hellman and Reinhard Wolf, who

[57] Viday Mahajan, Subhash Sharma, and Richard Bettis, "The Adoption of the M-Form Organizational Structure: A Test of Imitation Hypothesis," *Management Science* 34 (October 1988): 1188–1201.

[58] The similarities between the two fields are not completely a coincidence, as ideas about organizational learning have drawn substantially on research about individual learning. See March and Olsen, "New Institutionalism," 740; and Hedberg, "How Organizations Learn and Unlearn," 6.

[59] On generations, see Karl Mannheim, *Essays on the Sociology of Knowledge*, ed. Paul Kecskemeti (New York: Oxford University Press, 1952); and Alan B. Spitzer, "The Historical Problem of Generation," *American Historical Review* 78 (December 1973): 1353–1385.

[34]

posited that "the fact that the North Atlantic Treaty *Organization* exists will make it unlikely to disappear."[60]

It is arguable that drawing lessons only from such large events is not an optimal strategy for using information, as information received from lesser events is largely ignored. In some cases, though, focusing learning efforts on infrequent, large-scale events may not necessarily be suboptimal behavior. In some cases, such infrequent events are the best available sources of information for an organization. For example, a utility company wants to improve nuclear reactor safety but can get solid data only from real accidents, and an army wants to evaluate its military doctrine but can obtain credible feedback only from actual combat experience. In both cases, the organizations have to make the best from information sources that are very limited in number.[61]

A second similarity is that both social psychology and organization theory predict that a decision maker's own experiences are more likely to spark the drawing of new lessons than are the experiences of others. Events experienced first hand by an individual are predicted to be relatively more vivid and therefore more persuasive. Similarly, crises experienced firsthand by an organization are more likely to dislodge old beliefs and stimulate new ideas, as they more directly touch the organization itself.

From these similarities between the two theories grow the foundations of a theory of learning in international relations. The small set of high impact, vivid events that spur the drawing of new lessons I term *formative events*, as they form beliefs about international relations. Of course, the idea that political choices and outcomes are often driven by single, high-impact events is not a new one. The historian William Langer considered how societies are deeply affected by periodic crises:

> As historians we must be particularly concerned with the problem whether major changes in the psychology of a society or culture can be traced, even in part, to some severe trauma suffered in common, that is, with the question whether whole communities, like individuals, can be profoundly affected by some shattering experience. If it is indeed true that every society or culture has a "unique psychological fabric," deriving at least in part from past common experiences and attitudes, it seems reasonable to suppose that any great crisis, such as famine, pestilence, natural disaster, or war, should leave its mark on the group, the intensity and

---

[60] Gunther Hellman and Reinhard Wolf, "Neorealism, Neoliberal Institutionalism, and the Future of NATO," *Security Studies* 3 (Autumn 1993): 20; emphasis in original.

[61] James G. March, Lee S. Sproull, and Michal Tamuz, "Learning from Samples of One or Fewer," *Organization Science* 2 (February 1991): 1–13.

duration of the impact depending, of course, on the nature and magnitude of the crisis.[62]

Several scholars have examined the formative events proposition regarding American foreign policy, proposing that the lesson learned by Americans from the World War II experience was the failure of isolationism and the imperative of international engagement. This lesson expressed itself in the belief of the extreme dangers of appeasement and imperatives of opposing aggression, a belief that, it has been argued, was overturned following the formative Vietnam experience.[63]

The formative model, first given extensive theoretical discussion by Robert Jervis, is the most common political science approach to learning.[64] A wide array of formative events and their foreign policy impacts have been examined, including the Russo-Japanese War and its effects on Soviet perceptions of Japan, the effects of global economic crises on international economic policies, the Holocaust and its effects on Israeli foreign policy, and the Korean War and its effects on the American decision to escalate the war in Vietnam, to name a few examples.[65]

[62] William L. Langer, "The Next Assignment," *American Historical Review* 68 (January 1958), 291.

[63] Bruce Kuklick, "Tradition and Diplomatic Talent: The Case of the Cold Warriors," in *Recycling the Past*, ed. Leila Zenderland (Philadelphia: University of Pennsylvania Press, 1978), 116–131; Bruce Kuklick, "History as a Way of Learning," *American Quarterly* 22 (Fall 1970): 609–628; Michael Roskin, "From Pearl Harbor to Vietnam: Shifting Generational Paradigms and Foreign Policy," *Political Science Quarterly* 89 (Fall 1974): 563–588; Neil E. Cutler, "Generational Succession as a Source of Foreign Policy Attitudes: A Cohort Analysis of American Opinion, 1946–1966," *Journal of Peace Research* 7 (1970): 33–47; Graham T. Allison, "Cool It: The Foreign Policy of Young America," *Foreign Policy* 1 (Winter 1970/71): 144–160; Bruce Russett, "The Americans' Retreat from World Power," *Political Science Quarterly* 90 (Spring 1975): 1–21; John Mueller, "Pearl Harbor: Military Inconvenience, Political Disaster," *International Security* 16 (Winter 1991/92): 171–203. For a more skeptical view of the argument that the Vietnam experience resulted in long-term changes in the beliefs of the American public about foreign policy, see Eugene Wittkopf, *Faces of Internationalism: Public Opinion and American Foreign Policy* (Durham: Duke University Press, 1990); Ole R. Holsti, "Public Opinion and Containment," *Containing the Soviet Union: A Critique of US Policy*, ed. Terry L. Deibel and John Lewis Gaddis (Washington: Pergamon-Brassey, 1987), 20–58; and Ole R. Holsti and James N. Rosenau, *American Leadership in World Affairs* (Boston: Allen & Unwin, 1984).

[64] Jervis, *Perception and Misperception*, 217–287.

[65] Jonathan Haslam, "The Boundaries of Rational Calculation in Soviet Policy towards Japan," in *History, the White House, and the Kremlin*, ed. Fry, 38–50; Stephen D. Krasner, "State Power and the Structure of International Trade," *World Politics* 28 (April 1976): 341; Judith Goldstein, "Ideas, Institutions, and American Trade Policy," *International Organization* 42 (Winter 1988): 179–217; Judith Goldstein, "The Impact of Ideas on Trade Policy: The Origins of U.S. Agricultural and Manufacturing Policies," *International Organization* 43 (Winter 1989): 31–71; Michael Brecher, *Decisions in Israel's Foreign Policy* (New Haven: Yale University Press, 1975), 333–334, 514; Khong, *Analogies at War*. For a discussion of possible lessons learned from and during the Cuban Missile Crisis, see James G. Blight, *The Shattered Crystal Ball: Fear and Learning in the Cuban Missile Crisis* (Savage, Md.:

Scholars have focused on how formative events drive policy both through institutional[66] and individual learning.[67]

Additionally, decision makers often draw lessons from only their own experience, ignoring the arguably relevant experience of other states. For example, the Europeans dismissed as irrelevant the battle-field experiences of the American Civil War, though the tactics and technologies used in that war gave an early and revealing glimpse into what was to transpire a half century later in World War I on the European continent.[68] Curiously, lessons about domestic politics seem more likely to be drawn from the experiences of other nations, though the empirical evidence is mixed.[69]

The basic proposition, then, is that a few high-impact events in world

---

Rowman & Littlefield, 1990). For a more sophisticated, comparative assessment of the impacts of formative events versus the cumulation of small events on learning, see Karl W. Deutsch and Richard L. Merritt, "Effects of Events on National and International Images," in *International Behavior: A Social-Psychological Analysis*, ed. Herbert C. Kelman (New York: Holt, Rinehart and Winston, 1965), 132–187.

[66] See, for example, Goldstein, "American Trade Policy"; Goldstein, "Impact of Ideas on Trade Policy"; G. John Ikenberry, "Creating Yesterday's New World Order: Keynesian 'New Thinking' and the Anglo-American Postwar Settlement," in *Ideas and Foreign Policy: Beliefs, Institutions, and Political Change*, ed. Judith Goldstein and Robert O. Keohane (Ithaca: Cornell University Press, 1993); Condoleezza Rice, "The Soviet General Staff: An Institution's Response to Change," in *History, the White House, and the Kremlin*, ed. Fry, 91–105.

[67] See, for example, Khong, *Analogies at War*; and Kuklick, "Tradition and Diplomatic Talent." Examining sixteen international crises, Glenn Snyder and Paul Diesing found that decision makers tend to think in terms of historical analogies when making decisions in crises, though Raymond Cohen, using a completely different set of cases, found that decision makers did not refer to apparently available historical experiences. See *Conflict among Nations: Bargaining, Decision Making, and System Structure in International Crises* (Princeton: Princeton University Press, 1977), esp. 321; and Raymond Cohen, *Threat Perception in International Crisis* (Madison: University of Wisconsin Press, 1979), esp. 82–84.

[68] Jay Luvaas, *The Military Legacy of the Civil War: The European Inheritance* (Lawrence: University Press of Kansas, 1988). For a more optimistic view of the ability of states to draw lessons from the experiences of other states, see Colin J. Bennett, "How States Utilize Foreign Evidence," *Journal of Public Policy* 11 (January–March 1991): 31–54. David Brian Robertson argued that the process of drawing lessons from foreign experiences is often deeply politicized, in "Political Conflict and Lesson-Drawing," *Journal of Public Policy* 11 (January–March 1991): 55–78.

[69] On the spread of regime types and coups d'états, see James M. Lutz, "The Diffusion of Political Phenomena in Sub-Saharan Africa," *Journal of Political and Military Sociology* 17 (Spring 1989): 93–114; Gilbert M. Khadiagala, "Security in Southern Africa: Cross-National Learning," *Jerusalem Journal of International Relations* 14 (September 1992): 82–97; and James Lee Ray, *Democracy and International Conflict* (Columbia: University of South Carolina Press, 1995). On the spread of internal political conflict, see Rodger M. Govea and Gerald T. West, "Riot Contagion in Latin America," *Journal of Conflict Resolution* 25 (June 1981): 349–368; and Stuart Hall and Donald Rothchild, "The Contagion of Political Conflict in Africa and the World," *Journal of Conflict Resolution* 30 (December 1986): 716–735.

politics do form beliefs that, in turn, strongly influence thinking about international relations and foreign policy behavior. This is as opposed to the proposition that beliefs are formed and updated on the basis of all received information, a proposition that is closer to how a rational choice model of decision might view the learning process. Maintaining the a priori assumption that the set of belief-formative events is small precludes a comparative test between the formative events model and a model based on continual belief updating, of course, but this is an acceptable shortcoming, for three reasons. The first is that the continual updating model does not seem to be a realistic portrayal of human decision making. The experimental evidence indicates that largely for reasons of cognitive economy, the human mind operating either alone or within an organizational structure does not tend to perform the kind of information-processing tasks demanded by theories of statistical inference.[70] This behavior is not necessarily irrational, as crises may be the only source of high-quality information and because the costs of continually gathering information may be prohibitive. Also, if one conceives of rational choice as maximizing utility given certain choices and information, then information-gathering strategies ought not be viewed as either rational or nonrational but rather as prerational.

Second, the modeling tasks of testing a continual updating model are almost insuperable. The core of the difficulty is that mathematical relationships between data and likelihoods have to be derived beforehand so that predictions can be offered as to how decision makers are likely to act after receiving all kinds of information. This problem is especially acute in international politics, given the lack of conformity between pieces of information and events. For example, consider a decision maker who wants to know if imposing a selective tariff on motorcycle imports is likely to attract retaliatory tariffs. To use Bayesian analysis, she would have to be able to assign probabilities between events and this hypothesis. The difficulty of such a task is manifest: it is reasonable to assert that if she found out that an automobile tariff imposed five years ago attracted retaliation it would increase her assessment of the probability that the motorcycle tariff would attract retaliation, but by how much? Also, how could she assign prior probabilities to the hypothesis?

[70] For an empirical study which finds that psychological models describe decision making better than does a continual updating model, see Kaufmann, "Out of the Lab." Hopf (*Peripheral Visions*) found that the traditional deterrence model that makes continual assumptions of the updating type does not attract empirical support for Soviet intervention in the Third World.

Third, a model built on the a priori assumption that formative events drive learning can still be rich and offer a number of different learning predictions. The model can test different events as being potentially formative, and it can test for different lessons derived from a particular event. Additionally, any learning propositions can be tested competitively against other international relations theories offering predictions for the dependent variable.

So far, the discussion has focused on the question of when new lessons get drawn. This leaves the important question, What will the contents of these lessons look like? For organizations, the characteristic of an event most relevant to the drawing of new lessons is the degree to which the event was associated with success or failure. As previously discussed, one of the central ideas that has dominated organization theory is that organizations are oriented toward accomplishing certain goals, whether these goals are maximizing profits, winning wars, or passing a specific piece of legislation. Therefore, the lessons an organization is apt to learn from an event will probably be dominated by whether the event was an organizational success (such as record quarterly earnings or military victory) or defeat (net quarterly losses or defeat on the battlefield). Success is likely to stifle innovation and encourage the continuance of policies, whereas failure is likely to encourage innovation. In other words, organizations learn from successes to continue their policies and from failures to adopt new policies.[71]

This cluster of ideas about the learning process discussed so far are summarized in the following set of propositions.

Proposition 1. Beliefs are used in international politics to inform decisions in the face of uncertainty. Beliefs are derived from interpretations of past events (from Chapter 1).
Proposition 2. Learning in the international arena occurs infrequently and is driven by formative events. Events that have great impact, such as great successes or great failures, are more likely to be formative than are events of lesser impact.
Proposition 3. Events experienced directly are more likely to be formative than are events experienced vicariously.
Proposition 4. Successes encourage continuance of policy, and failures encourage innovation.[72]

[71] Sitkin, "Learning through Failure."
[72] A similar hypothesis was presented in Bennett, "Theories of Individual, Organizational, and Governmental Learning." The learning theory presented here is necessarily different from Russell Leng's Experiential Learning Realpolitik (ELR) model, which focuses on lessons drawn about the importance of resolve, an issue that has little application outside of Leng's empirical realm, crisis bargaining. See Leng, "When Will They Ever Learn?" *Journal of Conflict Resolution* 27 (1983): 379–419.

So far, formative events have been treated as given elements: given an experience in a formative event, then it is likely that lessons will be drawn from the event and acted on. I have discussed this question somewhat, for example, that vivid events are especially likely to be formative. This sidesteps the problem a bit, however, as it leaves the question, What events are likely to be vivid? Organization theory and social psychology can be used to provide general theoretical parameters for understanding what events are apt to be formative, but we still lack hypotheses that are specific enough to be falsifiable and testable.

Certainly, it is virtually impossible to construct a single set of falsifiable, testable learning hypotheses that can be applied to all areas of foreign policy. I present what might be considered the next best thing—a set of theoretical parameters that can be used on any given foreign policy area to predict what events are likely to be formative for that area. The determination of exactly which events are formative, though, needs to be conducted within the context of the foreign policy area under consideration. Some might argue that such an approach threatens the veracity of the results, as an important portion of the hypothesis to be tested is extracted from the data. Such observers might contend that a scientist trying to prove a formative events theory for a particular outcome could scan the records of history in search of a formative event and would eventually find some experience predating the outcome to which one could point as formative of beliefs. The ultimate implication is that the results of an empirical test of the formative events theory could be presented which appear to offer empirical support to the formative events proposition, when in fact the relationship is spurious.

Sensitive to this criticism, the empirical portion of this book attempts to provide rigorous, falsifiable tests of the proposition that formative events guide decisions. Quantitative tests are conducted on the sample to assess correlation; I buttress these with case studies to explore issues of causation more deeply. Additionally, the learning hypotheses are tested against an alternative, likely theory: realism. A different concern is the generalizability of the findings beyond the sample under examination here, that is, alliance choices. The generalizability of the findings is limited; although theoretical parameters are established deductively before examination of the data, some inductive measures inevitably must be taken to determine which events ought to have been formative. Such induction facilitates empirical tests but comes at the price of limiting generalizability.

[3]

Realism, Balance of Threat, and Alliances

The first modern realists unabashedly proclaimed the importance of power in world politics and the desire of all states to maximize their power. Most neorealists in recent years have tempered this claim somewhat, arguing that some states seek to maximize security rather than power.[1] For both types of realists, a state's foreign policy centers around its alliance choices: alliances are the primary foreign policy means by which a state can increase both its power and its security. Additionally, on a systemic level, alliances are the very machinery of the balance of power, a central component of realist theory. Accurately predicting alliance formation, therefore, is a crucial test for realism. It is in this area of international politics that I test the predictions of learning theory. This chapter presents the realist argument, discussing first a quasi-realist approach to understanding alliance behavior before laying out neorealism and an alternative, realist explanation of alliance behavior, balance of threat. The last of these is demonstrated to be preferable as an explanation of small power behavior, the empirical focus of this study. Balance of threat is tested against learning theory in the empirical chapters that follow.

SECURITY AS UTILITY FOR WAR

One theory of alliances which is attracting increasing attention seeks to build a model that is amenable to both formal analysis and quantita-

[1] Kenneth Waltz explicitly maintained that states' foreign policy aims can vary widely, in *Theory of International Politics* (New York: Random House, 1979). John J. Mearsheimer, on the other hand, maintains that all states seek power; see "The False Promise of

tive tests. Like realism, this theory sees security as an important component of the utility of states. Unlike realism, this approach defines a state's security as the utility for war it has with other states in the international system, proposing that if a state has a higher utility for war, it is more secure, and if it has a lower utility for war, it is less secure. Utility for war vis-à-vis one particular state is defined as the probability of defeating that state in war times the benefits captured by victory minus the probability of losing in war minus the costs of defeat. The fruits of victory are defined as the difference between the foreign policy preferences between the two states; the costs of defeat have the same absolute value as the fruits of victory, but are negative. Foreign policy differences are operationalized by observing the differences between the alliance portfolios of the two states. A state provides for its security by increasing domestic armament procurements or by forming military alliances. Increasing armaments increases security but decreases material welfare. Forming alliances leaves material welfare unaffected but decreases autonomy and may increase, decrease, or have no net effect on security, since joining an alliance definitely increases the number of friends a state has, but it might also increase the number of its enemies.[2]

By defining a state's security as its utility for war, though, this model seems to have missed the real meaning of security. It is not controversial to argue that a state is more secure if its chances of winning a prospective war are higher. Benefits of victory, however, are calculated by measuring the difference between the foreign policy positions of the two states: if a country is powerful, the greater the fruits of military victory, the higher its security. One counterintuitive implication is that a large state facing a small state gets more benefits from war if the small

International Institutions," *International Security* 19 (Winter 1994/95): 9. Randall Schweller has argued that current international relations theory overstates status quo maintenance as a foreign policy goal of states and that more attention needs to be paid to revisionist states. See Schweller, "Bandwagoning for Profit: Bringing the Revisionist State Back In," *International Security* 19 (Summer 1994): 72–107, and "Neorealism's Status Quo Bias," *Security Studies* 5 (Spring 1996).

[2] Michael T. Altfeld, "The Decision to Ally," *Western Political Quarterly* 37 (December 1984): 523–544. Altfeld's conceptualization of a state's utility calculus is taken from Bruce Bueno de Mesquita, *The War Trap* (New Haven: Yale University Press, 1981). Studies using a similar approach include Bruce D. Berkowitz, "Realignment in International Treaty Organizations," *International Studies Quarterly* 27 (1983): 77–96; Michael T. Altfeld and Won K. Paik, "Realignment in ITOs: A Closer Look," *International Studies Quarterly* 30 (1986): 107–114; Michael F. Altfeld and Bruce Bueno de Mesquita, "Choosing Sides in Wars," *International Studies Ouarterly* 23 (March 1979): 87–112; David Lalman and David Newman, "Alliance Formation and National Security," *International Interactions* 16 (1991): 239–253; and Grace E. Iusi Scarborough and Bruce Bueno de Mesquita, "Threat and Alignment Behavior," *International Interactions* 14 (1988): 85–93.

state is an enemy than if it is a friend, so the large state has a higher utility for war and is more secure if the small state is hostile than if it is friendly. There would seem to be a mismatch, then, between the basic idea of what constitutes security and this particular operationalization.

An additional problem is the model's use of alliance portfolios to measure foreign policy preferences. Such a measure makes no provision for the inclusion of territorial or other disputes as sources of enmity between states. One unfortunate effect of this reliance on alliance portfolios is that the model cannot efficiently distinguish between the relationship between two states that are relatively indifferent toward each other and those that are actively hostile. Additionally, the use of alliances as both dependent and independent variable further diminishes the precision of the measure. One hypothesis from the model is that as an alliance bears a higher cost in autonomy, the odds increase that the alliance will break up. The cost in autonomy of the alliance, however, is measured by a state's alliance portfolio, which is meant to reflect policies on a number of issues. Therefore, the measurement of the independent variable would not pick up a widening in the gap between foreign policy preferences until after the alliance was broken. This would incur one of two modeling problems: if the independent variable was measured before the dependent variable, the change in autonomy predicted to precede an alliance breakup could not be observed; alternatively, if the independent and dependent variables are measured at the same time, then the hypothesis would be very difficult to falsify, for when the dependent variable coded an alliance breaking up, the independent variable would necessarily measure a widening of foreign policy preferences between the two states, which is predicted to cause an alliance to break apart. In summary, the methodological problems of this model cast serious doubts on its ability to generate falsifiable, testable predictions of alliance behavior.

Though parts of this model—particularly its conceptualization of security—suffer from serious problems, some of its theoretical insights are interesting. A few more-recent works have kept the model's ideas about how arms and alliance affect the utility components of security, foreign policy autonomy, and welfare but have looked for sounder empirical tests. Thus far, however, empirical tests have used the looser case study format or have tested indirect implications of the model rather than testing the model's ability to predict alliance formation, producing only mixed empirical results.[3]

---

[3] For more recent theoretical work on this model, see James D. Morrow, "Alliances and Asymmetry: An Alternative to the Capability Aggregation Model of Alliances," *American Journal of Political Science* 35 (November 1991): 904–933; and Michael D. McGinnis, "A

NEOREALISM AND BALANCE OF THREAT

The conceptual sparseness of realism offers a good deal of room for interpretation by its scholarly adherents. Two strands of realism offering explanations of alliance preferences, neorealism and balance of threat, are outlined and assessed here.[4] Neorealism holds that the structure of the international order determines the behavior of states. Neorealism's primary modern proponent, Kenneth Waltz, proposed three key characteristics of system structure: the principle by which it is ordered (whether its power relations are hierarchically determined or if anarchy reigns), the specification of the functions of differentiated units, and the distribution of capabilities across units. He argued that the international system has been anarchic for the past several centuries and that all states have the same specified functions, so that variance in the distribution of power determines the character—in particular, the stability—of the international order.[5]

A shortcoming of neorealism is that it has little to say about the behavior of nations other than great powers. This is not surprising, given that if one accepts the neorealist argument that international

---

Rational Model of Regional Rivalry," *International Studies Quarterly* 34 (1990): 111–135. A set of case studies finding empirical support for the model is James D. Morrow, "Arms versus Allies: Trade-Offs in the Search for Security," *International Organization* 47 (Spring 1993): 207–233. Morrow, "Alliances and Asymmetry," and Gerald Sorokin, "Arms, Alliances, and Security Tradeoffs in Enduring Rivalries," *International Studies Quarterly* 38 (September 1994): 421–446, found quantitative empirical support for some implications of the model, though quantitative studies with more doubtful empirical results include B. A. Most and Randolph M. Siverson, "Substituting Arms and Alliances, 1870–1914: An Exploration in Comparative Foreign Policy," *New Directions in the Study of Foreign Policy*, ed. Charles F. Hermann, Charles W. Kegley Jr., and James N. Rosenau (Boston: Unwin Hyman, 1987); Paul Diehl, "Substitutes or Complements? The Effects of Alliances on Military Spending in Major Power Rivalries," *International Interactions* 19 (1994): 159–176; and John A. C. Conybeare, "Arms versus Alliances: The Capital Structure of Military Enterprise," *Journal of Conflict Resolution* 38 (June 1994): 215–235. I discuss this model within the context of this book's empirical findings in later chapters.

[4] To be sure, realism is not the only theory of international relations to offer explanations as to why states seek alliances, but realism represents the mainstream of international relations thought and therefore receives attention here as the primary alternative explanation to learning. For a list of several dozen alliance propositions found in the international relations literature, see Ole Holsti, P. Terrence Hopmann, and John D. Sullivan, *Unity and Disintegration in International Alliances* (New York: Wiley, 1973). One conventional proposition is that states with common political systems or ideologies tend to ally. For a limited, empirical test of this hypothesis, see Randolph M. Siverson and Juliann Emmons, "Birds of a Feather: Democratic Political Systems and Alliance Choices in the Twentieth Century," *Journal of Conflict Resolution* 35 (June 1991): 285–306. For an interesting critique of this argument, see Stephen M. Walt, *The Origins of Alliances* (Ithaca: Cornell University Press, 1987).

[5] Waltz, *Theory of International Politics*.

system structure is the key intervening variable determining important outcomes in international politics and that what is important about international system structure is the number of great powers, one can conclude with little difficulty that small powers can be safely left out of a theory of international politics. Waltz is quite blunt about his assessment of the irrelevance of small powers to international politics and international relations theory:

> The theory, like the story, of international politics is written in terms of the great powers of an era. . . . In international politics, as in any self-help system, the units of greatest capability set the scene of action for others as well as for themselves. In systems theory, structure is a generative notion; and the structure of a system is generated by the interactions of its principal parts. Theories that apply to self-help systems are written in terms of the systems' principal parts. It would be as ridiculous to construct a theory of international politics based on Malaysia and Costa Rica as it would be to construct an economic theory based on the minor firms in a sector of an economy. . . . A general theory of international politics is necessarily based on the great powers.[6]

The proposition that Waltz's realism permits the prediction of opposite alliance behaviors for great powers, chain-ganging and buck-passing, can be applied to the choice between neutrality and alliance which small powers face. Thomas Christensen and Jack Snyder argued that when the global power structure is multipolar, states chain-gang if they perceive the offense to be dominant on the battlefield and buck-pass if they perceive the defense to be dominant. Unfortunately, this important theoretical insight offers just limited purchase for making predictions. Their analysis applies only to environments of structural multipolarity, not bipolarity. They contend that superpower intervention in the periphery should be limited under conditions of bipolarity, but they do not predict the conditions under which states (particularly small powers) are more likely to prefer alliance with great powers. Further, methods of using and measuring "perceptions of offense-dominance" are still developing; Jack Levy has argued that periods of history are rarely clearly offense- or defense-dominant, and Jonathan Shimshoni has suggested reevaluation of the whole concept, given that offense- or defense-dominance is usually determined by military entrepreneurs, not the state of military technology.[7]

[6] Ibid., 72–73.
[7] Thomas J. Christensen and Jack Snyder, "Chain Gangs and Passed Bucks: Predicting Alliance Patterns in Multipolarity," *International Organization* 44 (Spring 1990): 137–168. David Lalman and David Newman argued that as international power becomes more

A realist explanation of alliance formation which refines Waltz's argument is balance of threat theory, presented by Stephen Walt. He asked whether states would, when faced with a threat, ally against the source of threat (balance) or with the source of threat (bandwagon), outlining a number of hypotheses predicting when states would be more likely to balance and when they would be more likely to band-wagon.[8] Walt's theory is a narrower version of the classic balance of power theory, which proposes that states join together to balance against political power to prevent domination of the international system by one state. Walt's less parsimonious version is that states balance against threat, though power is an important component of threat.[9] In studies of the Middle East and Southwest Asia, Walt found balancing to be more prevalent than bandwagoning. Another scholar, using Walt's theoretical framework, found balancing to dominate band-wagoning in the 1990–1991 Gulf crisis.[10] More sophisticated tests exam-

---

concentrated, the opportunities for alliance decrease, so the frequency of alliance ought to decrease, as well. Their findings are discussed in Chapter 5. Lalman and Newman, "Alliance Formation and National Security." For analyses of the offense/defense balance variable, see Jack S. Levy, "The Offensive/Defensive Balance of Military Technology: A Theoretical and Historical Analysis," *International Studies Quarterly* 28 (June 1984): 219–238; and Jonathan Shimshoni, "Technology, Military Advantage, and World War I," *International Security* 15 (Winter 1990/91): 187–215.

[8] Walt, *Origins of Alliances*. See also Stephen M. Walt, "Alliance Formation and the Balance of World Power," *International Security* 9 (Spring 1985): 3–41, and Walt, "Alliances in Theory and Practice: What Lies Ahead?" *Journal of International Affairs* 43 (Summer/Fall 1989). For a review of Walt's theory, see Glenn H. Snyder, "Alliances, Balance, and Stability," *International Organization* 45 (Winter 1991): 121–142. A different balance of threat theory, in which state leaders ally to balance against internal, domestic, and external threats was presented by Steven R. David, "Explaining Third World Alignment," *World Politics* 43 (January 1991): 233–256. See also Steven R. David, *Choosing Sides: Alignment and Realignment in the Third World* (Baltimore: Johns Hopkins University Press, 1991). For a related model, see Michael N. Barnett and Jack S. Levy, "Domestic Sources of Alliances and Alignments: The Case of Egypt, 1962–73," *International Organization* 45 (Summer 1991): 369–395, and Barnett and Levy, "Alliance Formation, Domestic Political Economy, and Third World Security," *Jerusalem Journal of International Relations* 14 (December 1992): 19–40; and Michael N. Barnett, *Confronting the Costs of War: Military Power, State, and Society in Egypt and Israel* (Princeton: Princeton University Press, 1992). A general theory of state behavior based on balancing internal and external threats has not yet emerged, though; these three scholars concede that their propositions are specific to Third World nations (Barnett and Levy, "Domestic Sources of Alliances and Alignments," 373; David, "Explaining Third World Alignment," 233).

[9] For classic discussions of the balance of power in history and theory, see Edward Vose Gulick, *Europe's Classical Balance of Power* (New York: W. W. Norton, 1967); Hans J. Morgenthau, *Politics among Nations* (New York: Alfred A. Knopf, 1949); and Herbert Butterfield and Martin Wight, eds., *Diplomatic Investigations* (Cambridge: Harvard University Press, 1966). Curiously, though, Walt maintains (*Origins of Alliances*, 263–265) that balance of threat theory is equally parsimonious as balance of power theory.

[10] Walt, *Origins of Alliances*; Stephen M. Walt, "Testing Theories of Alliance Formation: The Case of Southwest Asia," *International Organization* 42 (Spring 1988): 275–316; David

ining balance of threat as well as other theories of alliance behavior found only limited support for balance of threat predictions in the Gulf crisis and no support for these predictions in U.S.-European decisions about cooperation in the Persian Gulf in the early 1980s.[11] Some have noted that balance of threat does not explain the stability of NATO across the cold war, as the level of international threat has fluctuated.[12] Other scholars have argued that Walt has underestimated the prevalence of bandwagoning.[13]

Notice, though, that in addition to examining the origins of balancing and bandwagoning, Walt is also providing an answer to the question of why states seek to join alliances at all: they do so as an answer to a perceived threat, since as threat increases, the probability of alliance (whether it be with or against the source of the threat) increases, and as threat decreases, the probability of creating new alliances decreases and the probability of existing alliances breaking apart increases. In Walt's own words, "The greater the threat, the greater the probability that the vulnerable state will seek an alliance."[14] Walt, then, does not see the choice between chain-ganging and buck-passing as indeterminate in realist theory, for he argues that chain-ganging behavior dominates buck-passing behavior. In contrast to neorealism, balance of threat theory applies to the behavior of all states, because the basic logic applies regardless of a state's size or relative rank in the international system; Walt's empirical work includes analysis of small powers in the Middle East and Southwest Asia. Trygve Mathisen, a scholar of small power behavior, also applied balance of threat logic to nongreat pow-

---

Garnham, "Explaining Middle Eastern Alignments during the Gulf War," *Jerusalem Journal of International Relations* 13 (1991): 63–83. Walt also argued that balancing behavior dominated bandwagoning behavior in Europe in the thirties; see "Alliance, Threats, and U.S. Grand Strategy: A Reply to Kaufman and Labs," *Security Studies* 1 (Spring 1992): 448–482. One study purports to find evidence that balancing is just as frequent as bandwagoning, but it omits intentions, making it a test of balance of power rather than balance of threat. Further, its empirical results indicate that the *absence* of either balancing or bandwagoning is a far more prevalent outcome. Thomas R. Cusack and Richard J. Stoll, "Balancing Behavior in the Interstate System, 1816–1976," *International Interactions* 16 (1991): 255–270.

[11] Andrew Bennett, Joseph Lepgold, and Danny Unger, "Burden-Sharing in the Persian Gulf War," *International Organization* 48 (Winter 1994): 39–75; Charles A. Kupchan, "NATO and the Persian Gulf: Examining Intra-Alliance Behavior," *International Organization* 42 (Spring 1988): 317–346.

[12] John S. Duffield, "International Regimes and Alliance Behavior: Explaining NATO Conventional Force Levels, *International Organization* 46 (Autumn 1992): 819–855.

[13] Schweller, "Bandwagoning for Profit"; Paul Schroeder, "Historical Reality vs. Neorealist Theory," *International Security* 19 (Summer 1994): 108–148; Robert Kaufman, " 'To Balance or to Bandwagon?' Alignment Decisions in 1930s Europe," *Security Studies* 1 (Spring 1992): 417–447.

[14] Walt, *Origins of Alliances*, 26.

ers: "The main reason why a small power freely joins a military alliance is that it considers its security to be in danger and hopes that it can be better safeguarded in this way."[15]

Walt conceptualizes threat as the danger of future war posed by one state to another. A state looks at two characteristics of a potential threatener to understand the extent of the threat: the threatener's intentions, which are how the foreign policy goals of the threatening state would be advanced by successfully prosecuting war against the threatened state, and the threatener's war-waging capabilities, which describe the threatening state's confidence that it could win a war. Neither aggressive intentions nor material capabilities alone, however, are sufficient to constitute threat, as both the willingness and the ability to go to war must be present for threat to be credible. A composite measure of threat can account for this condition of necessity by multiplying intentions and capabilities. In this way, for example, a very powerful but friendly country would pose no threat (as a large capability index times an aggressive intentions index of zero equals a composite threat of zero), and a fiercely aggressive but small country poses little threat (a high aggressive intentions index times a low capabilities index equals a low composite threat).[16]

Though Walt does not present a specific coding system for calculating threat, he describes threat as being composed of aggressive intentions and three subcomponents of capability: geographic proximity, aggregate power, and offensive power. Aggressive intentions are just that: the appearance that the threatener is considering military action against the threatened to advance its foreign policy aims. Walt's analysis of capability is aimed at assessing what determines the probability

[15] Trygve Mathisen, *The Functions of Small States in the Strategies of the Great Powers* (Oslo: Scandinavian University Books, 1971), 257. Jack Levy argued that the balance of power applies only to great powers, but he was referring to the *implementation* of a balance of power collective security structure, rather than balance of power as an *explanation* of small power behavior. See Levy, *War in the Modern Great Power System, 1495–1975* (Lexington: University Press of Kentucky, 1983), 3, 176 n. Other analyses of small powers and the balance of power have tended to focus on whether small powers are safer as neutrals when there is balance or imbalance of power among great powers. See, for example, Efraim Karsh, *Neutrality and Small States* (London: Routledge, 1988); Hans Morgenthau, "The Resurrection of Neutrality in Europe," *American Political Science Review* 33, no. 3 (June 1939): 482–483; Bruce Hopper, "Sweden: A Case Study in Neutrality," *Foreign Affairs* 23, no. 3 (April 1945): 435–449.

[16] J. David Singer conceptualized threat in the same way: "To state the relationship in quasi-mathematical form: Threat-Perception = Estimated Capability × Estimated Intent," in "Threat-Perception and the Armament Tension Dilemma," *Journal of Conflict Resolution* 2 (1958): 93–94. One scholar has argued that belligerent acts can be more threatening in a context of low defense spending then a context of high defense spending. as such acts may be interpreted as indicating more belligerent intentions. Ido Oren, "The Indo-Pakistani Arms Competition," *Journal of Conflict Resolution* 38 (June 1994): 185–214.

that the threatening state will defeat the threatened state on the battle-field.[17] His distinction between aggregate power and military forces is a necessary one, as other scholarship has distinguished between the two as determinants of war outcomes. Some scholars have found that aggregate power does determine war outcomes, if one accounts for differences in states' capacities for extraction of resources from socie-ties.[18] From a different angle, others have found that standing military forces have a powerful effect on the likelihood of deterrence success, though aggregate power does not. This is consistent with the finding that deterrence is most likely to break down when an attacker feels it can win a swift war of maneuver, in which standing military forces are likely to be more important than is industrial capacity. This is relevant to the discussion here, because the probability of deterrence success is hypothesized to be related to the estimation of the likelihood of mili-tary victory, a central component of threat.[19]

Although Walt treats all threats as comparable, understanding how nations reply to threats requires the division of threat into two groups, which I label as direct threats and systemic threats. The difference between the two is the nature of the threatening state's ambitions. If the threatening state is making a specific demand of a state with the im-plicit or explicit promise of military action if the demand is not met, this is a direct threat. An example is Britain's demand in 1982 for Argentina to vacate the newly captured Falkland Islands—the British made a specific demand of Argentina with the promise of military action if Argentina did not comply. Of course, either a great or a small power can pose or be the target of a direct threat.

Systemic threat describes a situation in which a local power appears to be posing a general threat to the nations of the region, such that it seems to have broad ambitions for greater political power and/or territory.[20] The nations in the region feel a threat to their national

[17] Walt, *Origins of Alliances*, 22–28.

[18] A. F. K. Organski and Jacek Kugler, *The War Ledger* (Chicago: University of Chicago Press, 1980); Jacek Kugler and William Domke, "Comparing the Strength of Nations," *Comparative Political Studies* 19 (April 1986): 39–69. For a more sophisticated model, see Allan C. Stam, *Win, Lose, or Draw: Domestic Politics and the Crucible of War* (Ann Arbor: University of Michigan Press, 1996).

[19] Paul K. Huth, *Extended Deterrence and the Prevention of War* (New Haven: Yale Univer-sity Press, 1988); Paul Huth and Bruce Russett, "General Deterrence between Enduring Rivals: Testing Three Competing Models," *American Political Science Review* 87 (March 1993): 61–73; John J. Mearsheimer, *Conventional Deterrence* (Ithaca: Cornell University Press, 1983).

[20] This is different from Klaus Knorr's conceptualization of systemic threat, which "means that, over the longer run, no state-actor can ever be certain of its security [as other states' intentions and capabilities can change abruptly]." Knorr, "Threat Perception," in

security which is very real though not as specific as a direct threat in that the threatening nation does not make a particular demand. Such a threat concerns all powers in the region—even those with no direct disputes with the threatening power—because they may be drawn into a future, systemwide war. As Robert Gilpin noted in his study of such wars: "The conflict becomes total and in time is characterized by participation of all the major states and most of the minor states in the system. The tendency, in fact, is for every state in the system to be drawn into one or another of the opposing camps."[21] In its struggle with other great powers, a revisionist power may invade a neutral power to take advantage of the neutral's geographical location. World War II is a good example of how a war can expand to a number of countries that did not have specific political or territorial disputes with the belligerents.

Distinguishing between systemic and direct threat is important, for the type of threat a nation faces determines what policy responses are appropriate. If a small power faces a systemic threat, both balancing and bandwagoning are potential responses. Balancing is motivated by the desire both to increase the chances of deterring military action by the systemic threat and to increase the chances of successfully defending against military action if it should come. Bandwagoning can emerge from a defensive motivation, as a country may join the threatening state to avoid being invaded by it, or because of offensive motivation, as it may join the threatening state to share the spoils of conquest.[22]

One option for a state facing systemic threat which Walt appears to exclude is neutrality. He defines bandwagoning broadly, so that true neutrality is not an option for a threatened state. If, when faced with a threat, a state signs no formal alliance against the source of threat, then Walt considers this to be accommodation and therefore bandwagoning with the source of threat. For example, Walt deems Belgium's formal declaration of neutrality in the late 1930s as bandwagoning with Germany, although Belgium signed no alliance or nonaggression pact with Germany, nor did it attempt to appease Germany by making territorial or other concessions.[23] This conflation of three categories—

Historical Dimensions of National Security Problems, ed. Knorr (Lawrence: University Press of Kansas, 1976), 79.

[21] Robert Gilpin, *War and Change in World Politics* (Cambridge: Cambridge University Press, 1981), 199.

[22] Walt, *Origins of Alliances*, 21; Schweller, "Bandwagoning for Profit."

[23] Walt, *Origins of Alliances*, 31 n. On Belgium's exit from alliance with France and declaration of neutrality in the late thirties, see David Owen Kieft, *Belgium's Return to*

bandwagoning, balancing, and neutrality—into two—bandwagoning and balancing—is unjustified. Genuinely different consequences exist for a state that opts for formal neutrality as opposed to for one that bandwagons.[24] The international arena is not as zero-sum as Walt would imply; not every state need be classified as on one side or the other. Some states may accept buck-passing logic and attempt to avoid becoming embroiled in future military conflict by not taking sides. As Robert Osgood put it, "Every state must have an alliance policy, even if its purpose is only to avoid alliances."[25] One important difference is that the presence of a formal alliance is a very good indicator of the likelihood that one state will agree to defend another state if it is attacked. At the moment of truth in a military crisis, a formal alliance substantially increases the odds that an otherwise disinterested state will become involved because of the implications that breaking an alliance would have for that state's international reputation. The proposition that a tighter alliance bond between states increases the chances that the signatories will go to war to defend their alliance partners has been demonstrated by both quantitative, empirical research and formal, theoretical models.[26]

Additionally, if neutrality can be defined as alliance, then balance of threat has successfully made its principal claim—that the probability of alliance is positively correlated with the perceived level of threat—largely unfalsifiable. In a threatening environment, every state, even those that have formally declared neutrality, can be coded as having allied; it would be logically impossible to find evidence of a state not

Neutrality (Oxford: Clarendon, 1972); and Jane K. Miller, *Belgian Foreign Policy between Two Wars, 1919–1940* (New York: Bookman Associates, 1951).

[24] Other scholars have also made the point that states have real options besides balancing and bandwagoning. See Eric J. Labs, "Do Weak States Bandwagon?" *Security Studies* 1 (Spring 1992): 383–416; and Kaufman, "'To Balance or to Bandwagon?'" 417–447.

[25] Robert E. Osgood, *Alliances and American Foreign Policy* (Baltimore: Johns Hopkins University Press, 1968), 17.

[26] Empirical studies include J. David Singer and Melvin Small, "Formal Alliances, 1815–1939," *Journal of Peace Research* 3 (1966): 1–32; Paul Huth and Bruce Russett, "Deterrence Failure and Crisis Escalation," *International Studies Quarterly* 32 (1988): 29–45; and Randolph M. Siverson and Harvey Starr, *The Diffusion of War* (Ann Arbor: University of Michigan Press, 1991). For a view skeptical of the proposition that alliance commitments are honored, see Alan Ned Sabrosky, "Interstate Alliances: Their Reliability and the Expansion of War," in *The Correlates of War*, vol. 2, ed. J. David Singer (New York: Free Press, 1980), 161–198. One study found that countries are more likely to honor alliances with minor powers, the empirical focus of this study, than great powers. Randolph M. Siverson and Joel King, "Attributes of National Alliance Membership and War Participation, 1815–1965," *American Journal of Political Science* 24 (February 1980): 1–15. For a formal proof of the proposition that alliance commitments are likely to be honored, see James D. Morrow, "Alliances, Credibility, and Peacetime Costs," *Journal of Conflict Resolution* 38 (June 1994): 270–297. See also Osgood, ibid., 19–20.

allying in the face of threat, making the threat-alliance proposition unfalsifiable. To avoid this problem, it is necessary for a theory of alliance formation to include the possibility that no alliance is formed, that a state can genuinely opt for neutrality. A falsifiable theory would allow for a state facing systemic threat to remain neutral or ally, and if it allies, it could either balance or bandwagon.

A state facing a direct threat has options different from one facing a systemic threat. Allying with other states to balance against the direct threat is clearly an option for the threatened state. Similar to balancing against systemic threat, it offers the advantages of increasing the chances of deterrence and successful defense against attack. However, the other two responses to systemic threat, neutrality and bandwagoning, are not appropriate as responses to direct threat. As a response to systemic threat, neutrality's selling point is that by not taking sides, the neutral state might be able to avoid participation in a future war. In other words, neutrality minimizes the chances of entrapment (whereas alliance minimizes the chances of abandonment).[27] The key assumption of a policy of neutrality is that the threatening state has no direct interest in conquering the neutral state, that it might prefer to bypass the neutral to go after bigger game. In the case of a direct threat, however, this reasoning does not apply, as the threatened state is the target of a direct and specific demand. Staying out of alliances does not by itself remove the threatening state's motivation for attack; if the threat was credible to begin with, the threatening state will execute its promise of military action if the specific demand is not met.

Bandwagoning is also an inappropriate category as a response to a direct threat. When faced with a direct threat, a state certainly might adopt a policy of accommodation and give in to the demands of the threatener, as France did to Britain during the Fashoda Crisis. But accommodation is bandwagoning only if the action taken by the threatened state is to ally with the threatener; if the accommodating action takes another form, such as the exchange of territory, then it is not bandwagoning. This distinction is important, because direct threats usually occur over issues such as territory or political sovereignty, not demands to sign a defense alliance. Walt is quite specific on this point:

> Backing down in a confrontation is not the same as bandwagoning; states often make concessions to adversaries while continuing to balance against them. The Soviet Union backed down in the Cuban Missile Crisis and the

[27] See Michael Mandelbaum, *The Nuclear Revolution: International Politics before and after Hiroshima* (Cambridge: Cambridge University Press, 1981), 151–152; and Glenn H. Snyder, "The Dilemma in Alliance Politics," *World Politics* 36 (July 1984): 461–495.

United States made a series of concessions to Iran to obtain the release of U.S. hostages, but neither case qualifies as bandwagoning. Properly understood, bandwagoning means aligning with the strongest or most threatening state, thereby rendering it more powerful but also more benign (or so the bandwagoning state hopes). Broadening the definition in this way [by including all accommodation] is confusing and should be avoided.[28]

Neither bandwagoning nor neutrality, therefore, is an appropriate response to direct threat; appropriate responses include balancing and making concessions.

If bandwagoning is not an appropriate response, this poses a potential problem for some of Walt's empirical results. The data in his *Origins of Alliances* orient mostly on direct threats, such as the direct Israeli threat to Egypt, but his dependent variable is whether the threatened state balances or bandwagons. Therefore, Walt's finding that nearly all Middle Eastern alliances from 1955 to 1979 are examples of balancing rather than bandwagoning may have been determined by the inapplicability of the bandwagoning option for most of the states in his data set, not by the empirical validity of the proposition that when states can either balance or bandwagon, they are apt to balance.

I frame the alliance choice as between neutrality and alliance, rather than between neutrality, balancing, and bandwagoning. One possible criticism of this dichotomy of alliance and neutrality is that bandwagoning and balancing do not belong in a single category and that the superior taxonomy to both Walt's and the above dichotomies is a trichotomy of balancing, bandwagoning, and neutrality. While important theoretical and practical differences exist between bandwagoning and balancing, the difference between neutrality and all alliances is more important. It is not always a black-and-white question for a small power as to which great power is the threatening one and which is the defender of the status quo. In 1940, for example, Norway had to face the possibility of military action by either Britain or Nazi Germany; if Norway had allied with either one, it could have been coded after the fact as balancing, bandwagoning, or even both. Additionally, balancing and bandwagoning cannot be cleanly separated on the basis of foreign policy goals; states may bandwagon because they seek to protect national security or because they wish to share the spoils of victory—hence the distinction drawn between offensive and defensive bandwagoning.[29]

---

[28] Walt, "Alliances, Threats, and U.S. Grand Strategy," 471.
[29] Walt, *Origins of Alliances*, 19–21; and Garnham, "Explaining Middle Eastern Alignments," 64–65.

Traditional realism cannot predict when a state is more likely to follow buck-passing logic and remain neutral and when it is more likely to follow chain-ganging logic and ally. Learning theory is one answer to the question of how states make this choice, stating that formative experiences determine whether a state will ally or remain neutral. One realist theory that does offer falsifiable, testable propositions, though, is balance of threat theory. To offer a comparative test, I will examine the predictions of learning theory and balance of threat theory. The general balance of threat proposition I study in this book is:

Proposition 5. The greater the level of perceived international threat, the greater the likelihood that a state will seek an international alliance.

[4]

Cases, Hypotheses, and Variables

The empirical strategy of this book is to use both quantitative and case study methods to test two competing theories, learning and realism. This chapter spells out the specific hypotheses to be tested and covers nuts-and-bolts issues related to case selection and measurement of the variables. Some readers may find the discussion a bit extensive, but when outlining empirical method, I believe virtue lies in transparency. This is especially true for quantitative tests, as inadequate explanations of specifics can obscure important assumptions and preclude replication.

At the outset, a few words are in order about my choice of empirical strategy. One of the most divisive conflicts in political science and especially in international relations is methodological: some scholars view large sample tests using quantitative methods as the only worthwhile mode of empirical analysis, whereas others see case study analysis of one or a few cases as the best method. My view is that both methods are useful, each accomplishing some tasks that the other cannot. The depth and texture of case studies permit analysis of causation and exploration for new ideas which is difficult to accomplish using quantitative studies. Large n quantitative studies, on the other hand, permit the simultaneous and mathematical application of several hypotheses to a set of empirical phenomena, and the use of large samples substantially improves the generalizability of empirical results.[1]

So far, the literature on learning in international relations has mostly used case study methods. Some studies (including a number of histori-

---

[1] Christopher H. Achen and Duncan Snidal, "Rational Deterrence Theory and Comparative Case Studies," *World Politics* 41 (January 1989): 143–169.

cal works) have proceeded inductively, examining the historical record and then pointing to examples of learning as they are uncovered.[2] Others have built a theoretical structure for understanding learning before examining a few cases. In this latter category, however, the case study technique is often applied in a rather rough-and-ready, somewhat inductive manner, because theory is laid out as a set of general parameters without specific, falsifiable predictions.[3] The limitation of this approach is that its generality threatens the falsifiability of the test: slack in the theory might permit the researcher too much leeway in finding the evidence necessary to support the theory.

Probably the best and most rigorous test of a learning theory using case study methods is Yuen Foong Khong's *Analogies at War*.[4] He first carefully develops a learning model based on the individual use of analogies, drawing heavily (and deductively) on the theoretical and experimental literature in psychology. He devotes the rest of his book to testing the theory on the American decisions to escalate the Vietnam War, made in February and June of 1965. His tests are impressive because he compares the fit of his own analogies model to alternative explanations (such as realism) and because he makes extensive use of interviews and archival materials to provide an extremely deep and textured account of both decisions. Khong convincingly proves the importance of analogies in both decisions, showing that his analogies model is superior to alternative explanations at predicting the American policy choices. But Khong analyzes only two decisions, which severely limits the generalizability of his findings. At the end of the book, the reader is persuaded of the importance of analogies in guiding the American escalation of the Vietnam War, but given only two cases, which use the same decision makers in the same country in the same war in the same year, this reader is likely to be skeptical that a strong case has been made for the importance of analogies for military escalation in general, much less in international relations.

On the other side of the methodological spectrum are studies that analyze learning by using quantitative methods. To my knowledge, at this writing only three studies of learning use quantitative methods: a study of crisis bargaining by Russell Leng, a small portion of Paul Huth's study of extended immediate deterrence, and one part of

[2] See, for example, Ernest May, *"Lessons" of the Past: The Use and Misuse of History in American Foreign Policy* (London: Oxford University Press, 1973); and Abraham F. Lowenthal, *The Dominican Intervention* (Cambridge: Harvard University Press, 1972).

[3] See, for example, Glenn Snyder and Paul Diesing, *Conflict among Nations: Bargaining, Decision Making, and System Structure in International Crises* (Princeton: Princeton University Press, 1977).

[4] Yuen Foong Khong, *Analogies at War* (Princeton: Princeton University Press, 1992).

Edward Rhodes's critique of the bureaucratic politics model as applied to procurement decisions of the American navy.[5] I will use Leng's work as a foil for a methodological discussion because learning is his primary focus. After a fairly brief theoretical discussion, Leng proposes essentially that a state will learn realpolitik lessons from crisis experiences, so that from a diplomatic defeat at the hands of a particular adversary, it will learn that a more belligerent strategy is warranted in the next confrontation with that adversary. He applied his propositions to six pairs of states, each of which interacted three times, meaning that each state has two opportunities to apply a lesson, thus yielding a total data set of twenty-four decisions. Leng's method offers some advantages over Khong's method. Both Leng and Khong present at the broadest level some very general theoretical ideas about learning, though Khong's discussion is much more extensive. Leng, however, proposes some prior, deductive hypotheses that are general enough to apply to an entire class of cases (learning about crisis bargaining strategies) but narrow enough such that they are falsifiable and can be tested. Khong's construction of hypotheses is more inductive: from his deduced theoretical parameters he builds hypotheses specific to the two cases he is examining. He effectively protects the falsifiability of his test by presenting alternative hypotheses to learning and by discussing what kinds of evidence would constitute support for the various hypotheses. But his hypotheses are very context-specific, and he does not formally present hypotheses that could be applied to other escalation decisions. Since Leng's hypotheses are broad enough to apply to an entire class of foreign policy decisions, it is possible to test them on a larger sample, which improves our confidence in the generalizability of his findings.

A shortcoming in Leng's empirical approach (due perhaps to space limitations of an article-length manuscript) is the absence of discussion of any cases. He presents some quantitative evidence that offers correlative support for a number of his propositions, but he offers no

[5] Russell Leng, "When Will They Ever Learn?" *Journal of Conflict Resolution* 27 (September 1983): 379–419; Paul K. Huth, *Extended Deterrence and the Prevention of War* (New Haven: Yale University Press, 1988); and Edward Rhodes, "Do Bureaucratic Politics Matter? Some Disconfirming Findings from the Case of the U.S. Navy," *World Politics* 47 (October 1994): 1–41. Khong (ibid., 50) characterizes the works of Jervis, May, and Snyder and Diesing as large n studies. However, Jervis uses anecdotes in an unsystematic manner for illustration only. May tests only four cases (U.S. policy in World War II, the Korean War, the cold war, and the Vietnam War). Snyder and Diesing look at sixteen cases but analyze learning in a rather loose, inductive fashion rather than by first presenting falsifiable hypotheses and coding rules and then testing the data. Robert Jervis, *Perception and Misperception in International Politics* (Princeton: Princeton University Press, 1976); May, *"Lessons" of the Past*; Snyder and Diesing, *Conflict among Nations*.

historical discussion of any of the cases themselves. The concern is that foreign policy behavior that is consistent with the learning predictions may be due to factors other than the application of lessons from previous crises. A few quotes from political leaders about how some past crises cast a shadow over current deliberations would at least begin the argument that learning is a good explanation of what is going on. Further, the learning hypotheses are not tested against any alternative explanations of crisis-bargaining behavior.

In the empirical approach taken here, I try to use the best parts of Khong's and Leng's approaches. The general empirical goals are to provide empirical results that have high amounts of both external and internal validity, to improve confidence that the postulated theoretical explanation is the true cause of the observed behavior and that the results can be generalized outside of the data set analyzed here. Like in Khong's work, a theory of learning is built on ideas and empirical evidence from decision sciences before data are examined. Also like Khong, I test the predictions of the learning theory against an alternative explanation, realism. Like Leng, I analyze a large number of cases in a quantitative fashion to assess support for the hypotheses; here, however, these quantitative tests are buttressed with a few case studies to explore more directly the posited causal relationships among the variables.

ALLIANCES

An alliance is a formal and mutual commitment to contribute military assistance in the event one of the alliance partners is attacked.[6] And, here, I focus on alliances to the exclusion of lesser forms of political alignment, such as nonaggression pacts or military consultation arrangements. A formal alliance as expressed in a treaty is qualitatively distinct from a general congruence of interests, as the formality of a treaty creates tight bonds between the signatories. Hans Morgenthau has remarked, "When the common interests are inchoate in terms of policy and action, a treaty of alliance is required to make them explicit and operative." Further, a commitment formalized in a

---

[6] This is similar to Arnold Wolfers's definition of an alliance as "a promise of mutual military assistance between two or more sovereign states." Wolfers, "Alliances," in *International Encylopedia of the Social Sciences*, ed. David L. Sills (New York: Macmillan, 1968), 268. See also Glenn H. Snyder, "Alliances, Balance, and Stability," *International Organization* 45 (Winter 1991): 123.

treaty is more likely to be honored, because failure to do so would jeopardize the state's future reputation as an ally; other forms of alignment, such as nonaggression pacts or consultation agreements, do not carry the same reputational stakes as does a mutual defense treaty.[7]

Learning theory suggests that individuals tend to draw simple, broad lessons to facilitate their application to future decisions. This theoretical insight encourages the construction of simple modeling parameters by laying out a small set of possible lessons that a decision maker could learn from an experience. The model assumes that the lessons nations draw about alliance policy revolve around the choice between neutrality or alliance, so that a nation can learn either that neutrality or that alliance is desirable, where an alliance is operationally defined as a mutual defense treaty. Of course, characterizing a state's alliance policy as for either alliance or neutrality is something of a simplification. The alliance choices a state faces might be more completely conceptualized as a spectrum, along which are different degrees of neutrality and alliance, rather than as an either/or choice. Even in terms of such a specification, though, the act of signing a mutual defense treaty is a unique dividing place along the spectrum, as relations between states that have such a treaty are qualitatively different from those between states that do not have such a treaty. I assume, then, that the choice between alliance and neutrality is an important decision (though not the only one) a state must make when fashioning its alliance policy.[8]

An additional dimension to alliance policy which is not taken up at length in this book is the choice of allies. The quantitative results presented in the next chapter focus on the choice between alliance and neutrality as opposed to the choice between specific countries as potential allies. Addressing the issue of how inferences are drawn about specific countries is rather difficult, because few of the structural similarities are required for quantitative tests. Political circumstances often limit the availability of allies, thus a nation that was available as an ally during the formative event may not be available as a potential ally afterward. Learning about specific countries as allies is an important question, though, one I discuss at the end of Chapter 5.

---

[7] Hans Morgenthau, "Alliances in Theory and Practice," in *Alliance Policy in the Cold War*, ed. Arnold Wolfers (Baltimore: Johns Hopkins University Press, 1959), 188. See also George Liska, *Nations in Alliance* (Baltimore: Johns Hopkins University Press, 1962), 3. For empirical research that supports the proposition that alliances are honored, see Chapter 3.

[8] Liska, *Nations in Alliance*, 32–33.

FORMATIVE EVENTS

The learning theory in this book focuses on lessons drawn from what are termed *formative events*. The first task in the deduction of specific learning propositions, then, is the determination of which experiences are formative of beliefs about the desirability of either alliance or neutrality. Explicitly, a peacetime military alliance is a policy response to the problem of war, so lessons about alliances are most likely to be drawn from experiences in wars. The theoretical discussion in the previous chapter, however, leads us to believe that not all wars are likely to be formative of beliefs; only the most vivid of conflicts will probably disturb old beliefs and inspire the drawing of new lessons.

Of the set of all wars, I will assume that only the largest of wars, which I call *systemic wars* because they involve most of the international system and usually all the great powers, are formative of beliefs about alliances and neutrality. Systemic wars in which great powers fight each other for very high political stakes are generally the most earth-shaking events in world politics; in the words of historian Sally Marks, they "often provide the punctuation marks of history, primarily because they force drastic realignments in the relationships among states."[9] A number of theories in international relations highlight the importance of systemic wars as defining events in international relations.[10] The political and material impacts of these wars make them the most likely of events to be vivid and therefore formative of beliefs about international relations. Even a state that avoids participation in a world war raging around it will draw important lessons from its experience, just as a driver who walks away from an auto accident uninjured because he wore his seat belt is more likely to wear his seat belt in the future.

Some scholars have suggested that systemic wars are not conceptually distinct in *cause* from other wars, but the argument here is that

[9] Sally Marks, *The Illusion of Peace: International Relations in Europe, 1918–1933* (New York: St. Martin's, 1976), 1. On the impact of the Napoleonic Wars, see Paul W. Schroeder, *The Transformation of European Politics, 1763–1848* (Oxford: Clarendon, 1994). On the impact of World War I, see Jack J. Roth, ed., *World War I: A Turning Point in Modern History* (New York: Alfred A. Knopf, 1967); and John Mueller, *Retreat from Doomsday: The Obsolescence of Major War* (New York: Basic Books, 1989).

[10] For arguments as to the qualitative distinctiveness of this type of war, see Robert Gilpin, *War and Change in World Politics* (Cambridge: Cambridge University Press, 1981); Jack S. Levy, *War in the Modern Great Power System, 1495–1975* (Lexington: University Press of Kentucky, 1983); Immanuel Wallerstein, *The Politics of the World-Economy* (Cambridge: Cambridge University Press, 1984); William R. Thompson, *On Global War: Historical-Structural Approaches to World Politics* (Columbia: University of South Carolina Press, 1988); and George Modelski, *Long Cycles in World Politics* (Seattle: University of Washington Press, 1987).

systemic wars are conceptually distinct in terms of *effect*. Bruce Bueno de Mesquita, the main proponent of the argument that systemic wars are not distinct in cause, highlighted the unique impacts of such wars:

> While the human toll of such disputes is monstrous, the importance of great wars does not stem only from their destructiveness. Such global disputes often may reshape the international environment, rearranging political and social institutions in ways that are much more consequential than the cumulative impact of many lesser conflicts. The origins of the modern state system, for instance, are generally attributed to the resolution of the Thirty Years War in 1648. Similarly, the gradual rise of self-determination and decolonization in the twentieth century is often explained as a consequence of the First World War.[11]

Lesser wars, on the other hand, are less likely to be systematically formative of beliefs. The impacts of such wars vary more widely than those of systemic wars, such that many are not formative of beliefs. Some nonsystemic wars may be significant enough in consequences to be formative of a nation's beliefs. But on balance, internal validity is better protected by excluding all lesser wars as possible formative events and thereby risking excluding a few formative events than by assuming that all lesser wars are formative events and including several events that are not formative. A second reason why I focus on learning from systemic wars is that states are more apt to draw lessons about alliances from systemic wars than they are from lesser wars. The greater scale and tendency for systemic wars to be battles between coalitions make alliance choices a more important element of states' foreign policy in systemic wars than in lesser wars, in which alliances often play a lesser role.

A skeptic might find these theoretical arguments insufficient and still worry about the exclusion of lesser wars as possible formative events. If this concern is valid, then we would expect that the empirical results would be biased against learning theory, as it would mean that the reality of the learning process is more complicated than the simple learning model used to measure it (because lessons get drawn from more events than just systemic wars). Therefore, if the empirical results for the simple model indicate strong support for learning theory, then this allays the concern that lesser wars are unjustifiably excluded from the class of formative events. Additionally, the case studies in later chapters will provide an additional mechanism for assessing the possibility that lesser wars were formative.

[11] Bruce Bueno de Mesquita, "Big Wars, Little Wars: Avoiding Selection Bias," *International Interactions* 16 (1990): 159–160.

The empirical focus of this book is on the alliance decisions of small powers. The justification for the focus on small powers rests on two propositions. First, the same set of learning hypotheses cannot be applied to both small powers and great powers, because these two groups of nations think about alliances and world wars in qualitatively different ways and therefore ask fundamentally different kinds of questions when drawing inferences about alliance policy from world wars. Second, small power alliance behavior is of special interest to understanding both alliances and learning, encouraging the strategy of focusing on small powers and giving great power alliance choices relatively brief treatment.

Small Powers and Great Powers are Different

My main empirical goal here is to provide a larger sample test of learning hypotheses on state behavior. Building a data set large enough to permit quantitative analysis introduces the risk of including cases in the sample which are not really part of the population. For example, if one were testing hypotheses on naval spending, the data set ought not to include landlocked nations. This problem is especially salient when analyzing how actors learn. The theory proposes that lessons are drawn from experiences, but outside the laboratory, the experiences that different individuals have in the same event can vary widely. If there are two groups of learners each of which can learn from a differ-ent set of possible lessons, then a single hypothesis predicting what lesson a learner should draw could not be applied to both groups. Assume, for example, that there is an event E from which lessons are drawn and that three actors—A, B, and C—are drawing lessons from the event. Given their roles in the event, possible lessons for actors A and B are lessons L_1 and L_2, whereas possible lessons for actor C are lessons L_3 and L_4. Actors A, B, and C cannot be grouped together for a test of a single learning hypothesis. If hypothesis H_1 predicts that under one condition an actor might draw lesson L_1 while under an-other condition he might draw lesson L_2, then H_1 could be applied to actors A and B: since both actors can learn either L_1 or L_2, it is possible to gather empirical evidence that either falsifies or supports H_1. How-ever, H_1 should not be tested on actor C, because it would be impossi-ble to gather evidence in support of H_1, since C cannot learn L_1 or L_2 no matter what the conditions. To draw an analogy with American football, different players are likely to draw lessons about different parts of an adversary's team following a game depending on the position each plays. The placekicker is likely to draw a lesson about the opponent's special teams; the quarterback, about the nature and quality of the opposing team's defense; and the safety, about the speed and sure-handedness of the opponent's wide receivers.

Similarly, the questions that nations seek to answer when drawing lessons are likely to vary from nation to nation, depending on what aspects of the experience are most important to each, which in turn is determined largely by the goals of each. The modeling task required by testing a theory of learning is to outline a group of nations that ought to ask similar questions about an experience, so that they are all likely to draw from the same set of possible lessons and can therefore be grouped for a test of learning hypotheses. One way to create such a group is to think about how nations in the international system might be categorized according to foreign policy goals. Two kinds of nations with fundamentally different foreign policy aims are great and small powers. A small power tends to accept the structure of the international system and work within it to pursue its foreign policy goals, whereas a great power actively seeks to shape the structure of the international system to advance its national interests. The situation can be compared with perfect and imperfect competition in market economics. If a firm is an oligopolist and therefore has a large share of the market, it experiences imperfect competition, as its pricing behavior affects market prices. If the firm is small, it experiences perfect competition, as its pricing behavior does not affect the market price. The great power–small power distinction is comparable: just as the oligopolist is a price-giver and the small firm is a price-taker, the great power is a structure-giver and the small power is a structure-taker.[12]

Some might take this point further, arguing that small powers are mere puppets of great powers and have no freedom in making foreign policy. It is certainly true that being less powerful makes small powers

[12] Kenneth Waltz focused on great powers because they determine system structure: "In international politics, as in any self-help system, the units of greatest capability set the scene of action for others as well as for themselves." *Theory of International Politics* (New York: Random House, 1979), 72. Raymond Aron phrased it thus: "The status of great nation confers certain rights: no matter of importance can be treated in a system without all the great nations being consulted." *Peace and War: A Theory of International Relations*, trans. Richard Howard and Annette Baker Fox (Garden City, N.Y.: Doubleday, 1966), 58. See also Hans A. Mouritzen, "Defensive Acquiescence: Making the Best Out of Dependence," in *Small States in Europe and Dependence*, ed. Otmar Höll (Vienna: Braumüller, 1983), 240. Similarly, George Liska argued that "a minor state is mostly a 'consumer' rather than a 'producer' of security under the collective system; it follows rather than initiates joint action against aggression." *International Equilibrium* (Cambridge: Harvard University Press, 1957), 25.

more vulnerable to outside influences and restricts their options, but this does not necessarily mean that they are not independent actors. If a small power's foreign policy is steered in a particular direction by the threat of sanctions from a great power, then the small power is just as sovereign (or helpless) as a great power who wishes to attack a small power but is dissuaded by the extended deterrent imposed by a rival great power. The difference is in freedom of action, not independence, and it is one of degree, not kind. Small powers still have real choices to make, and the propositions for small power behavior presented here predict how these decisions are made. Most analysts of small power foreign policy agree with the broad point that small powers have the freedom to make some real choices about their foreign policies, despite some limits on foreign policy options.[13] As an empirical matter, if small powers were really just puppets, then nearly none would be neutral, for each would probably be bought or threatened into joining an alliance with a great power suitor who wanted to increase the power of its bloc. Of course, the twentieth century offers refutation of this claim, as lots of small powers have remained unallied with great powers. Lastly, guidelines in the empirical tests ensure that only states' preferences are being measured, as opposed to unwanted actions imposed from without. Sovereign nations whose foreign policies were directly dictated by a great power, including several in Eastern Europe after World War II, are excluded from the data set. Also, the dependent variable measures the preferences of small powers rather than actual alliance membership, which alleviates the problem that great power machinations might distort the measurement of small power beliefs. The case studies in later chapters provide a good opportunity to assess more closely the claim that small powers have no foreign policy sovereignty; I summarize and discuss these findings in Chapter 9.

As structure-takers, small powers are likely to have less-complicated security concerns than do great powers. A small power focuses mostly on threats to its national territory, whereas a great power must also consider the security of adjacent and overseas territories that it believes are instrumental to the security of its homeland and national interests.[14]

---

[13] See Trygve Mathisen, *The Functions of Small States in the Strategies of the Great Powers* (Oslo: Scandinavian University Books, 1971); Annette Baker Fox, *The Power of Small States: Diplomacy in World War II* (Chicago: University of Chicago Press, 1959); Karl Mueller, "Strategy, Asymmetric Deterrence, and Accommodation: Middle Powers and Security in Modern Europe," Ph.D. diss., Princeton University, 1991; Robert L. Rothstein, *Alliances and Small Powers* (New York: Columbia University Press, 1968).

[14] Mathisen, *Functions of Small States*, 61. Michael Desch distinguishes between the foreign policies of great and small powers by pointing out that great powers must attempt to defend themselves, intrinsically valuable areas, and extrinsically valuable

The security concerns of small powers are therefore more likely to be one-dimensional than are those of great powers. These differences in foreign policy interests have direct implications for how great and small powers are likely to draw lessons from their experiences in systemic wars. Great powers determine which coalition of powers wins or loses the war, whereas small powers have comparatively little effect on who wins or loses. Great powers also have more direct interest in who wins the war. For a great power, a defeat in a systemic war, even if it does not mean conquest of the homeland of the great power, can mean loss of control of external foreign policy interests that are crucial to the nation's power base. The goals of a great power, then, are usually dominated by winning the war, because it has both the capability to affect the outcome of the war and a direct interest in the outcome of the war. The goals of the small power, on the other hand, center more on directly protecting the security of the homeland, which is not necessarily defined by who wins and who loses the war. A small power does not have the kind of extended foreign policy interests that a great power must maintain, so its goals in a systemic war are limited to its own national security. This emphasis on the national security of the homeland is especially central for small powers because the national sovereignty and independence of a small power is more likely to be threatened or destroyed in a systemic war than are the sovereignty and independence of a great power. Therefore, a small power is likely to focus its learning on only the question of how the security of the nation itself fared in the war, whereas a great power is likely to consider a number of additional issues, such as what factors determined the outcome of the war and how the great power's extended foreign policy interests were affected by the war.

Small Powers Are the Appropriate Empirical Focus

I focus on the alliance choices of small powers for a number of reasons. First, the empirical strategy of building deductive, generally applicable, and falsifiable propositions lends itself quite well to small powers. Because learning hypotheses need to be tested on a group of actors who can learn from the same set of lessons, such a group is often defined by actors who share the same basic foreign policy goals, evaluating their past actions in similar terms. If most have the same goal, then they will tend to ask the same question: Did our strategy choice

---

areas, whereas small powers must worry about defending only themselves. "The Keys That Lock Up the World," *International Security* 14 (Summer 1989): 86–121.

help us reach or prevent us from reaching that goal? Small powers often have the same, relatively simple aims regarding the formative events under examination here, systemic wars: national security in the strict sense of defending just the national borders. Therefore, they are all likely to learn from the same set of lessons: essentially, alliance protects the national security, or neutrality protects the national security.[15]

The foreign policies of great powers, on the other hand, do not lend themselves easily to the application of such hypotheses. Although great powers are as likely as small powers to act on the basis of lessons drawn from past experiences, their diverse goals, strategies, and foreign policies defy the creation of a single hypothesis that applies to all great powers. The foreign policies of great powers are more complex and multidimensional, as they must concern themselves with maintaining a whole network of international interests as well as with protecting the immediate security of their own borders. These complexities undermine attempts at predicting for the group how great powers draw lessons, especially given that almost as many great power grand strategies have existed as have great powers. Jack Snyder's study of overexpansion demonstrates this limitation. He tests three theories of overexpansion—a realist explanation, a domestic political explanation, and a cognitive explanation, which includes elements of learning. Of the three, his theoretical discussion of the cognitive theory is the most general, providing only the broad strokes of social psychology to lay out the basic ideas of the theory. Further, the learning propositions he tests are quite idiosyncratic to each case—great power behaviors defy being grouped together under a single learning hypothesis.[16] Great power learning is better treated on a more individual, contextual basis than by application of general hypotheses to all great powers. Chapter 5 presents a brief discussion of great power alliance choices.

An additional reason to prefer examination of small powers is that since alliance policy is more important to the foreign policy of a small power than to a great power during a systemic war, small powers are more likely to learn about their alliance policies from a systemic war. A small power is much more dependent on its allies for successful deterrence and/or defense than is a great power. The most a small power can do by itself if threatened by a great power is make its conquest

---

[15] Chapter 7 discusses a few small powers who had different, offensive motivations. For these cases, the learning propositions (which assumed defensive motivations) not surprisingly provide a relatively poor fit.

[16] Jack Snyder, *Myths of Empire: Domestic Politics and International Ambition* (Ithaca: Cornell University Press, 1991). Snyder finds little support for his cognitive model.

inconvenient or unfruitful, whereas a great power has at least a reasonable chance of fending off an attack by itself. Since alliances are more important for small powers than for great powers in systemic wars, small powers are more likely to attribute success or failure in a systemic war to alliance policies. Great powers, on the other hand, will give more weight to other questions, such as military strategy or economic resources, when attempting to attribute success or failure to individual causes.

The peacetime alliance policy of a small power is also more likely than that of a great power to be driven by security concerns. Alliance choices have greater gravity for a small power; as Efraim Karsh noted, "For the great power, neutrality often constitutes a question of simple costs and benefits, whereas for the small state, neutrality can be a matter of existence."[17] A great power has more internal resources to use in response to an external threat, so it would be more likely to let nonsecurity considerations, such as issues of foreign economic policy, affect its alliance policy decisions.[18] This means that lessons about security (the model assumes that the main lessons from a systemic war are security-oriented) are more likely to determine the alliance policy of a small power than of a great power. Therefore, exclusion of great powers increases our confidence that a finding that formative events have little or no impact on peacetime alliance choices undercuts the validity of the theory.

On a different level, a test of small power alliance behavior is more *interesting* than a test of great power behavior, for two reasons. First, enough small powers exist to permit the fruitful application of quantitative tests. The use of quantitative and case study methods offers important advantages, and I perform both kinds of tests on small power behavior. The low number of great powers and difficulty in comparing great power learning with a single hypothesis, on the other hand, make the application of quantitative tests to great power behavior quite problematic. Second, small power behavior provides a more interesting testing ground for comparison of learning and realism

---

[17] Efraim Karsh, *Neutrality and Small States* (London: Routledge, 1988), 4.

[18] James Morrow makes this same point: "Minor powers have low levels of security and high levels of autonomy and so try to form alliances that increase their security at the cost of some autonomy. . . . The situation is different for major powers. They possess high levels of both autonomy and security. They have no overriding interest to raise either autonomy or security; some desire to enhance their security, while others are content with theirs. As a group, major powers will not be driven to pursue exclusively autonomy or security in their alliances." James D. Morrow, "Alliances and Asymmetry: An Alternative to the Capability Aggregation Model of Alliances," *American Journal of Political Science* 35 (November 1991): 913.

than does great power behavior. Realism has a hard time explaining some genuinely interesting puzzles about small power behavior, such as why under the same threat some small powers prefer neutrality, whereas others prefer alliance. For great powers, however, though learning predictions make generally correct predictions about their alliance choices, these predictions are not terribly counterintuitive or unanticipated by realism. Illustration of this point is provided in Chapter 5, where learning hypotheses are applied to a number of cases of great power alliance choices.

This modeling decision to focus on small powers might invite the criticism that an artificial distinction between great and small powers has been introduced and that the systematic exclusion of great powers might preclude drawing conclusions about all states. In a limited sense, this is true; to maintain the internal validity of the test, the hypotheses will be tailored to fit the kinds of questions that small powers will probably ask about a formative event, so that the empirical findings will not shed light directly on the validity of the hypotheses as applied to great powers. But the empirical findings will have implications for the general learning *theory* as well as for the specific hypotheses. The basic principles of the learning theory are generic to human and organizational decision making, so conclusions about decision-making processes taken from analysis of small power behavior can be applied to the behavior of great powers. There is literature that addresses small powers as a special class of states, but these theories of small power foreign policy behavior tend to focus on the different place held in the international system by small powers rather than posit that small powers make foreign policy in a manner that is qualitatively distinct from how great powers do so.[19]

Of course, great powers' decision-making processes are likely to have some systematic differences from those of small powers. Given that great powers' foreign policies are more complex and that their interests are more extended, their decisions—as well as the organizational machinery that makes the decisions—are likely to be more complex. Still, the basic structures of the decision-making apparatus are about the same for great and small powers, especially for big decisions of foreign policy, ones usually made by a few individuals at the top of the organizational pyramid. In fact, we might expect learning theory to be *more* applicable to great powers than to small powers. The great

[19] See, for example, Fox, *Power of Small States*; Robert O. Keohane, "Lilliputians' Dilemmas: Small States in International Politics," *International Organization* 23 (Spring 1969): 291–310; Karsh, *Neutrality and Small States*; Mathisen, *Functions of Small States*; Mueller, "Strategy, Asymmetric Deterrence, and Accommodation."

power foreign policy–making process is likely to differ from small power foreign policy–making in two important regards: great power decision makers are apt to face more uncertainty because the decisions they make are more complicated and must account for more factors, and a great power probably has a more extensive organizational apparatus for making foreign policy than does a small power. Given these two differences, we would expect that learning, a theory which assumes that uncertainty complicates the making of foreign policy and which incorporates organization theory into its tenets, ought to be *more* accurate in its predictions of great power behavior, whereas realism, a theory that assumes a certain decision-making environment and that nations are unitary actors, ought to be *less* accurate for great powers than for small powers. Therefore, small power behavior is in some ways the tougher test for learning theory (though admittedly an easier group on which to apply learning *hypotheses*), and if learning predictions attract empirical support in this realm, then this is particularly powerful support for the learning theory.

Because the model uses systemic wars as formative events, the focus is on the preference of small powers for alliance with only great powers. Limiting the dependent variable to alliance preferences with great powers mitigates the problem of excluding nonsystemic wars as potential formative events, as only a portion of the potential alliance partners that a small power would consider as a response to a direct threat would be great powers, whereas nearly all the potential alliance partners that a small power would consider as a response to a systemic threat would be great powers. Of course, small powers might draw lessons from nonsystemic wars about alliances with other small powers, but this area of learning is not examined here, and not accounting for this kind of learning does not introduce bias into the study of learning about alliances with great powers from systemic wars.

An alliance of small powers is likely to be credible as a response to a great power threat only if the alliance has several members. Such multimember, small power alliances are, however, more difficult to form and hold together, as the absence of a single larger state to impose its preferences introduces coordination problems, as does the simple fact that more members increases the possibility of disagreement among the members as to the structure and policy of the alliance. As a result, such small power alliances tend to be no more than loose configurations of states, such as the northern European neutrals in the 1930s, southeastern Europe in the 1930s, and Scandinavia during the cold war. More important, whether a small power is allied with a great power is often a defining characteristic of that nation's foreign policy,

[69]

and the decision to enter or exit a great power alliance constitutes a genuine restructuring of foreign policy, as distinct from the ebb and flow of policy which occurs within a given foreign policy orientation.[20]

Learning

In a systemic war, a small power attempts to be allied or neutral. A small power is defined as attempting to be allied if it has a mutual defense pact with a belligerent great power as the war breaks out or if it joins one of the warring coalitions without being attacked first. Otherwise, it is attempting neutrality. Organization theory predicts that failure and success constitute the dominating themes when lessons are drawn, specifically that failure encourages innovation and success promotes policy continuance. *Failure* and *success* are defined as follows:

If a small power attempts neutrality in a systemic war, the experience is considered a success if it is not invaded during the war. Otherwise, it is a failure.

If a small power attempts being allied, an experience constitutes success if the nation is on the winning side and is not invaded; it is also a success if it is invaded but acquires more population in postwar territorial settlement than it lost in the war. Otherwise, it is a failure.

Population works reasonably well as an indicator of success and failure because it allows a rough comparison between war costs (lives lost) and war benefits (territory gained).

It is assumed that a formative event (systemic war, in this application) is a watershed, such that previous formative events are dominated by the most recent formative event in terms of belief formation. The organization theory idea that crises create new myths that replace old myths supports this assumption, which is necessary to avoid infinite regress in determining which event is formative. I offer two different propositions about how formative events drive learning and, in

---

[20] K. J. Holsti, *Why Nations Realign: Foreign Policy Restructuring in the Postwar World* (London: George Allen & Unwin, 1982). Beliefs are likely to be especially important in determining such major foreign policy decisions. Ole Holsti, "Foreign Policy Formation Viewed Cognitively," in *Structure of Decision*, ed. Robert Axelrod (Princeton: Princeton University Press, 1976), 29–30.

turn, behavior. The first proposition is that a state will learn whether alliance pays based on its own experience in systemic war, and in the following years, it will behave in accordance with this lesson.

Hypothesis 1. A small power can attempt a policy of alliance with a great power or neutrality in a systemic war. If the small power experiences failure, then it will switch policies following that war; if the small power achieves success, then it will continue that policy.[21]

Note that this hypothesis proposes that a state draws conclusions about international dynamics based only on its own experiences, as its own experiences are assumed to be more vivid to it than are those of other states. A different learning hypothesis is that all states do not view their own experience as idiosyncratic and garner the same lesson from a systemwide experience, regardless of individual experience. If it is assumed that a state's own experience is not idiosyncratic and that the experiences of other nations have application to a state's own foreign policy choices, then learning from the experiences of all small powers in a formative event would be more unbiased than learning just from one's own experience. On the other hand, if it is assumed that a state's experience is uniquely instructive about its own foreign policy, then equally weighting lessons from the experiences of all small powers with lessons from one's own experience would introduce bias. This study does not attempt to answer this question of whether other states' experiences are objectively relevant, choosing instead to examine which sort of learning—oriented toward one's own experience or vicarious—is more prevalent.

Relaxing the assumption that states view their own experiences as idiosyncratic means that a small power would weight the experiences of all small powers for a formative event equally in determining a composite lesson about the relative merits of alliance and neutrality. Therefore, a formative event produces one systemwide lesson that is learned by all small powers. Note that this second, systemic learning hypothesis retains the vividness effect assumption that beliefs are formed from a few salient events but does not assume that the national experience is more vivid than the experiences of other states. The lesson

[21] The general argument that individuals are more likely to learn from firsthand experiences was made by Jervis in *Perception and Misperception*, 239–243. A form of this argument as applied to small power alliances was made by Donald E. Nuechterlein, "Small States in Alliances: Iceland, Thailand, Australia," *Orbis* 13 (Summer 1969): 600–623. This study expands on Nuechterlein's work by building the hypotheses from broader areas of decision theory, comparing their predictions to those of realism, and testing the hypotheses quantitatively on a larger number of cases.

can range from strongly advocating alliance to indifference between neutrality and alliance, to strongly advocating neutrality.

Hypothesis 2. A systemic war will produce a systemwide lesson on the effectiveness of alliance with a great power based on the experiences of all small powers. The systemwide lesson affects equally the alliance behavior of all small powers following the war.

One potential problem every study of learning faces is the possible observance of behavior consistent with the predictions of a learning hypothesis, although this result was produced by a process other than that envisioned in the learning theory. Three alternative explanations to learning—structural adjustment, evolutionary selection, and domestic political change—deserve specific treatment.[22] The first of these, structural adjustment, is the argument that rational, timely, and appropriate changes are made to changes in the international environment. For example, a shift to a more maneuver-oriented military strategy might be a structural adjustment in response to the appearance of tanks. But this explanation is in some ways not distinct from the formative events theory of learning—the formative events model also sees changes in policy as being motivated by the receipt of new information. The main difference is that the formative events model predicts that changes ought to be observed only when certain kinds of information are received, specifically information from the experience of a formative event. This may imply suboptimal behavior, as structural changes do not always cause formative events to announce their arrival, so appropriate policy changes might not be made in step with structural changes. Therefore, examples of states acting on the basis of lessons drawn from formative events rather than from structural changes would be evidence in favor of the formative events learning model and evidence against the structural adaptation model.

The second alternative explanation is evolutionary selection. According to this argument, we might observe actors at time $t + 1$ acting differently from actors at time t because of some event x that occurred at time t, but not because the actors have observed x and changed their behavior. Rather actors may be incapable of changing their behaviors, and those that practiced inferior behavior were eliminated from the environment, whereas those that practiced superior behavior remained

---

[22] For a discussion of alternative explanations, see Levy, "Learning and Foreign Policy"; and William W. Jarosz with Joseph S. Nye Jr., "The Shadow of the Past: Learning from History in National Security Decision Making," in *Behavior, Society, and International Conflict*, vol. 3, ed. Philip E. Tetlock, Jo L. Husbands, Robert Jervis, Paul C. Stern, and Charles Tilly (New York: Oxford University Press, 1993).

and thrived. If the unit of analysis is a state, however, and the behavior of the same group of states is observed at times t and t + 1, then evolutionary selection of states can be eliminated as a possible alternative explanation.

The third explanation is a domestic politics explanation. This proposition is similar to the evolutionary selection argument except that it is a vision of evolutionary selection within the state rather than between states. This argument holds that decision makers do not themselves actually learn, but the replacement of leaders makes it appear that learning has taken place. The assumption is that leaders do not change their beliefs even after having experienced a formative event, but they may be replaced with leaders whose ideas are preferred because they are more in line with the lessons offered by the formative event. Therefore, a sort of national political ecosystem of politicians exists, within which evolutionary selection takes place.

Two comments about the domestic politics explanation are in order. First, if this is an accurate description of what happens, then it is still a description of a learning process. If the public at large sees from an experience that a particular policy is undesirable and then votes or by some other means puts a new leader or group of leaders in power, then it provides an example of drawing lessons from history and then acting on these lessons. Of course, it is learning at a level different from that where leaders themselves draw lessons from the event and change policy, but it is learning nonetheless. Second, this is really an argument for a more sophisticated model of learning in foreign policy than an argument that learning is not an important part of the making of foreign policy. If formative experiences cause changes in policy through domestic political shifts, then a model needs to incorporate ideas about domestic politics as well as ideas about decision making. The main task of this book is not the construction of such a model but rather the construction and empirical testing of a more basic model of learning and foreign policy. Chapter 8, however, presents a preliminary model that incorporates both decision making and domestic political factors.

Realism

Although learning predicts that formative experiences determine whether a small power will prefer alliance with a great power, balance of threat theory predicts that a small power is more likely to prefer alliance with a great power—whether it be a revisionist or status quo great power—when the prospect of such a systemic war appears imminent. The prospect of such a great power war concerns all small powers in the region because their geographical proximity risks their involvement. In its struggle with other great powers, a revisionist great power may invade a neutral small power to take advantage of the small power's geographical location, even if the neutral power has no specific dispute with the revisionist. Balance of threat theory would predict that if systemwide war appears to be impending, a small power would either join with the revisionist power to avoid being overrun and/or to share in the spoils of victory or ally with the defending powers to attempt to balance against the revisionist threat. Even though a specific threat may not be posed to the small power in question, it perceives a threat to its security as arising from a systemwide conflict. The logic of balance of threat theory predicts that the small power would prefer alliance in the face of such a threat.

Hypothesis 3. A small power is more likely to prefer alliance with a great power than no alliance with a great power if it perceives that a systemic war in its region is imminent.

Realist principles can be used to produce an argument opposite to that of balance of threat—neutrality—so that if small powers perceived a systemic war to impend, they would probably exit alliances in an attempt to avoid involvement in the coming war. This study tests the dominant realist hypothesis that threats increase the likelihood of alliance. Again, the learning hypotheses provide a solution to realism's falsifiability problem, proposing that whether states subscribe to realist alliance logic or realist neutrality logic depends on the beliefs they have about alliances and neutrality, which in turn are constructed from lessons of past experiences.

The relative military status of the small power should affect its perception of threat and therefore the likelihood of its willingness to prefer alliance. Realism predicts that a relatively strong small power may feel that it will be left alone in a major war; even if its military capabilities are not large enough to prevent conquest from a great power, they may be sufficient to inflict enough costs on a great power to dissuade it from attacking.[23] Conversely, a very small country will probably not feel that it can inflict enough costs on a great power invader to dissuade it from attacking.

Hypothesis 3a. If a small power perceives that a systemic war is imminent, the greater the military advantage that the potential great power revisionist has

---

[23] See Mueller, "Strategy, Asymmetric Deterrence, and Accommodation."

over the small power, the greater the likelihood that the small power will prefer alliance with a great power.

Additionally, balance of threat theory predicts that geography plays an important role in mediating threat.[24] If a small power is geographically exposed to an apparently revisionist great power, it is more likely to think that it will be drawn into a systemic war than if it rests at the geographical perimeter of the system. The exposed small power, therefore, perceives a greater threat and is more likely to prefer alliance. Scholars of small power foreign policy often distinguish between "buffer" small powers and "rimstate" small powers, the former lying between great powers and the latter resting adjacent to only one. Generally, buffers are thought to be in greater danger than rimstates.[25]

Hypothesis 3b. If a small power perceives that a systemic war is imminent, it is more likely to prefer great power alliance if it is geographically exposed to the potential revisionist than if it is not.

The dependent variable is limited to one form of third-party assistance, mutual alliances with great powers. If a small power can count on one-way defense commitments made to it by one or more great powers, it will be less likely to prefer a mutually committing alliance with a great power. In such a case, the small power has acquired great power extended deterrence without increasing the chances of its entanglement in a war.

Hypothesis 3c. If a small power perceives that a systemic war is imminent, it is less likely to prefer great power alliance if one or more great powers have made nonalliance defense commitments to it.

A small power could also be faced with a direct threat, which is defined as a specific threat made to the target over a particular political or territorial issue. Such a threat could come from one or more states, great or small. Balance of threat theory predicts that the presence of such a threat would increase the probability that the threatened small power would prefer an alliance with a great power to balance against the threat.

[24] Stephen M. Walt, *The Origins of Alliances* (Ithaca: Cornell University Press, 1987), 23–24.
[25] Mathisen, *Functions of Small States*, 105–106; Karsh, *Neutrality and Small States*, 81–84.

Hypothesis 4. The probability that a small power will prefer alliance with a great power is positively correlated with the level of direct threat the small power perceives.

Balance of threat theory would predict that if the small power in question has alliances with other small powers or nonalliance defense commitments from great powers, the external threat is effectively lessened, so the need to ally with a great power to deal with the direct threat is diminished.

Hypothesis 4a. If faced with a direct threat, the greater a small power's alliances with other small powers or nonalliance great power commitments, the less likely it will be to seek great power alliance.

A remaining question is how balance of threat and learning relate to each other in their predictions. A persistent balance of threat advocate might argue that learning is just a particular operationalization of balance of threat theory, in that it proposes that a state adopts a policy of neutrality or alliance based on its conception of how that policy deals with threats, leaving the same bottom line as balance of threat theory— that states ally in response to threats. Strictly speaking, this is partly true: the learning theory outlined here maintains that the problem to which a policy of neutrality or alliance is addressed is threat from the international environment. Learning, however, predicts that an experience provides the state with beliefs about how to deal with threat, whether to accept the logic of buck-passing or chain-ganging, whereas balance of threat assumes that the universal response to threat is always to ally, whether with it or against it. Also, balance of threat focuses on short-term reactions to changes in the international environment, whereas learning focuses on how larger ideas about grand strategy are formulated. After a formative event, learning predicts that a state that learned a lesson favoring alliance would prefer alliance with a great power even without any current threat in the international environment, because such an orientation is in accord with a broad belief in the utility of alliance in dealing with threats when they arrive. A balance of threat advocate might contend that this case is one of a state balancing against a possible future threat, therefore validating her theory. But if this were true, then all states would always prefer alliance, because the international anarchy assumed by realism means that a future threat is always possible. If she argued that states do not always prefer alliance because different states have different views on how to address possible future threats, then this would beg the question of where these different views come from, a question that learning answers by proposing that past experiences determine how states come to view the best way of dealing with future threats.

Another issue in the comparison of realism and learning is whether a theory predicting rational behavior (realism) clashes with a theory predicting nonrational behavior (learning). Learning's primary critique of realism, though, is not that realism makes unreasonable, rationalist assumptions about the decision-making abilities of leaders but that it wrongly frames a decision problem by assuming that alliance is the only possible reply to threat. Learning argues that more than one reply to threat exists (neutrality and alliance) and that decision makers choose a reply by using a certain decision strategy, namely, drawing a lesson from the most recent formative event. Is the formative learning strategy itself nonrational? In at least some cases, we would expect that focusing on a single previous event might lead to playing down or ignoring other relevant evidence, meaning that formative event learning is inconsistent with scientific induction. But if one assumes that rationality is concerned with making choices given certain information, then formative event learning can only be termed prerational and not nonrational.

CASES

The general strategy in constructing the data set has been to collect a group of decisions in which the actors had approximately the same choices; this encouraged limiting the test to small powers and to learning from systemic wars. This guiding principle encourages the examination of learning after formative events that offered fundamentally similar kinds of possible lessons. Here, I examine systemic wars as a class of formative events. For the quantitative tests, data was collected for peacetime behavior of small powers following the two systemic wars in the twentieth century, World War I and II. Since the emergence of the modern nation-state system in 1815, the only other possible candidate would be small power behavior following the Napoleonic Wars. However, the international structure in Europe which followed the final defeat of Napoleonic France was one in which the small powers had very little freedom of action in alliance policy, as the great powers virtually controlled international relations through the Concert of Europe. For example, the great powers *created* the countries of Switzerland and Belgium in the nineteenth century, stipulating in treaties that the international community would recognize both countries as neutrals.[26] Twentieth-century politics have afforded small powers much greater freedom of choice. Therefore, the decision environments faced by nineteenth-century small powers were fundamentally different from those of their twentieth-century counterparts because they had less real freedom of choice in their alliance policies.

To be included in the data set, a country must be a nongreat power member of the Correlates of War data set during and following the formative event and located in a primary theater of conflict during the formative event (for World War I, Europe was the only primary theater; for World War II, Europe, the Middle East, and Southeast Asia were the primary theaters). Additionally, the government must not be a puppet controlled by an outside power. This excludes a number of Eastern European nations after World War II because of Soviet military domination, Greece after World War I because the 1917 Allied-sponsored coup there distorted its learning during World War I, and Greece in the late forties because of the extensive American control of politics in Greece until elections were held in 1950. Post–World War II Yugoslavia was included because it, as distinct from other small powers in Eastern Europe, did not experience direct interference from the Soviet Union in the formation of its government and policies. For the post–World War I period, members of the data set included Albania, Belgium, Bulgaria, Denmark, the Netherlands, Norway, Portugal, Romania, Spain, Sweden, Switzerland, and Turkey. For the post–World War II period, members included Australia, Belgium, Denmark, Egypt, Finland, Greece, Iran, Iraq, Ireland, Luxembourg, the Netherlands, New Zealand, Norway, Portugal, Spain, Sweden, Switzerland, Thailand, Turkey, and Yugoslavia.[27]

The learning hypotheses make the prediction that alliance preferences for a state for the years following a formative event will be in accordance with the lesson of the formative event. It is necessary, however, to collect more than one observation per small power per formative event to test for the possibility that a state's alliance policy varied across time during a postevent period, as well as for the possibility that levels of threat varied across time. The modeling question, then, is, In which years of a post–formative event period should data be coded? The general guideline for selecting the years of observation

[26] Liska, *International Equilibrium*, 46–47; Karsh, *Neutrality and Small States*, 18. Paul Schroeder has argued that European states learned from the Napoleonic Wars that the old, eighteenth-century focus on balancing against one aggressor needed to be abandoned and that, instead, the great powers should focus on creating a durable structure for peace. *Transformation of European Politics*, esp. 581.

[27] On the Correlates of War project, see Melvin Small and J. David Singer, *Resort to Arms: International and Civil Wars, 1816–1980* (Beverly Hills: Sage, 1982).

was to include years with different levels and sources of threat to provide a richer test of the balance of threat hypotheses.[28] Observation years were spaced apart evenly, the first being a few years after the end of the formative event to account for the staggered emergence of the postwar order. For each case, behavior was coded at six-year intervals for four points in time: in the post–World War I period, at 1921, 1927, 1933, and 1939; and in the post–World War II period, at 1949, 1955, 1961, and 1967. The onset of World War II makes post-1939 codings for World War I lessons inappropriate, given the assumption that the most recent formative event dominates beliefs. For the post–World War II period, codings were limited to 1967 to keep a comparable time frame with the post–World War I period, about two decades (the approximate length of a generation). These years reflect different conditions in the international environment. For the interwar period, 1921 represents the nadir of German economic and military power and Italy before the rise of Mussolini; 1927 reflects substantial turmoil and instability in the Balkans and the first years of Mussolini; 1933 represents new conditions in the Balkans; and 1939 contains the months preceding the outbreak of world war. For the postwar period, 1949 represents a Stalinist Soviet Union overshadowing a frantically rebuilding Europe; 1955, a relaxation of the U.S.-Soviet conflict; 1961, the heating up of the cold war after a number of dangerous international crises; and 1967, the start of another waning of the cold war.

Determining how far apart to set the observation years is an important decision, as there are risks of degrading the validity of the estimates of the model. Given the need to collect data to catch variations in the level of threat, one could argue for collecting data for every time period for which data is available. For this model, that would be yearly, as the threat hypotheses are operationalized using annual defense spending figures. Observations were taken six years apart, however, because there are good reasons to suspect autocorrelation in codings of alliance preferences for consecutive years, as states may not genuinely reevaluate important decisions every year. Inclusion of more and more observation years per country diminishes the credibility of the claim that each of the observation years is a separate case, introducing the risk of artificially inflating the size of the data set with the potential for distorting empirical results. Given that one can only guess at the nature of the autocorrelation, which probably varies from case to case, I prefer

[28] Spacing apart the times of observation is known as *systematic sampling*. See John R. Freeman, "Systematic Sampling, Temporal Aggregation, and the Study of Political Relationships," in *Political Analysis*, ed. J. A. Stimson (Ann Arbor: University of Michigan Press, 1990).

to forgo a formal test of the hypothesis that the dependent variable is autocorrelated and space apart the observation years to reduce the distorting effects of autocorrelation and improve confidence in the model's estimates. Additionally, if the learning hypotheses are valid, there ought to be high autocorrelation in the dependent variables, because decision makers are not changing alliance policies between formative events. This means that an attempt to "correct" for autocorrelation by adjusting the functional form of the model might substantially bias the results toward downplaying the significance of learning. Spacing apart years for which data was collected ought not to degrade significantly the validity of the model's estimates, as inclusion of more observation years would not substantially enrich the empirical findings. If anything, taking infrequent observations makes the test of learning theory stronger, for taking more and more frequent observations would make learning appear to be increasingly powerful as an explanation of the dependent variable because of inflation of the data set. Therefore, if learning appears to be a powerful explanation of behavior even when observations of behavior are made at intervals of several years rather than annually, then this is strong evidence of the power of learning theory. The observation years chosen catch all the direct and systemic threats, as well as all the small power preferences for great power alliances—in other words, no one-year blips of threat or alliance preference fall between observation years.[29]

I will use a data set of 127 cases (4 observations per country in each post–formative event period: 12 countries in the post–World War I period and 20 countries in the post–World War II period, minus the 1949 Greece case), and will conduct quantitative analysis and confidence tests on the basis of a sample size of 127. Though the model does not provide a test of the hypothesis that the dependent variable is autocorrelated, rigorous tests reasonably unbiased from autocorrelation are provided for the balance of threat and learning hypotheses which extract as much information as possible from the records of history without distorting conclusions by substantially inflating the data set. Of course, it cannot be claimed that absolutely no bias due to sample size exists in the results, given that it is impossible

---

[29] As described below, threat was assessed on the basis of primary and secondary historical sources. One might argue that coding for threat in 1949 leaves out the Soviet threat to Turkey in 1946, meaning that the significance of direct threat is underestimated. However, since the USSR is coded as posing a systemic threat to Turkey in 1949, one of the balance of threat variables can be used to explain Turkey's preference of alliance in the late 1940s.

to determine what size sample both wastes no information and is perfectly unbiased. To check on the possibility of introduction of bias because of inflated sample size, I perform quantitative tests on data sets with different intervals to explore the robustness of the empirical results.

VARIABLES

This section lays out the equation used in the quantitative tests, explaining the operationalizations and coding rules for the variables. The dependent variable is dichotomous; during the year in question, it is coded as 1 if the small power preferred a mutual alliance with a great power (following the Correlates of War list of great powers) committing the parties to military action (as opposed to nonaggression treaties or agreements to consult in the event of war), and 0 if not. For example, in 1955 Belgium is given a coding of 1 because it is a member of the North Atlantic Treaty Organization (NATO) of which the United States (a great power) is a member; Sweden, on the other hand, is given a coding of 0 in 1955 because it is not a member of either NATO or the Warsaw Pact and was not a member of nor was it seeking membership in any other military alliances with a great power. Coding for the dependent variable was made on the basis of primary and secondary historical sources.[30] Though the presence of an alliance can be considered adequate evidence that a small power prefers alliance (with a few exceptions discussed above, such as Eastern Europe after World War II), the absence of any alliances between a small power and any great powers does not necessarily indicate the preference on the part of the small power for neutrality—it may be the case that the small power seeks alignment with a great power but there is no willing great power. To deal with this possibility, the foreign policy preferences of all small powers that were not in an alliance with a great power were checked, and a handful of small powers were coded as preferring alliance with a great power even though they had not formally entered any alliance.[31] The codings of the dependent variable are presented in Table 1. Once again, observations were taken for the years 1921, 1927, 1933, 1939, 1949, 1955, 1961, and 1967.

When the dependent variable is 0 or 1, a model such as logit which

[30] Sources are listed in the bibliography.

[31] These small powers included Spain, Iraq, and Iran, all in the post–World War II period. These coding decisions were made on the basis of primary and secondary historical sources.

Table 1. Small powers' preferences for neutrality and alliance

Country	Years when neutrality preferred	Years when alliance preferred (allies and/or desired allies)
Albania	1921	1927, 1933, 1939 (Italy, U.K., France)
Australia	—	1949, 1955, 1961, 1967 (U.S.)
Belgium	1939	1921, 1927, 1933, 1949, 1955, 1961, 1967 (U.K., France, NATO)
Bulgaria	1921, 1927, 1933, 1939	—
Denmark	1921, 1927, 1933, 1939	1949, 1955, 1961, 1967 (NATO)
Egypt	1955, 1961, 1967	1949 (U.K.)
Finland	1949, 1955, 1961, 1967	—
Greece	—	1955, 1961, 1967 (NATO)
Iran	—	1949, 1955, 1961, 1967 (U.S.)
Iraq	1961, 1967	1949, 1955 (U.S.)
Ireland	1949, 1955, 1961, 1967	—
Luxembourg	—	1949, 1955, 1961, 1967 (NATO)
Netherlands	1921, 1927, 1933, 1939	1949, 1955, 1961, 1967 (NATO)
New Zealand	—	1949, 1955, 1961, 1967 (U.S.)
Norway	1921, 1927, 1933, 1939	1949, 1955, 1961, 1967 (U.S.)
Portugal	—	1921, 1927, 1933, 1939, 1949, 1955, 1961, 1967 (U.K., NATO)
Romania	1921, 1939	1927, 1933 (France)
Spain	1921, 1927, 1933, 1939	1949, 1955, 1961, 1967 (NATO)
Sweden	1921, 1927, 1933, 1939, 1949, 1955, 1961, 1967	—
Switzerland	1921, 1927, 1933, 1939, 1949, 1955, 1961, 1967	—
Thailand	—	1949, 1955, 1961, 1967 (U.S.)
Turkey	1921, 1927, 1933	1939, 1949, 1955, 1961, 1967 (U.K., France, NATO)
Yugoslavia	1949, 1955, 1961, 1967	—
Total number of country-year cases	60	67

estimates the probability that the dependent variable is 1 is appropriate.[32] The logit equation to be estimated is as follows:

$$\text{Pr(prefer alliance)} = \frac{1}{1 + e^{-X\beta}} \tag{1}$$

[32] A functional form very similar to logit is probit. This study used logit because the effects of individual variables are easier to assess with logit than with probit. Analysis of the data with a probit form, however, produces essentially similar results as with logit. On logit and probit, see Eric A. Hanushek and John E. Jackson, *Statistical Methods for Social Scientists* (San Diego: Academic Press, 1977), 179–216; John H. Aldrich and Forrest D. Nelson, *Linear Probability, Logit, and Probit Models* (Beverly Hills: Sage, 1984); and Gary King, *Unifying Political Methodology* (Cambridge: Cambridge University Press, 1989).

$$X\beta = K + \beta_1(INDL) + \beta_2(SYSL) + \beta_3(DTMB) + \beta_4(DCOM) + \beta_5(STRS)$$
$$+ \beta_6(STRS)(GEOG) + \beta_7(STMB) + \beta_8(STMB)(GEOG) + \beta_9(SCOM)$$

where   Pr(prefer alliance) = probability a small power will prefer alliance with a great power; the estimates are bounded at 0 and 1, though the actual codings are 0 or 1

INDL = individual learning variable; 0 or 1

SYSL = system learning variable; continuous, bounded between 0 and 1

DTMB = direct threat military balance; continuous, with a lower bound of 0

DCOM = amelioration of direct military balance from commitments other than great power alliances; continuous, with a lower bound of 0

STRS = for systemic threat revisionist share of great power resources; continuous, with a lower bound of 0

STMB = systemic threat military balance between revisionist and small power; continuous, with a lower bound of 0

GEOG = geographical exposure variable; 0 or 1

SCOM = amelioration of systemic threat military balance from great power commitments other than alliances; continuous, with a lower bound of 0

I discuss the operational measures for each variable below.

The individual learning hypothesis was expressed as a dichotomous variable, given a value of 1 if the historical lesson advocated alliance (if the country was allied and succeeded or was neutral and failed) or 0 if the lesson advocated neutrality (if the country was allied and failed or was neutral and succeeded). Hypothesis 1 proposes that the coefficient for this variable, β_1, should be positive. The lessons garnered by states for each of the postwar periods are displayed in Table 2.

Hypothesis 2 posits that each formative event provides one systemwide lesson on great power alliances which is followed by each small power. The content of the lesson is determined by the collective experiences of all the relevant small powers in that formative event. This value is a number from 0 to 1 which indicates the content of the lesson, the extent to which it advocates neutrality or alliance. A value of 0 would be the strongest lesson for neutrality, a value of 0.5 would indicate a lesson favoring neither, and a value of 1 would indicate the

Table 2. World war experiences and predicted individual lessons for postwar choices between alliance and neutrality

Nation	Formative event	Experience	Predicted individual lesson
Albania	World War I	Failed neutral	Alliance
Australia	World War II	Successful ally	Alliance
Belgium	World War I	Failed neutral	Alliance
Belgium	World War II	Failed neutral	Alliance
Bulgaria	World War I	Failed ally	Neutrality
Denmark	World War I	Successful neutral	Neutrality
Denmark	World War II	Failed neutral	Alliance
Egypt	World War II	Failed ally	Neutrality
Finland	World War II	Failed ally	Neutrality
Greece	World War II	Failed neutral	Alliance
Iran	World War II	Failed neutral	Alliance
Iraq	World War II	Failed ally	Neutrality
Ireland	World War II	Successful neutral	Neutrality
Luxembourg	World War II	Failed neutral	Alliance
Netherlands	World War I	Successful neutral	Neutrality
Netherlands	World War II	Failed neutral	Alliance
New Zealand	World War II	Successful ally	Alliance
Norway	World War I	Successful neutral	Neutrality
Norway	World War II	Failed neutral	Alliance
Portugal	World War I	Successful ally	Alliance
Portugal	World War II	Successful ally	Alliance
Rumania	World War I	Successful ally	Alliance
Spain	World War I	Successful neutral	Neutrality
Spain	World War II	Successful neutral	Neutrality
Sweden	World War I	Successful neutral	Neutrality
Sweden	World War II	Successful neutral	Neutrality
Switzerland	World War I	Successful neutral	Neutrality
Switzerland	World War II	Successful neutral	Neutrality
Thailand	World War II	Failed neutral	Alliance
Turkey	World War I	Failed ally	Neutrality
Turkey	World War II	Successful ally	Alliance
Yugoslavia	World War II	Failed neutral	Alliance

Notes: The totals are fifteen lessons of neutrality and seventeen lessons of alliance:

Wartime policy	Wartime experience	
	Failure	Success
Neutrality	11	10
Alliance	5	6

strongest lesson favoring great power alliance. The fraction is constructed as follows:

$$\text{systemic learning value} = \frac{\text{sum of failed neutral and successful allied small powers for that event}}{\text{number of small powers for that event}}$$

For World War I, there were 2 failed neutrals and 2 successful allied nations out of a total of 12 small powers, producing a systemwide learning fraction of 0.33 for interwar cases. This lesson moderately favors neutrality. For World War II, there were 9 failed neutrals and 4 successful allied states out of a total of 20 nations, producing a value of 0.65 for post–World War II cases. This lesson moderately favors great power alliance. Hypothesis 2 implies that $\beta 2$ will be positive.

The first category of threat is systemic threat, present when a revisionist great power poses a general threat to the international system. Building a measure of systemic threat requires a measure that detects when states perceive an imminent great power war as likely. Under one coding scheme, great power war was seen as more likely to be imminent if alliances tighten and interaction among alliance groups decreases. These activities were considered to be signs that great power elites saw the possibility of war in the immediate future.[33] Application of this coding scheme to the empirical question at hand is problematic, as alliance decisions would constitute the dependent and independent variables, threatening falsifiability. Further, alliance interactions might not be uniformly perceived by all states, for neutrals, because they are outside these diplomatic loops, might not receive the signals of increased communication between allies and decreased communication between alliance groups. Instead of alliance tightness, militarized great power crises were used as the indicators of imminent great power war. This variable was coded as dichotomous: if a great power initiated a militarized crisis with another great power or with a regional ally of another great power in the year of observation or the previous year, then all small powers in that region during the observation year were considered to perceive this great power as potentially revisionist, and the possibility of an imminent great power war, high. Otherwise, small powers were considered to be seeing great power war as not imminent.

One possible criticism of the use of great power militarized crises as indicators of the imminence of systemic war is that wars that transform international system structure occasionally erupt over issues of essentially low consequence. Therefore, high-stakes political crises between great powers might be ineffective "warnings" of imminent systemic war and poor indicators of perceived threat.[34] The threat perceived by small powers emerges, however, not from the postwar effects on inter-

[33] Bruce Bueno de Mesquita, "Measuring Systemic Polarity," *Journal of Conflict Resolution* 19 (1975): 187–216; A. F. K. Organski and Jacek Kugler, *The War Ledger* (Chicago: University of Chicago Press, 1980).

[34] Bruce Bueno de Mesquita, "Pride of Place: The Origins of German Hegemony," *World Politics* 43 (October 1990): 28–52; Bueno de Mesquita, "Big Wars, Little Wars," 159–169.

national structure but from the direct threats to security resulting from the war itself. Wars fought between two status quo states over issues of relatively low intrinsic significance are therefore not likely to threaten small powers, for neither power is apt to fight the sort of total war which would threaten small powers, even if system structure changes after the war.

In half of the eight observation years in the data set, systemic threat was coded as present for at least some small powers. For the post–World War I years, Germany qualifies as a perceived potential revisionist in 1939 because of its annexation of the Sudetenland in 1938 and invasion of Czechoslovakia in 1939. The Soviet Union qualifies as a perceived potential revisionist in Europe in 1949 because of the Berlin blockade and in 1961 because of the Berlin deadline crisis. China counts as a potential revisionist in East Asia in 1955 because of its actions and threats against the American ally Taiwan.

If a great power war is perceived as imminent because of such a militarized crisis, then it is assumed that small powers will perceive the probability of an actual outbreak of war to depend on the relative share of great power capabilities held by the potential revisionist, because a greater share of great power resources gives the revisionist a better chance of winning. For each of the potential great power revisionists, the systemic threat resource share values were recorded as the average of the revisionist's share of each of the Correlates of War's six measures of material capabilities among the great powers: military spending, military troop levels, total population, urban population, energy consumption, and iron and steel consumption (if there is no revisionist threat, this variable is coded as 0). Hypothesis 3 proposes that this measure is positively correlated with the probability that the small power will prefer alliance, therefore predicting that β_5 will be positive.

Some have argued that the military capability component of threat is better assessed by examining a state's standing military forces rather than its gross power. Of course, military capability must be measured in relative rather than absolute terms. Empirical research has found that standing military forces are more important than long-term, war-fighting capabilities in a state's calculus of war outcomes. One way to capture the relative capability of standing military forces is to use the ratio of military spending of the threatener, the state perceived as being a potential revisionist, to the threatened, where a ratio of 0 indicates no threat.[35] Using troop levels is problematic for small powers, as some countries rely heavily on reserve or militia forces for defense. The

[35] Correlates of War data on military spending were used.

contribution of these forces is difficult to assess except on a case-by-case basis, because their quality and the speed with which they could be committed to the national defense vary widely.

Balance of threat theory would predict that as this ratio increases, so does the probability that a small power will prefer alliance with a great power. However, there is probably a diminishing return to increases in fear from increases in capability; for example, the level of fear may double as the ratio increases from $2:1$ to $4:1$, but it is not likely to double as the ratio increases from $100:1$ to $200:1$. A simple transformation indicating diminishing marginal returns but maintaining monotonicity is to take the square root of this military spending ratio, which is the systemic threat military balance variable. Hypothesis 3a predicts that β_3 will be positive.

Hypothesis 3b predicts that geographic exposure to a systemic threat increases the probability of preferring alliance. This is operationalized as a dummy variable. If a great power lies between the small power and the potential revisionist, than the small power is coded as unexposed, and the geographic exposure variable is coded as 0; otherwise the small power is exposed, and the variable is coded as 1. The geographic exposure variable is included as an interactive term with the resource share and revisionist military balance variables, as realism would predict that if a small power is geographically exposed, it will feel more threatened by a more powerful revisionist. Therefore, Hypothesis 3b predicts that β_6 and β_8 will be positive.

Hypothesis 3c proposes that great power commitments other than mutual alliances (such as one-way extended deterrent arrangements) ought to ameliorate the systemic threat and therefore decrease the probability that a small power will seek a mutual alliance with a great power in the face of a systemic threat. The contribution of allied forces (forces of great powers which are committed to the defense of the small power in an arrangement other than a mutual alliance) needs to be considered separately from the defender's military forces, since if the defender is attacked, it cannot count on the full contribution of allied forces because allies also need to worry about the defense of their own countries. In other words, one allied soldier is worth less for the defense of the target than is one of the small power's soldiers. The methodological task is to devise a scheme that assesses separately the contribution of allied forces and the contribution of the small power's own military to the security of the small power. If no such nonmutual alliance commitments exist and if T represents the military resources of the threateners and D represents the resources of the defender, then T/D represents the military balance between the two. As this value grows, so does the threat posed to the defender. If we assumed that allied forces could be counted on completely and so could be considered as if they were the forces of the defending country, then the military balance would be $T/(D + A)$, as the forces of the allies (A) could simply be added to the forces of the defender in assessing the size of the force available to protect the defender. Therefore, the larger the allied force, the lower is $T/(D + A)$ and the lower the threat. Because we should not make the assumption that allied forces make a contribution equal to that of defending forces, the amelioration of the threat offered by allied forces needs to be evaluated as a separate term, so that a separate coefficient can be estimated for the contribution it makes to decreasing threat. C is the amelioration of the military balance offered by allied forces. Since allied forces always make the balance of forces better for the defender (in other words, they never make a completely negligible contribution or increase the threat), C will always decrease T/D, so

$$\frac{T}{D} - C = \frac{T}{D + A}$$

Multiplying both sides by $D(D + A)$ yields

$$T(D + A) - CD(D + A) = TD$$

which reduces to

$$C = \frac{TA}{D(D_{,} + A)} \tag{2}$$

This is the independent contribution to the military balance offered by allied forces, which will be evaluated as a separate term. The square root of this value was used to create the systemic threat commitments variable. Hypothesis 3c predicts that $\beta 9$ will be negative.

Concerning direct threats, a small power was considered threatened if one or more other powers (small or great) presented demands for the revision of territorial borders or challenges to the sovereignty of the ruling government of the target in the year in question and if the target perceived these demands to carry the risk of military conflict in the near future. Klaus Knorr provided a broader definition of direct threat: "If a state-actor is or feels threatened by another, he anticipates—with some degree of probability—the loss of something of value, such as territory and population, restriction or loss of sovereignty, economic assets, and

Table 3. Direct threats and commitments other than great power alliances

Threatened nation	Threatening nations	Year	Nongreat power allies/nonallied great power defenders
Albania	Yugoslavia, Greece	1921	Italy
Albania	Yugoslavia, Greece	1927, 1933	
Albania	Italy, Greece	1939	
Egypt	Israel	1955	Syria, Lebanon, Iraq, Yemen, and Jordan
Egypt	Israel	1961	1955 allies plus United Arab Emirates and Tunisia
Egypt	Israel	1967	1961 allies plus Morocco and Kuwait
Iran	USSR	1949, 1955	
Iran	USSR	1961	U.S.
Romania	USSR	1927, 1933	Yugoslavia, Poland, Czechoslovakia
Romania	Hungary	1939	Yugoslavia, Poland, U.K., France
Turkey	U.K., France, Italy, Greece	1921	
Turkey	Greece	1927	
Yugoslavia	USSR, Albania, Romania, Bulgaria, Hungary	1949	

political constitution."[36] The coding rule in this study is limited to demands for territory. Anticipation of the complete loss of sovereignty in the special case of the threat to conquer the target is also included. Lesser threats to sovereignty, such as economic penetration by another state, are left out, as responses other than military alliance are usually more appropriate. Hypothesis 4 predicts that the coefficient, β_3, ought to be positive. Codings for direct threats are listed in Table 3.

A separate value for the testing of Hypothesis 4a consists of the amelioration of the dyadic threat military balance offered by small power alliances and nonalliance commitments from great powers. This value was computed in a similar fashion as was the systemic threat commitments variable. Hypothesis 4a predicts that this coefficient β_4 will be negative.

[36] Klaus Knorr, "Threat Perception," in *Historical Dimensions of National Security Problems,* ed. Knorr (Lawrence: University Press of Kansas, 1976), 78.

[5]

Quantitative Results

This chapter describes the results of quantitative, empirical tests of the model presented in Chapter 4. Included in this chapter are robustness tests of the model which assess the claim that the model is arranged in an idiosyncratic manner rigged to produce a certain set of empirical results. These tests alter some of the specifications of the model to see if small changes lead to substantial changes in the empirical results. Included as a test is an application of the learning and realist hypotheses to great power alliance choices in the twentieth century.

EMPIRICAL RESULTS

The dependent variable describes whether the small power in question during the year in question chose alliance with a great power. The population of cases included periodic observations of the alliance choices of small powers in the years following World Wars I and II. Since the dependent variable is dichotomous, logit regression estimation using a maximum likelihood estimator was employed (the model to be estimated is equation [1] in Chapter 4). The results of the logit estimation are shown in Table 4.

Overall, the equation does quite well in predicting the alliance choices of states. In 90 percent of the cases, the model predicted alliance choices correctly.[1] More specifically, Table 4 indicates quite clearly

---

[1] The contingency table is a different measure of global fit for a model with a dichotomous dependent variable. It is not used here, for in explaining the variance of the dependent variable, it groups most of the cases near 0 or 1 because of the heavy dominance of a single, dichotomous independent variable, individual learning. This makes the

Table 4. Logit estimation of the causes of small power alliance choices after World Wars I and II

Variable	Estimated coefficient	Standard error	Significance level
Learning			
Individual	4.80	0.796	<0.0005
Systemic	5.78	2.37	0.008
Direct threat			
Military balance	−0.0119	0.155	—
Nonalliance commitments	−0.111	0.189	—
Systemic threat			
Resource share	0.0784	0.0496	0.06
Resource share × geography	−0.192	0.0725	0.01[a]
Military balance	−0.0467	0.0395	—
Military balance × geography	0.227	0.112	0.02
Nonalliance			
Commitments	−0.659	1.23	—
Constant	−5.07	1.42	<0.0005

Notes:

n = 127

Log-likelihood(0) = −87.387

Log-likelihood function = −36.102

Likelihood ratio test = 103.470 with 9 df

Predicted behavior	Actual behavior	
	Neutrality	Alliance
Neutrality	53	6
Alliance	7	61

Number of correct predictions: 114

Percentage of correct predictions: 90 percent

[a] The sign of the estimate is not in the predicted direction, but the estimate is statistically significant at the 0.01 level for a two-tailed significance test. All other significance tests are one-tailed.

that both the individual and the systemic learning variables had statistically and substantively significant impacts on the dependent variable. This is strong empirical support for Hypotheses 1 and 2, even with the conservative assumption that the standard errors are likely to be underestimated given autocorrelation in the dependent variable.

Assessing the distinct, individual effects of these two learning variables, however, is a more difficult question. The indicated significance of the systemic variable can be misleading, because the empirical results would still show the predictions of the systemic learning variables

---

contingency table's plotting of decile performance scores against a 45-degree reference line less useful and possibly misleading.

as doing well even if decision makers learned only according to their own lessons and not at all by systemic lessons, since individual lessons compose systemic lessons. For example, if systemic learning had no real effect and half the individual lessons were for neutrality, it would appear that systemic learning would be having some effect because half of the sample did, as predicted, prefer neutrality, although systemic experiences had been irrelevant to the forming of preferences. Such a phenomenon is not inconceivable with this data set: for each post–formative event group of cases, the fraction of cases for which the small power preferred alliance roughly approximated the predicted fraction of the systemic learning variable, which expresses the degree to which alliance was favored by the systemic lesson (for post–World War I cases, 23 percent of the nations preferred alliance, and the systemic learning variable was coded at 0.33; for post–World War II cases, 68 percent of the nations preferred alliance, and the systemic learning variable was coded at 0.65).

One way to separate out the effects is to see if the individual learning hypothesis is successful at predicting individual cases, particularly for those nations that had preferences in opposition to the systemic lesson derived from the formative experience. The empirical results point to individual learning as a powerful explanation of the dependent variable—by itself, the individual learning variable correctly predicts 111 out of 127 cases, compared with the entire model predicting 114 correctly, with the systemic learning variable alone predicting only 89 cases correctly. Further, of the cases for which the predictions of individual learning were at odds with those of systemic learning (40 cases), the individual learning variable correctly predicted 80 percent of these cases versus 20 percent for the systemic learning variable. This result is consistent with the research on crisis bargaining and reputation which argues that when a nation assesses its adversary's reputation, it does not draw lessons from the adversary's behavior in interactions between the adversary and third states.[2]

By contrast, the effects of changes in the levels of international threat have only marginal effects on the dependent variable. A model including all the threat variables and neither of the learning variables makes only 51 percent correct predictions of the dependent variable. This is not very impressive given the dichotomous nature of the dependent variable; flipping a coin would on average make 50 percent correct

---

[2] Paul K. Huth, *Extended Deterrence and the Prevention of War* (New Haven: Yale University Press, 1988); and Glenn H. Snyder and Paul Diesing, *Conflict Among Nations: Bargaining, Decision Making, and System Structure in International Crises* (Princeton: Princeton University Press, 1977).

predictions. The estimates for the direct threat variables are clearly not statistically significant, offering evidence against Hypotheses 4 and 4a. Of the systemic threat variables, the military balance variables appear to have little substantive and limited statistical significance, providing evidence against Hypothesis 3a. Since there are several proxy variables for the systemic threat proposition, though, analysis of the individual effects of the different variables is necessary. One way of estimating the contribution of individual terms toward explaining the dependent variable in maximum likelihood estimation is to assess the degree to which they affect the likelihood score of the estimation, which is an indication of the likelihood that the model produced the data observed. Adding variables will never diminish a likelihood score, but adding variables to the model which have a systematic effect on the dependent variable will raise the likelihood score significantly more than adding variables that have no systematic effect. The likelihood ratio test evaluates whether the contribution to the likelihood score from the addition of one or more variables is significant and therefore whether the added variables are meaningful factors affecting the dependent variable.[3] The likelihood ratio test statistic (LRTS) can be evaluated on a chi-square distribution, having m degrees of freedom, where m equals the difference in the number of terms of the two model specifications under comparison. For equation (1), likelihood ratio tests reveal that the two systemic threat military balance variables (the systemic threat military balance term itself and the term composed of the systemic threat military balance variable multiplied by the geographic exposure variable) and the direct threat variables add so little to explaining the dependent variable that they can be justifiably excluded.[4] Such a test also reveals that inclusion of the systemic threat resource share and the systemic threat nonalliance commitments variables are justified.[5]

[3] On this test, see Gary King, *Unifying Political Methodology* (Cambridge: Cambridge University Press, 1989), 84–87. The likelihood ratio test statistic (LRTS) is calculated as follows:

$$LRTS = 2[\ln L - \ln L(R)]$$

Where   L = likelihood of the model which is unrestricted, having the greater number of terms;

   L(R) = likelihood of the model which is restricted, having the lesser number of terms.

[4] The LRTS is 5.39, which is greater than the value for the 0.20 level in a chi-square distribution with 4 degrees of freedom, meaning that we can estimate with confidence that little systematic relationship exists between these 4 variables and the dependent variable.

[5] The LRTS for comparing the model in equation (1) with a model including just the two learning variables is 14.8, which is significant at the 0.05 level with 7 degrees of freedom. The LRTS for a comparison of a model containing just the learning variables and one containing the learning variables as well as the two resource share terms and the

These tests point to two initial conclusions regarding the influence of systemic threat on the dependent variable, alliance choices. First, we can be reasonably confident that systemic threat does have a statistically significant effect on the dependent variable. Second, the data indicate that as a proxy variable, the systemic threat military balance variable does not have a statistically significant effect on the dependent variable; the systemic threat resource share, however, does have a significant effect. Since the military balance variable is a measure of the relation of military strength between the revisionist and small power, this finding indicates that the size of the small power does not affect the way in which it reacts to emerging systemic threats. The unimportance of the systemic threat military balance variables is confirmed by examining logit analysis of a model that excludes those variables from analysis. These results are shown in Table 5, which illustrates that exclusion of these two independent variables does not substantially alter the estimates.

The high standard error for the estimate of the systemic threat nonalliance commitments variable offers evidence against Hypothesis 3c. As predicted, states that are geographically unexposed to a systemic threat are more likely to prefer alliance with a great power than if there were no systemic threat, and the greater the resource share of the revisionist power, the greater the likelihood that they will prefer such an alliance. An important caveat to this finding is that the estimate has limited statistical significance (only at the 0.10 level). If the threatened small power is geographically exposed to the systemic threat (74 percent of those states coded as facing a systemic threat were coded as being geographically exposed), then the net effect is for the small power to be *less* likely to prefer alliance with the great power than if there were no systemic threat. Again, when a small power is geographically exposed to a systemic threat, the geographical exposure variable is coded as 1, so the net coefficient for the resource share held by a great power posing a systemic threat is b(resource share) + b[(resource share) * (geography)] = 0.0422 −0.0736 = −0.0314. This is evidence against Hypothesis 3b, which predicts that when a systemic threat appears, the probability that a small power will prefer alliance ought to increase; the sign of the coefficient is opposite that predicted by the hypothesis, which indicates that the data point to a relationship opposite that predicted by balance of threat theory. Further, as the revisionist's share of great power resources increases, the chances of the small

---

systemic threat nonalliance commitments variable is 9.394, which exceeds the chi-square value for the 0.05 level at 3 degrees of freedom, 7.815.

Table 5. Logit estimation of the causes of small power alliance choices excluding systemic threat military balance variables

Variable	Estimated coefficient	Standard error	Significance level
Learning			
Individual	4.29	0.650	<0.0005
Systemic	4.72	2.12	0.02
Systemic threat			
Resource share	0.0422	0.0327	0.10
Resource share × geography	−0.0736	0.0385	0.06[a]
Nonalliance commitments	−0.542	0.747	—
Constant	−4.39	1.23	<0.0005

Notes:
n = 127
Log-likelihood(0) = −87.387
Log-likelihood function = −38.797
Likelihood ratio test = 98.0798 with 5 df

Predicted behavior	Actual Behavior	
	Neutrality	Alliance
Neutrality	53	7
Alliance	7	60

number of correct predictions: 113

percentage of correct predictions: 89 percent

[a] The sign of the estimate is not in predicted direction, but the estimate is statistically significant at the 0.06 level for a two-tailed significance test. All other significance tests are one-tailed.

power preferring neutrality increase even further, again in opposition to the predictions of balance of threat theory. These findings are not dismissable as stochastic hiccups—a likelihood ratio test supports the inclusion of both the systemic threat resource share terms (the variable by itself and the variable multiplied by the geography exposure variable) and the systemic threat nonalliance commitments variable. The real effect in this sample, then, is that for geographically exposed states, the presence of a systemic threat decreases the likelihood that a small power will prefer alliance. Certainly, this finding is at odds with the predictions of balance of threat theory, which proposes that status quo states will tend to ally together to balance against a state bent on systemic hegemony or territorial expansion. It does, however, seem to offer empirical support for the proposition that when faced with a systemic threat, small powers tend to accept buck-passing/neutrality logic rather than balance/bandwagon/chain-ganging logic.

So far, discussion has focused on statistical significance. The next task is assessment of the relative magnitudes of the effects of the learning and threat variables. Direct comparison of coefficient estimates as a means of assessing explanatory power is difficult in this case, given the logit specification of the model and the variety of units used in measurement. A more fruitful approach is to think specifically about the predictions of the two theories under examination. Balance of threat theory predicts that in a high-threat environment, a state will be more likely to choose alliance rather than neutrality regardless of its lesson, and in a low-threat environment, a state will be more likely to choose neutrality rather than alliance regardless of its lesson. Learning theory, on the other hand, provides that regardless of the level of external threat, a state is likely to choose alliance if its lesson advocates alliance and to choose neutrality if its lesson advocates neutrality. These predictions can be tested by comparing the predicted values for the dependent variable at high and low levels of threat and with lessons of alliance and neutrality. This method of assessing explanatory power is useful because it provides a comparison of cases in which the two theories make opposing predictions.

The focus here will be on individual learning, because that appears to be the more powerful of the two learning explanations, and systemic threat, as direct threat is not statistically significant. I will examine the systemic threat resource share variable because the systemic threat military balance variable is not systematically related to the dependent variable. To examine how predictions for the dependent variable change as the values change for individual learning and systemic threat resource share, the other independent variables need to be set constant. I will assume that no direct threat or nonalliance commitments exist from great powers and that the small power is geographically exposed to any systemic threat. To isolate the effects of individual learning, the comparison will further assume that the systemic lesson favors neither neutrality nor alliance; therefore, the systemic threat value will be set at 0.5 (where a value of 1 indicates that the systemic lesson strongly favors alliance and a value of 0 means that the systemic lesson strongly favors neutrality). The coefficient estimates from Table 5 will be used, and these offer the following formulation:

$$\Pr(\text{prefer alliance}) = f\big[-4.39 + 4.29(\text{INDL}) + 4.72(\text{systemic learning}) + 0.0422(\text{systemic threat resource share}) - 0.0736(\text{systemic threat resource share} \times \text{geography})\big]$$

In the analysis I consider five different systemic threat environments: the 1939 Nazi German threat, the 1949 Soviet threat, the 1955 Chinese threat, the 1961 Soviet threat, and an environment of no threat. For each environment, I then compare the predictions for the dependent vari-

Table 6. Predictions of small powers' alliance choices given different levels of systemic threat and different individual lessons

Year	Systemic threatener (resource share)	Predicted probability of choosing alliance with an individual lesson of neutrality (individual learning = 0)	Predicted probability of choosing alliance with an individual lesson of alliance (individual learning = 1)
1939	Germany (23.4)	0.060	0.816
1949	USSR (34.9)	0.042	0.754
1955	China (20.4)	0.065	0.829
1961	USSR (28.3)	0.051	0.791
—	No systemic threat (0)	0.117	0.902

Note: Table entries are predictions for the dependent variable, based on coefficient estimates in Table 5.

ables for the case of an individual lesson favoring neutrality and an individual lesson favoring alliance, presenting these in Table 6. If the level of threat is the most important factor driving states' alliance decisions, then in environments of high threat (the first four rows) the dependent variable prediction should be close to 1, indicating a high probability of preference for alliance; conversely, in a low-threat environment (the bottom row), the dependent variable prediction should be close to 0, signifying a high probability of preference for neutrality. If a state's individual formative experience is the primary factor determining its alliance choices, then we would expect that with an individual lesson of alliance (the right column) the dependent variable prediction should be close to 1, indicating a high probability of preference for alliance; conversely, with an individual lesson favoring neutrality (the left column) the dependent variable should be close to 0, denoting a high probability of preference for neutrality.

As predicted by learning theory, the likelihood of a state choosing alliance or neutrality is strongly determined by the nature of the individual lesson: all entries in the right column are close to 1, and all those in the left column are close to 0. Table 4 also indicates that the level of threat is not an important factor determining preference for alliance or neutrality, as the probability of preference for alliance in a high-threat environment is high only when the lesson favors alliance, and the probability of preference for alliance is low (meaning necessarily that the probability of preference for neutrality is high) only when the individual lesson favors neutrality. Interestingly, the marginal effect of increases in threat is opposite that predicted by balance of threat theory, since as the level of threat increases (in other words, in comparing the top four rows of high-threat environments to the low-threat environment in the last row), the probability a state will prefer alliance *decreases*. This is especially interesting given that in all cases the hypothetical small power is assumed to be geographically exposed, its perceived level of threat thus heightened by the logic of balance of threat theory. In sum, in this critical test comparing opposing predictions of the balance of threat and learning theories, learning theory explains why states prefer alliance or neutrality, as the empirical evidence offers strong support for Hypothesis 1. Further, this evidence offers no support for Hypothesis 3, showing that small powers tend to follow logic opposite to balance of threat theory and to pass the buck when facing a threat rather than balance against or bandwagon with it.

Individual-level learning, then, is an accurate and powerful predictor of the dependent variable. These results also point to the considerable parsimony of the individual learning hypothesis—about 90 percent of the cases can be predicted correctly with the use of a single, simple proposition. This finding has encouraging implications for further exploration of learning in international relations. The hypotheses under examination are certainly great simplifications of the actual process of learning; states are complex entities, and the task of drawing inferences may be the most complicated of decision tasks faced by foreign policy–makers. The results here, however, show that highly complex models are not the only way to describe the learning process and that simple models of learning can tell us much about international politics.

SPECIFICATION TESTS

The equation analyzed in Table 4 represents the model that I feel best tests the learning and balance of threat explanations of small power alliance behavior. But I recognize that the model rests on a number of assumptions that might be subject to dispute. In this section, I will test the robustness of the empirical findings by exploring different specifications of the model and different coding rules for the data. The general approach is to consider what criticisms would be made by an observer who was skeptical of the empirical findings, namely, that the data support the learning hypotheses. In other words, I will explore the arguments that might be made by a critic who believes that I may have relied on an improbable and fragile set of assumptions in order to produce the strongest results possible. A dramatic change in the empirical results because of small changes in the specification of the model would point to the fragility of the results just presented. But a lack of such changes in the empirical results would boost our confidence in the findings.

Test 1: Fewer Observations per Formative Event

One possible criticism of the data set is that by taking a number of observations for the period following each formative event, the data set is artificially inflated, as decisions about whether to be allied or remain neutral might not be taken every six years. If so, measuring alliance decisions every six years might inflate the estimate of the strength of the individual lessons, for a single decision would be observed more than once. One way to test for this possibility is to split the data set into halves, thereby doubling the amount of time between observations and regressing only one-half of the data set at a time. If there is artifical inflation of the data set when observations are made for behavior at six-year intervals, then increasing the time of the interval between observations ought to show different results. Table 7 compares the coefficient estimates and standard errors for regressions of the full data set—for observations taken in the years 1921, 1927, 1933, 1939, 1949, 1955, 1961, and 1967—and for separate regressions for each half of the data set, in one of which observations were taken for 1921, 1933, 1949, and 1961, and in the other, for 1927, 1939, 1955, and 1967. For the latter half, multicollinearity among the systemic threat proxy variables was too high to permit inclusion of all of them in the same equation, so the regression was run with only the systemic threat resource share and military balance variables. As Table 7 clearly indicates, similar empirical conclusions as to the importance of the learning variables and the insignificance of the threat variables are drawn when the data set is split into halves and the interval between observations is increased to twelve years.

A persistent critic might argue that putting even a twelve-year lag between observations does not make them distinct phenomena if the state is acting on the same lesson. In other words, one might posit, learning from a single formative event can be observed only once; *any* additional measurement invites autocorrelation into the analysis and artificially inflates the data set. To explore this possibility, I divided the data set even further, into quarters. Each quarter of the data set includes one set of observations for one year following each of the two formative events, paired so as to have a similar space of time after the formative event: 1921 and 1949, 1927 and 1955, 1933 and 1961, and 1939 and 1967.

Table 7. Sensitivity analysis of logit estimates for alliance choices, varying the time between observations at 6 and 12 years

Variables	(1)	(2)	(3)
Learning			
Individual	4.80 (0.796)*****	9.45 (4.22)***	4.28 (0.952)*****
Systemic	5.78 (2.37)****	23.0 (13.8)*	4.31 (3.91)
Direct threat			
Military balance	0.012 (0.155)	−0.233 (0.412)	0.440 (1.07)
Nonalliance commitments	−0.111 (0.189)	−0.037 (0.439)	−0.166 (1.44)
Systemic threat			
Resource share	0.078 (0.050)*	0.084 (0.076)	−0.067 (0.127)
Resource share			
× geography	−0.192 (0.072)[a]	−0.399 (0.219)[a]	—
Military balance	−0.047 (0.040)	−0.109 (0.073)	−0.027 (0.178)
Military balance			
× geography	0.227 (0.112)***	0.411 (0.324)	—
Nonalliance commitments	−0.659 (1.23)	—	−0.862 (2.02)
Constant	−5.07 (1.42)*****	−15.0 (8.84)**	−4.02 (1.88)**
n	127	63	64
Percentage of correct			
predictions	88	90	88

Notes:
Table entries are coefficient estimates, with standard errors given in parentheses.
Column headings are as follows:
(1) years of observation are 1921, 1927, 1933, 1939, 1949, 1955, 1961, and 1967
(2) years of observation are 1921, 1933, 1949, and 1961
(3) years of observation are 1927, 1939, 1955, and 1967
  *Significant at the 0.10 level
  **Significant at the 0.05 level
  ***Significant at the 0.025 level
  ****Significant at the 0.01 level
  *****Significant at the 0.0005 level
[a] sign of the estimate is not in the predicted direction, but the estimate is significant at the 0.10 level or higher for a two-tailed test.

This test is especially strong because it takes only a single observation per formative event, removing virtually all autocorrelation among observations. If the explanatory power of the learning hypotheses has been exaggerated by including four observation years per formative event, then this subdivision ought to show a substantially diminished explanatory power for the learning variables. Table 8 displays the coefficient estimates, model performance, and individual learning performance for the full data set, the two data halves displayed in Table 7, and each of the data quarters.

The performance of the individual learning hypothesis is impressive. It correctly predicts a substantial percentage of observations for each

Table 8. Sensitivity analyses of logit estimates for alliance choices, varying the time between observations at 6, 12, and 28 years

Variable	(1)	(2)	(3)	(4)	(5)	(6)	(7)
Learning							
Individual	4.80*****	9.45***	4.28****	4.19***	4.07****	5.82****	4.47***
	(0.796)	(4.22)	(0.952)	(1.78)	(1.35)	(1.97)	(1.52)
Systemic	5.78****	23.0*	4.31	11.77*	4.78	2.39	−0.169
	(2.37)	(13.8)	(3.91)	(6.08)	(4.32)	(7.26)	(10.9)
Direct Threat							
Military balance	0.0119	−0.233	0.440	−0.258	0.437	1.10	0.170
	(0.155)	(0.412)	(1.07)	(0.202)	(1.27)	(6.01)	(0.944)
DCOM	−0.111	−0.037	−0.166	−0.434	0.0305	−0.788	—
	(0.189)	(0.439)	(1.44)	(2.02)	(2.05)	(6.75)	
Systemic Threat							
Resource share	0.0784*	0.0837	−0.067	—	—	—	—
	(0.0496)	(0.0755)	(0.127)				
Resource share × geography	−0.192*	−0.399ᵃ	—	—	—	—	—
	(0.0725)	(0.219)					
Military balance	−0.047	−0.109	−0.0265	−0.0547	8.74	0.0648	0.0057
	(0.0395)	(0.0727)	(0.178)	(0.0951)	(61,200)	(0.0751)	(0.285)
Military balance × geography	0.227***	0.411	—	0.0151	—	−0.131	−0.0071
	(0.112)	(0.324)		(0.0959)		(0.141)	(0.196)
SCOM	−0.659	—	−0.862	—	—	—	−0.780
	(1.23)		(2.02)				(1.23)
Constant	−5.1*****	−15.0**	−4.39**	−7.62***	−4.40**	−4.42	−1.80
	(1.42)	(8.84)	(2.41)	(3.70)	(2.57)	(3.76)	(6.67)
n	127	63	64	31	32	32	32
Loglikelihood (0)	−87.8	−43.6	−22.2	−21.5	−21.9	−22.1	−22.2
% correct for model	88	90	88	90	91	94	91
% correct for INDL	87	87	88	81	91	94	84

Notes:
Entries in rows with equation terms are coefficient estimates; numbers in parentheses are standard errors.
Column headings are as follows:
(1) years of observation are 1921, 1927, 1933, 1939, 1949, 1955, 1961, and 1967
(2) years of observation are 1921, 1933, 1949, and 1961
(3) years of observation are 1927, 1939, 1955, and 1967
(4) years of observation are 1921, and 1949
(5) years of observation are 1927, and 1955
(6) years of observation are 1933, and 1961
(7) years of observation are 1939, and 1967
DCOM = nonalliance commitments for direct threat
INDL = individual learning variable
SCOM = nonalliance commitments for systemic threat
*Significant at the 0.10 level
**Significant at the 0.05 level
***Significant at the 0.025 level
****Significant at the 0.01 level
*****Significant at the 0.0005 level
ᵃThe sign of the estimate is not in the predicted direction, but the estimate is statistically significant at the 0.10 level or higher for a two-tailed significance test. All other significance tests are one-tailed.

[101]

permutation of the data set, and it is the only hypothesis that maintains consistently high statistical and substantive significance for each permutation. Further, the strength of the individual learning variable is shown when the data set is quartered, a particularly strong test as virtually all possible autocorrelation is removed.

Test 2: Combining Systemic and Direct Threat

Another possible criticism of the data set is that the distinction between systemic and direct threat is an artificial one, the introduction of which artificially reduces the coefficient estimates for the threat variables. One way to assess such a criticism is to combine the direct and systemic threat measures into a single set of variables. For this to work, the systemic and direct threats must be expressed in common units. There are two possible ways of combining these variables: express both in terms of the military balance of the threatener to the threatened, or express threat in a dichotomous variable, with 1 reflecting the presence of threat, and 0, its absence. Commitments other than great power alliances can be relatively easily combined into one variable using the formula in equation (2) in Chapter 4. Two regressions were run to explore this possibility: one using a continuous measure of threat and commitment (ratios of defense spending, similar to the military balance variables), and the other using dichotomous measures (1 indicating the presence of a threat or a commitment). The results are presented in Table 9.

When combined, the threat-military balance variables are not significant, although the systemic threat variables were significant in Table 4. This points to the general conclusion that separating the threats inflates the importance of threat, indicating that, if anything, threat is more important when it is divided into two categories. The commitments variable is significant in both forms in Table 9, and the sign is in the predicted direction, which signifies that when small powers have other sorts of external commitments available, they are relatively less likely to pursue alliances with great powers. The variables do have a solid measure of substantive significance: if a small power faces no threat, has a systemic lesson favoring neither neutrality nor alliance, and has an individual lesson favoring alliance, the probability that it will prefer alliance with a great power drops from 0.90 to 0.61 if it has a commitment other than a great power alliance (using the coefficient estimates of the dichotomous measures).[6]

---

[6] These probabilities were calculated on the basis of the coefficient estimates in column (1) of Table 9.

Table 9. Sensitivity analyses of logit estimates: continuous and dichotomous measures of combined threat

Variable name	(1)	(2)
Learning		
Individual	4.17 (0.629)***	4.07 (0.616)***
Systemic	4.48 (1.94)**	4.58 (1.94)**
Threat		
CCTMB	0.0149 (0.0295)	—
CCOMM	−1.83 (0.0883)**	—
DCTMB	—	0.0040 (0.631)
DCOMM	—	−1.74 (1.02)*
Constant	−4.29 (1.15)***	−4.18 (1.15)***

Notes:

n = 127

Table entries are coefficient estimates, with standard errors given in parentheses.

Column headings are as follows:

(1) regression with continuous measures of combined threat

(2) regression with dichotomous measures of combined threat

*Significant at the 0.05 level

**Significant at the 0.025 level

***Significant at the 0.0005 level

All significance tests are one-tailed

CCTMB = continuous measure of combined threat-military balance; CCOMM = continuous measure of commitments other than great power alliances; DCTMB = dichotomous measure of combined threat-military balance; DCOMM = dichotomous measure of commitments other than great power alliances.

Test 3: *Differing Assumptions about the Soviet Threat*

Making coding decisions in hindsight about the presence of threat can be difficult, especially if military action was never actually taken. This is especially true for codings of systemic threat, as indications of intentions that threaten the entire region are often more vague than are intentions of a single state toward another single state over a specific issue. Coding Nazi Germany as a systemic threat to Europe in 1939 is a relatively safe decision, given Hitler's very thinly veiled aggressive ambitions and, of course, the eventual arrival of war. For the question of Soviet intentions after World War II, however, the issue is much hazier. The Soviet Union never did go to war with any Western powers during the cold war; the debate about the true nature of Soviet intentions and ambitions toward Europe and the United States during the cold war is one of the great questions of contemporary history.[7] Of

[7] The literature discussing the nature of the post–World War II Soviet threat is far too extensive to be given justice here. For an illuminating historiographical review of the debate, see Richard A. Melanson, *Writing History and Making Policy* (Lanham, Md.:

course, the coding scheme presented in Chapter 4 takes a position in this debate, arguing the relatively centrist position that in the eyes of the nations of Europe, the USSR presented a systemic threat in 1949 and 1961 but did not in 1955 or 1967.

It is worthwhile to consider, however, whether balance of threat theory would attract more empirical support if different coding decisions were made to reflect different assumptions about the Soviet threat or, more accurate, perceptions of the Soviet threat. There are almost as many opinions about Soviet intentions as there are historians, though two schools of thought can be seen to represent the two ends of the spectrum. The revisionist school claims that the Soviet Union never posed an aggressive threat to Western Europe and that its primary foreign policy goals were to maintain and protect a security buffer in Eastern Europe to ensure national Soviet security. The implication of this might be that the Soviet Union should be coded as never posing a threat to Europe after World War II; however, such an empirical assumption would not improve the performance of balance of threat theory, because no explanation remains for the creation and durability of NATO. In the context of this study, a more interesting comparison is to consider the other side of the spectrum: a fairly constant Soviet threat to Europe throughout the cold war era. To explore this possibility, I modified the data set so that a Soviet threat to Europe was coded as present throughout the cold war, from 1949 to 1967. The model in equation (1) was then regressed on this modified data set, the results of which are presented in Table 10.

As is evident in Table 10, coding the USSR as a constant threat to Europe throughout the cold war does not alter the substantive conclusion that learning is still the dominant explanation of the dependent variable, that external threat has only marginal effects on the dependent variable, and that those effects of threat may in fact be in a direction opposite to that predicted by balance of threat theory.

Test 4: Learning about Specific Countries

This study tests the proposition that small powers draw general lessons about neutrality and alliance. Another possibility is that they draw lessons instead about specific nations as potential allies. If small powers did learn about particular nations, then we would expect that

---

University Press of America, 1983). For a more recent review by a prominent, antirevisionist cold war historian, see John Lewis Gaddis, "The Tragedy of Cold War History," *Diplomatic History* 17 (Winter 1993): 1–16.

Table 10. Sensitivity analysis of logit estimates: different assumptions about the Soviet threat after World War II

Variables	(1)	(2)
Learning		
Individual	4.80 (0.796)******	4.66 (0.770)******
Systemic	5.78 (2.37)****	6.93 (2.62)*****
Direct threat		
Military balance	0.012 (0.155)	−0.0307 (0.159)
Nonalliance commitments	−0.111 (0.189)	−0.114 (0.193)
Systemic threat		
Resource share	0.078 (0.050)*	−0.0174 (0.0389)
Resource share × geography	−0.192 (0.072)[a]	−0.111 (0.0577)[a]
Military balance	−0.047 (0.040)	−0.0040 (0.0383)
Military balance × geography	0.227 (0.112)***	0.182 (0.109)**
Nonalliance commitments	−0.659 (1.23)	−0.638 (1.23)
Constant	−5.07 (1.42)******	−5.20 (1.42)******
Percentage of correct predictions	90	89

Notes:
Table entries are coefficient estimates, with standard errors given in parentheses; $n = 127$.
Column headings are as follows:
(1) standard data set—systemic Soviet threat coded as present in 1949 and 1961
(2) modified data set—systemic Soviet threat coded as present in 1949, 1955, 1961, and 1967
   *Significant at the 0.10 level
  **Significant at the 0.05 level
  ***Significant at the 0.025 level
 ****Significant at the 0.01 level
 *****Significant at the 0.005 level
******Significant at the 0.0005 level
[a]The sign of the estimate is not in the predicted direction, but the estimate is statistically significant at the 0.06 level or higher for a two-tailed significance test. All other significance tests are one-tailed.

from a formative experience a small power would draw lessons about which nations are the most valuable allies. This question is a bit tricky, as in drawing lessons about a *specific* nation as a potential ally, a power is concerned with both the potential ally's military capabilities/competence and its credibility as an ally (that is, the probability that it will honor its alliance commitments).[8] If small powers were drawing lessons from wars, then capabilities-driven learning would encourage them to shun alliances with the losers and seek alliance with the winners. Capabilities are drastically transformed from wartime to peacetime, however, when most of the vanquished's war-making capacity

[8] On the distinction between drawing lessons about credibility and drawing lessons about capabilities, see Ted Hopf, *Peripheral Visions: Deterrence Theory and American Foreign Policy in the Third World, 1965–1990* (Ann Arbor: University of Michigan Press, 1994).

lies in ruins, with the rest tightly regulated by the victors, and the victors demobilize to appease war-weary populations. Therefore, small powers are not likely to emphasize wartime performance over the material capabilities that they can actually observe in the peacetime years following the war. On the other hand, if learning focused on the question of resolve, then small powers would want to ally with those nations that honored their commitments and shun alliance with those that did not. On this issue, deriving predictions for either of the world wars is difficult. In the case of World War I, war erupted in part because all parties honored their commitments: the Russians defended the Serbs, the Germans defended the Austrians, the French did not abandon the Russians, and the British came to the rescue of the Belgians and the French. Similar circumstances describe World War II: the British and the French honored their commitments to Poland in September 1939, the Germans came to the rescue of the Italians during the disastrous campaign in the Balkans in 1941 (though they turned on the Russians, with whom they had signed a nonaggression pact), and none of the Allies signed a separate peace with the Axis.

A different way to think about learning about specific allies is to examine a different class of formative events: militarized crises involving great powers. If small powers draw lessons about the resolve of specific allies, then we would expect that after a great power crisis, the allies of the (diplomatically) defeated great power would tend toward neutrality or alliance with the victor, neutrals would tend toward alliance with the victorious great power, and allies of the victor would maintain their existing alliance ties. This argument is most often applied to the reactions following the string of British and French defeats in the middle and late 1930s, which included the ineffectively contested Italian invasion of Ethiopia, the German remilitarization of the Rhineland, the German annexation of Austria, the appeasement of Germany at the 1938 Munich conference concerning the fate of the Sudetenland, and the eventual invasion of Czechoslovakia. These diplomatic defeats did have some effects on small power behavior, most notably the crumbling of the Little Entente between France and Eastern European powers and the shift from some faith in the League of Nations as an effective guarantor of collective security toward more unilateral neutrality on the part of several neutral states.[9] Elsewhere in Europe, however, the predicted effects did not materialize. Historical research points to a complex array of domestic political factors driving

[9] Robert L. Rothstein, *Alliances and Small Powers* (New York: Columbia University Press, 1968); Nils Örvik, *The Decline of Neutrality, 1914–1941* (Oslo: Johan Grundt Tanum Forlag, 1953), 177–190.

the 1936 break between Belgium and France rather than a loss of faith in French resolve over the reoccupation of the Rhineland.[10] Additionally, the British-Portuguese alliance remained intact, and the predicted bandwagon effects did not appear, as neutral nations refrained from flocking to the German camp, with the arguable exception of Hungary. Turkey even began to negotiate an alliance with Britain and France in mid-1939.

There appears to be even less crisis-driven learning in the post–World War II period. In 1949, the United States demonstrated its resolve to defend its extended foreign policy interests in Europe: it stood by West Berlin through the Soviet blockade in the first major showdown between East and West. This resolve was further demonstrated in its strong response to the invasion of South Korea. These events occurred after the signing of the Brussels Treaty and the expression of interest in the formation of an Atlantic security structure, so the appearance of these treaties ought not be attributed to lessons learned from these two events. The entrances of Greece and Turkey into NATO can be considered to be only limited empirical support, because both had been in the Western camp since the end of World War II. Though it might be too much to expect the Communist-dominated nations in Eastern Europe to flee the Soviet camp, what is missing is any movement on the part of Yugoslavia, Finland, Sweden, Ireland, or Switzerland toward joining NATO after the Soviets lifted the blockade on Berlin in 1949. Similarly, the U.S. victories over the Soviet Union in the Berlin deadline crisis of 1961 and the Cuban Missile Crisis of 1962 also failed to move any European neutrals into NATO, any Warsaw Pact nations into neutrality, or Cuba away from Soviet influence. In short, then, there is some support for the proposition that great power crises can serve as formative events for small powers but have much less effect than world wars as formative events.

Test 5: Great Powers

Some critics might contend that the exclusion of great powers from the data set limits the generalizability of the results because small powers are simply not very important in world politics and that a theory that cannot be applied to the behavior of great powers is of very limited interest. I discussed this issue at some theoretical length in the previous chapter: the main thrust of the argument is that testing the formative events theory on great power behavior faces methodological

---

[10] David Owen Kieft, *Belgium's Return to Neutrality* (Oxford: Clarendon, 1972).

(though not theoretical) difficulties, warranting a focus on small powers given the empirical goals of this study. The general principles of the formative events theory are applicable, however, to decision making in general, which means that the theory-affirming empirical results presented in this chapter offer some support for the proposition that the formative events theory can be applied to great power behavior as well. This section presents a brief application of the ideas in the formative event theory to great power alliance behavior after World Wars I and II. These are not meant to be taken for complete case studies. Assessing the role of learning in great power alliance decisions in the twentieth century is itself a book-length project, as the low number of cases and the difficulty of comparing great power learning require case studies, which themselves would have to be extensive given that the primary and secondary sources addressing great power foreign policy decisions in the twentieth century are almost indigestibly extensive. The discussion that follows is meant to show only a preliminary, empirical plausibility that the formative events learning theory can explain great power alliance behavior.

Britain and France. British reliance on history to inform alliance decisions reaches back before this century. For example, in 1814 Lord Castlereagh supported a British alliance with Prussia based on the lesson he drew from the Napoleonic Wars that Prussia was the only available Continental power that could provide a check on future French territorial ambitions.[11] After the First World War, in constructing a new system of collective security, the British sought to avoid repeating the mistakes of the Congress of Vienna, so much so that they commissioned a historian to produce a study of the issue.[12] Britain was sympathetic to German recovery, concerned more with the revival of British markets than with the revival of Prussian imperialism. Unlike the French, who even in victory were still gripped by a mortal fear of Germany, the British did not fear a moderate renewal of German power in the context of reconstructing British trade and economic networks. Indeed, differences between the British and French about matters such as Germany impeded progress toward an Anglo-French security understanding. The British view was grounded in its historical experience as the great power balancer of Europe, as "the defeat of Germany could be looked upon as just another episode in the tradition where the

---

[11] Harold Nicolson, *The Congress of Vienna* (London: Constable, 1946), 120.
[12] Henry Kissinger, *Diplomacy* (New York: Simon and Schuster, 1994), 240.

defeats of Spain, the Dutch, and Napoleon were precedents."[13] Britain retained its traditional desire to maintain the balance of power in Europe by keeping its hands free, that is, avoiding too rigid alliance commitments that might prevent it from playing the role of balancer against any rising Continental hegemon.[14] This traditional British belief in the balance of power was coupled with a new lesson from 1914—fear of repeating Sarajevo. British appeasement of Germany in the 1930s was in many ways the shadow of 1914: they feared that backing Germany into a corner (a result of building a tightly bound, anti-German bloc) would force another world war.[15]

The experiment in appeasement in the 1930s was seen as a failure and contributed to British desires after the war to establish strong alliance ties with the United States. Interestingly, former prime minister Clement Attlee attributed the shocking Labour victory in the first postwar British elections to public memory of Munich and assignation of blame to the ruling Tories. In later years, Prime Minister Anthony Eden interpreted Abdel Nasser's seizure of the Suez Canal as equivocable to Hitler's aggression in the 1930s, thereby warranting a firm response.[16] The influence of the lessons of the two world wars on British thinking about alliance policy is expressed well by Michael Howard, perhaps Britain's leading, contemporary military historian, who in the preface to his *Continental Commitment* reflected:

> But the book is dated in another more subtle way. I can now see that, without any conscious intent, I was, in writing it, conducting an argument

[13] René Albrecht-Carrié, *A Diplomatic History of Europe since the Congress of Vienna*, rev. ed. (New York: Harper & Row, 1973), 388. See also P. A. Reynolds, *British Foreign Policy in the Inter-War Years* (London: Longmans, Green, 1954), 16.

[14] Keith Middlemas, *The Strategy of Appeasement* (Chicago: Quadrangle Books, 1972), 17.

[15] Robert G. Kaufman, "'To Balance or to Bandwagon?' Alignment Decisions in 1930s Europe," *Security Studies* 1 (Spring 1992): 427, 437; Larry William Fuchser, *Neville Chamberlain and Appeasement* (New York: W. W. Norton, 1982), esp. 7; Martin Gilbert and Richard Gott, *The Appeasers* (Cambridge, Mass.: Riverside Press, 1963), esp. 111; Williamson Murray, "The Collapse of Empire: British Strategy, 1919–1945," *The Making of Strategy: Rulers, States, and War*, ed. Williamson Murray, MacGregor Knox, and Alvin Bernstein (Cambridge: Cambridge University Press, 1994), 393; and Robert Jervis, *Perception and Misperception in International Politics* (Princeton: Princeton University Press, 1976), 267.

[16] Leon D. Epstein, *Britain—Uneasy Ally* (Chicago: University of Chicago Press, 1954), 134, 134n; *Clem Atlee: The Granada Historical Records Interview* (Granada, 1967), cited in Peter Hennessy, *Never Again: Britain, 1945–51* (London: Jonathan Cape, 1992), 67. Hennessy himself, however, is skeptical that Munich determined the 1945 Labour victory (*Never Again*, 56–86). For a review of the literature on the lessons of Munich, see Robert J. Beck, "Munich's Lessons Reconsidered," *International Security* 14 (Fall 1989): 161–191. On the Suez Crisis, see Anthony Eden, *Full Circle: The Memoirs of Anthony Eden* (Boston: Houghton Mifflin, 1960), 518–521.

with that older generation of naval and military historians, from Julian Corbett to Herbert Richmond and Liddell Hart, who had urged the need for maritime strategy, a specific "British Way in Warfare" based on the avoidance of any Continental Commitment. The experience of the Western Front in 1914–1918 had led an entire generation, whose most articulate spokesman was Liddell Hart, to eschew a "continental" strategy as an aberration from a historic norm. My own generation's experience of the Second World War and its aftermath indicated the contrary: no continental adversary could be defeated without a military decision on the mainland of Europe and Britain could wield no influence either in war or in peace unless she was prepared to make a major contribution to that decision. A subsequent, more dispassionate generation may therefore see this book with its implicit conclusions as a tract for the times, promoting my own convictions as to the importance of NATO in Britain's security, and as flawed in its analysis as the books of Liddell Hart.[17]

The case of France is also rather straightforward. A central lesson of the World War I experience for the French was clearly the importance of allies. The crucial importance of Britain, then Russia, and finally the United States in staving off German forces and eventually achieving victory was indisputable; without allies, France certainly would have been defeated by Germany. Indeed, it is not difficult to imagine a rather swift and crushing defeat for France in the autumn of 1914 absent the Russian attack on East Prussia or the contributions of the British Expeditionary Force. The French experience during wartime transformed its traditional obsession with security into an obsession with securing alliances; indeed, though there were deep conflicts over strategy in France in the interwar period, there was consensus on the need for allies.[18] Clemenceau and his successors committed themselves to linking French security to an Anglo-American guarantee. When initial Anglo-American commitments collapsed beneath the isolationist sentiment of the American Senate, the French pushed the British to make a

---

[17] Michael Howard, *The Continental Commitment: The Dilemma of British Defence Policy in the Era of the Two World Wars*, rev. ed. (London: Ashfield Press, 1989), 8. Howard is referring to Basil Henry Liddell Hart, one of the leading British military analysts of the interwar period. His aversion to a British Continental commitment can be traced to his own horrific experiences on the Western Front during World War I. See Brian Bond, *Liddell Hart: A Study of His Military Thought* (New Brunswick: Rutgers University Press, 1977), and John J. Mearsheimer, *Liddell Hart and the Weight of History* (Ithaca: Cornell University Press, 1988).

[18] Arnold Wolfers, *Britain and France between Two Wars* (New York: Harcourt, Brace, 1940), 16; Douglas Porch, "Arms and Alliances: French Grand Strategy and Policy in 1914 and 1940," in *Grand Strategy in War and Peace*, ed. Paul Kennedy (New Haven: Yale University Press, 1991), 136; and Robert A. Doughty, "The Illusion of Security: France, 1919–1940," in *Making of Strategy*, ed. Murray, Knox, and Bernstein, 471–472.

guarantee to defend France and to agree to a military convention that would define in specific terms the nature of the British defense; the latter of these demands caused the British to balk, partly because of their own historical experiences.[19]

The French also learned to appreciate the importance of allies in the East. A 1917 French position paper discussing postwar settlements argued that history had taught France the importance of Eastern allies in countering Germany, pointing specifically to the importance of postwar alliances with an independent Poland and an independent Czechoslovakia. These ideas were eventually realized in the Little Entente, a series of alliances established in the 1920s between France and a number of East European states.[20] Later, France took advantage of the deepening split between the Soviet Union and Nazi Germany in the mid-1930s to sign a defense pact with the Soviet Union in 1935.[21]

France's experience in World War II reinforced the belief in the importance of alliance, as reflected in its postwar alliance with Britain and eventual entry into NATO. France acted against this lesson in the 1960s when it formally exited NATO's integrated military structure, though it remained a signatory of the North Atlantic Treaty. This decision reflected a perception of reduced Soviet threat and shifts in French domestic politics toward a greater emphasis on independence.[22]

Central to both French and British alliance policies in the interwar period are the actions they took vis-à-vis Nazi Germany in the middle and late 1930s. Thomas Christensen and Jack Snyder characterized these alliance policies as buck-passing, in that they sought to pass the buck of balancing against Nazi Germany to others. This might be considered evidence against the learning proposition, especially for France, which learned the importance of maintaining tight alliance ties in World War I, though it ought to be noted that neither Britain nor France during these years sought to retreat into isolationist neutrality. Christensen and Snyder argue that the key independent variable that explains this buck-passing behavior is the perception about whether the offense is dominant on the battlefield; because Britain and France

[19] Jacques Néré, *The Foreign Policy of France from 1914 to 1945* (London: Routledge & Kegan Paul, 1975), 11–31; E. H. Carr, *International Relations since the Peace Treaties* (London: Macmillan, 1937), 25–30.

[20] Piotr S. Wandycz, *France and Her Eastern Allies, 1919–1925* (Minneapolis: University of Minnesota Press, 1962).

[21] William Evans Scott, *Alliance against Hitler: The Origins of the Franco-Soviet Pact* (Durham: Duke University Press, 1962); Jiri Hochman, *The Soviet Union and the Failure of Collective Security, 1934–1938* (Ithaca: Cornell University Press, 1984).

[22] Helga Haftendorn, "The NATO Crisis of 1966–67: Lessons from the Past and Perspectives for the Future," working paper (Berlin: Center on Transatlantic Foreign and Security Studies, Free University of Berlin, 1994).

perceived the defense to be dominant, they felt safe in passing the buck. Significantly, however, Christensen and Snyder point to both countries' World War I experiences as playing large roles in shaping their beliefs that the defense would dominate the next war.[23]

The United States. A number of scholars have argued that American foreign policy has been guided by formative events in this century. Occasional foreign policy crises have caused American foreign policy to bounce between isolationism and internationalism.[24] John Lewis Gaddis, a leading scholar of American foreign policy during the cold war, explained the effects of World War II on American foreign policy thus:

> World War II had produced a revolution in United States foreign policy. Prior to that conflict, most Americans believed that their country could best protect itself by minimizing political entanglements overseas. Events of 1939–40 persuaded leaders of the Roosevelt Administration that they had been wrong; Pearl Harbor convinced remaining skeptics. From then on, American policy-makers would seek security through involvement, not isolation. . . . Lessons of the past greatly influenced Washington's vision of the future. Determined to avoid mistakes which, in their view, had caused World War II, American planners sought to disarm defeated enemies, give peoples of the world the right to shape their own future, revive world trade, and replace the League of Nations with a new and more effective collective security organization.[25]

A critic of learning might argue that this predictive success is balanced by the failure to predict the American turn to isolation after World War I. After all, one could argue, the United States entered that war with an essentially similar goal, to maintain the balance of power against great power aggression, and the postwar behavior was opposite to that of post–World War II, although the outcome was essentially the same. The isolationist backlash after World War I was probably due to widespread American dissatisfaction with the outcome. The eventual rejection of American entry into the League of Nations reflected a

[23] Thomas J. Christensen and Jack Snyder, "Chain Gangs and Passed Bucks: Predicting Alliance Patterns in Multipolarity," *International Organization* 44 (Spring 1990): 159, 162. On the French case, see Richard D. Challener, *The French Theory of the Nation in Arms* (New York: Columbia University Press, 1955), esp. 140–183.

[24] See, for example, Michael Roskin, "From Pearl Harbor to Vietnam: Shifting Generational Paradigms and Foreign Policy," *Political Science Quarterly* 89 (Fall 1974): 563–588.

[25] John Lewis Gaddis, *The United States and the Origins of the Cold War, 1941–1947* (New York: Columbia University Press, 1972), 353–354. See also Kissinger, *Diplomacy*, 456.

deep and widespread reluctance toward a permanent involvement in European affairs. In one sense, then, the American reaction to the outcome of World War I was a response to a perceived failure of policy, thereby in line with learning theory. Yet such an interpretation requires a very context-dependent definition of failure, as the actual outcome was roughly similar to the World War II outcome, which was interpreted as a success.

Italy. Italy joined the Allied Powers in World War I for expansionist reasons: the Allies had to promise the Italians favorable treatment in the postwar territorial settlements to induce their entry. After war's end, the predominant perception among Italians was that Italy had not received its share of territorial compensation due a victor. Dissatisfaction with the Italian role in the world was one concern the Fascists exploited in their rise to power in the early 1920s. Benito Mussolini's distrust of the idealist League of Nations and belief in the importance of power encouraged him to propose in 1933 the Four Power Pact, which, though not an alliance, would have created a new Concert of Europe, allowing the four largest nations in Europe to direct international affairs.

Italy's hunger for empire and expansion only grew as the 1930s progressed. The successes in Spain and Ethiopia whetted Mussolini's appetite for future adventures, and in May 1939 Germany and Italy signed the Pact of Steel, an offensive alliance. As war broke out between Germany, Britain, and France, Mussolini saw it as an opportunity for the emergence of a real Italian empire, based on replacing France in Africa. As Germany made short work of France in 1940, Italy declared war on Britain and France. Italy clearly did not learn the lesson from World War I that entering a belligerent coalition for territorial expansion does not pay, in spite of the fact that Italians were disappointed with their share of the spoils after the war. If anything, Mussolini was *more* ambitious than Sidney Sonnino had been in 1915, foreseeing the war as hastening Italy's rise to being one of the two or three most powerful countries in the world. Interestingly, Mussolini drew the lesson that the unsatisfactory settlement was due to timid diplomacy, which in turn was a function of internal weakness; he used this argument to help carry him to power in 1922.[26]

[26] René Albrecht-Carrié, *Italy from Napoleon to Mussolini* (New York: Columbia University Press, 1950); MacGregor Knox, "Conquest, Foreign and Domestic, in Fascist Italy and Nazi Germany," *Journal of Modern History* 56 (March 1984): 26; H. James Burgwyn, *The Legend of the Mutilated Victory: Italy, the Great War, and the Paris Peace Conference, 1915–1919* (Westport, Conn.: Greenwood, 1993), 318–319; Brian R. Sullivan, "The Strategy of

Germany. Germany offers little as a testing ground for learning. Germany's post–World War II foreign policy was not really the choice of an independent state, as both the Federal Republic of Germany (FRG) and the German Democratic Republic were created as states to enter the blocs of NATO and the Warsaw Pact, respectively. Further, the expansionist aims of Hitler's Germany provide a poor match with the primarily defensively motivated aims of both states (especially the FRG), so post–World War II German leaders would be unlikely to draw on lessons from the Nazi experience to guide decisions on alliances. Of course, these leaders drew the very broad lesson that aggressive expansionism does not pay, not a terribly counterintuitive observation.

One could argue that German alliance decisions in the interwar period provide a good testing ground. Germany's pre–World War I policy was built around steadfast support for its Austrian ally. Indeed, many observers agree that it was this virtually unqualified support during the crisis in the summer of 1914 that was one of the leading, proximate causes of the outbreak of World War I. Following the experience of defeat in World War I, learning theory would encourage the prediction that Germany would view alliances as increasing the risk of entanglement and allies as contributing little to military victory. These lessons would have been difficult for Germany to apply in the interwar years, however: in the 1920s, Germany had no available allies due to its international isolation, and its foreign policy goals had shifted to a fundamentally defensive orientation, as it sought to rebuild economically, maintain internal political stability, and minimize external (particularly French) intervention in German affairs. Germany did engage in extensive political, economic, and military cooperation with the Soviet Union in the 1920s and early 1930s, primarily as a means to circumvent the armament restrictions of the Versailles Treaty, though it declined the Soviet offer in 1924 to create a military alliance between the two states.[27] Hitler's rebuilding of German power in the 1930s was, of course, a reorientation toward an aggressive, expansionist foreign policy. Could the lessons of World War I have been applied once again? The Nazis would probably not have drawn lessons from the World War I experience about how to *avoid* war. Hitler was quite unconcerned with preserving peace; indeed, one of the core elements of his foreign policy was a recognition of the central importance of war. This was the most extreme form of militarism: not only was war an acceptable

---

Decisive Weight: Italy, 1882–1922," in *Making of Strategy*, ed. Murray, Knox, and Bernstein, 304–351.

[27] Hochman, *Soviet Union and the Failure of Collective Security*, esp. 16.

means of foreign policy, it was viewed as an eventually essential path toward achieving the larger goal of more living space for the Aryan race. As a diplomatic tool, Hitler viewed war as a preferred approach, not just a last resort. Therefore, the prospect of entanglement in war posed no problem and the Nazis did not see the outbreak of war in 1914 as a diplomatic disaster—the true tragedy to them was the alleged "stab in the back" of the German war effort by the Jews and other groups. Alternatively, the Germans could have looked to World War I for lessons about whether allies help win a war. However, German dissatisfaction with the Austrian contribution in the First World War would not necessarily be a reason *not* to enter into an alliance; it simply highlights the importance of being independent when entering war. Indeed, Germany was alone in facing the Allies in the first year of World War II; Italy did not enter the conflict until the summer of 1940. One lesson Hitler drew from the First World War was that the kaiser made a mistake in facing a coalition including Britain as well as France. This motivated his attempts to form an alliance with Britain in the 1930s.[28]

The Soviet Union. The Soviet Union is also less useful for the examination of learning and alliance propositions. Analyzing Russia's entry into World War I to discern a lesson about alliances is a muddy task: it entered the war to save its Balkan ally, Serbia, from destruction at the hands of Austria. Also, its alliance with France failed to deter German entry after Russian mobilization. Given the eventually disastrous outcome for czarist Russia, the experience would seem to be a lesson against alliances. Yet one could argue that Russia saw its alliance with France as a means to enhance its war-fighting ability against Germany, not as a deterrent tool. In that light, the Russians might look favorably on the French alliance, which at least staved off defeat at the hands of the Germans for three years; without the western front, Germany could probably have finished off Russia much faster. The interpretation of these experiences is complicated, however, by the Bolshevik Revolution. The Bolsheviks had completely different ideas about foreign policy: they first saw it as a waste of time, as workers' revolutions would soon sweep Europe and invalidate the idea of nations and nationalism. When it became apparent that such events were not about to transpire, they gradually adopted more conventional for-

---

[28] Gordon A. Craig, *From Bismarck to Adenauer: Aspects of German Statecraft* (Baltimore: Johns Hopkins University Press, 1958); Gerhard L. Weinberg, *The Foreign Policy of Hitler's Germany: Diplomatic Revolution in Europe, 1933–36* (Chicago: University of Chicago Press, 1970); Reynolds, *British Foreign Policy in the Inter-War Years*, 99.

eign policies. Like czarist Russia, the Soviets had a general and pervasive concern about security, hence their eagerness to cooperate with Germany as far back as the early 1920s. After World War II, the Soviet Union sought allies in East Europe in particular, even at the cost of intervening to install and maintain pliable, Communist leaderships. Realism would predict this behavior, as the Soviets feared both a renewal of German power and a broad threat from the West. Learning would also predict the Soviet desire to create a bulwark of satellites in Eastern Europe, as a lesson drawn from the experience of the 1941 German invasion.

Japan. Like Italy, Japan's entry into World War I on the side of the Allies was motivated by expansion. Diplomatically, the war was a success for Japan, and in the postwar negotiations Japan achieved her foremost demand, control of the Shantung peninsula in China, formally a German territory.[29] Learning theory, then, would predict that Japan would ally with a belligerent bloc in wartime to help facilitate an expansionist foreign policy agenda. Japanese foreign policy in the 1930s certainly reflected this lesson, as Japan joined Fascist Italy and Nazi Germany in a drive to establish an empire in eastern Asia and the western Pacific. Testing for the impact of Japan's World War II experience on its postwar alliance decisions is problematic. Its foreign policy sovereignty varied from nonexistent to limited at best in the early years after the war. More important, Japan's postwar foreign policy goals were fundamentally different from its prewar goals: it abandoned its imperial ambitions for a basic status quo power orientation. Lessons about the foreign policy tools used to achieve expansionist goals are not appropriate for fashioning a status quo foreign policy, so Japan would have been unlikely to look to either its World War I or World War II experiences for guidance.

Discussion. This quick and admittedly shallow survey of learning and great power alliance behavior in the twentieth century shows that learning does moderately well. Learning is mostly correct in predicting the behavior of interwar Japan, the postwar United States, postwar and interwar Britain, and postwar and interwar France, with arguable exceptions over French Gaullism and French and British buck-passing in the mid- to late 1930s. Learning does poorly in predicting interwar Italian behavior and interwar American behavior. Interwar German

---

[29] Masamichi Royama, *Foreign Policy of Japan, 1914–1939* (Westport, Conn.: Greenwood, 1941), 17–29.

and Soviet behavior do not easily present themselves for tests of learning theory, although Germany's efforts to ally with Britain in the 1930s might be seen as motivated by lessons from World War I, and the Soviet desire for an Eastern European buffer zone realized in the creation of the Warsaw Pact was driven in part by its experience with German invasion.

Jack Snyder found that great powers' decisions about empire tended not to be guided by lessons from past experiences.[30] In his study of Germany, Britain, Japan, the United States, and the Soviet Union, he found that domestic politics provided a stronger explanation of why some great powers engaged in overexpansion and others did not; when historical analogies were made, the choice of analogy seemed to have been driven by domestic political factors rather than formative experiences. Though Snyder's dependent variable is somewhat different from either alliance/neutrality or isolation/engagement, he is still looking at a primary aspect of the foreign policies of these great powers, which raises doubts about the impact of formative events on great power foreign policy. Snyder's test of the learning hypothesis is a bit loose, however; he does not predict a priori from what events lessons ought to be drawn or what the content of lessons drawn ought to look like. He also does not provide a scheme for testing whether a lesson guided policy (in particular, whether the indicator of learning ought to be the statements of foreign policy–makers or foreign policy behavior). The preliminary nature of Snyder's test encourages the execution of more elaborate tests in the future to discern the role of learning in great power foreign policy.

How do balance of threat predictions perform for the great power alliance choices? Some of these nations, particularly Italy, Japan, and Germany in the interwar period, were aggressor powers rather than status quo powers; they were more interested in manufacturing threats than coping with them, so balance of threat theory offers little guidance. Of course, one could argue that these nations' decisions to enter alliances is evidence in support of a very traditional realism that views states as entering alliances to maximize their power. Among the defensively minded states, nearly all preferred alliance after both world wars, with the exception of the United States and the partial exception of Britain, both in the interwar period.

Whether one deems these predictions as successes for balance of threat depends on how one codes the level of threat. For small powers,

[30] Jack Snyder, *Myths of Empire: Domestic Politics and International Ambition* (Ithaca: Cornell University Press, 1991).

I have coded the German threat as relatively low in the interwar period until the mid-1930s, which means that France's paranoia about allies in the immediate post–World War I years is not correctly predicted by balance of threat. Of course, the French themselves said they felt threatened by Germany and no doubt genuinely did feel threatened; the base of their concerns was the irremediable advantage in population Germany had in the early 1920s and would maintain for several years, thus giving them an advantage in people over France. Britain and the United States were less concerned about an immediate renewal of the German threat and hence were less interested in maintaining alliance ties. A balance of threat advocate might argue that this confirms that perceptions of threat motivate alliance preferences, but it also begs the question, Where do perceptions of threat come from? One answer is that wartime experiences play a large role in determining threat perception. France had suffered more than Britain and much more than the United States during the war. France was, therefore, much more sensitive to threat, even though just after World War I, Germany lay in ruins and had been virtually emasculated militarily.[31] After World War II, France, Italy, West Germany, Britain, the United States, and Japan all preferred alliance in the face of the Soviet threat, which, like learning theory, balance of threat correctly predicts. Of course, if one assumes that these alliances are maintained even as the Soviet threat dips at various points in the cold war, this is evidence for learning theory and against balance of threat theory. Soviet willingness in the early interwar period to cooperate is at odds with a balance of threat prediction: the White Army counterrevolutionaries had been defeated, and Germany posed no threat (though, ironically, military cooperation with the USSR would help create a German threat as it enabled the Germans to make substantial progress in rearmament even under the Versailles strictures), so their eagerness for alliance with Germany was not made in a threatening international environment.

OTHER ALLIANCE SCHOLARSHIP USING QUANTITATIVE METHODS

Much of the earlier alliance literature using quantitative methods examined the links between alliances and war.[32] There is, however, a

[31] Challener, *French Theory of the Nation in Arms*, 138–140; Wolfers, *Britain and France between Two Wars*, 11–13.
[32] See, for example, Jack S. Levy, "Alliance Formation and War Behavior: An Analysis of the Great Powers, 1495–1975," *Journal of Conflict Resolution* 25 (December 1981): 581–613; Paul Huth and Bruce Russett, "What Makes Deterrence Work? Cases from 1900 to

body of quantitative alliance scholarship which finds support for the argument that current conditions in the international environment drive alliance decisions.[33] These findings are at odds with the results presented here, which deemphasize the role of current international conditions in driving alliance decisions. There are a number of possible explanations for this discrepancy. First, many of these other studies used the security-as-utility-for-war coding scheme, which differs from the system presented here of measuring threat. Chapter 3 presented some criticisms of this scheme, especially as applied to predicting alliance behavior. The considerable differences in coding rules might explain the different results. Second, the tests conducted in some of these studies were somewhat different from those conducted here. For example, two studies asked the question, Does the presence of the alliance decrease or increase the security of the members? a question different from that asked here, What causes states to prefer alliance or neutrality?[34] Third, in this book I provide a comparative test of theories, whereas these other works test only a single theory. If a comparative test of theories reveals little empirical support for a particular explanation, this must cast doubt on encouraging empirical results from tests conducted on that explanation alone.

This book sheds light on the claim of one study that the global distribution of power affects the propensity of states to seek alliances and that this explains why alliances were more likely after World War II than after World War I.[35] The results presented here offer the alternative explanation that the individual experiences of states during these wars motivated a greater propensity for neutrality after World War I and a greater propensity for alliance after World War II. The learning

---

1980," *World Politics* 36 (July 1984): 496–526; Randolph M. Siverson and Michael Sullivan, "Alliances and War: A New Examination of an Old Problem," *Conflict Management and Peace Science* 8 (Fall 1984): 1–15; Charles W. Kegley Jr. and Gregory A. Raymond, *When Trust Breaks Down: Alliance Norms and World Politics* (Columbia: University of South Carolina Press, 1990); James Lee Ray, "Friends as Foes: International Conflict and Wars between Formal Allies," in *Prisoners of War? Nation-States in the Modern Era*, ed. Charles S. Gochman and Alan Ned Sabrosky (Lexington, Mass.: Lexington Books, 1990), 73–91; and Frank Whelan Waymans, "Alliances and War: A Time-Series Analysis," in *Prisoners of War*, ed. Gochman and Sabrosky, 95–113.

[33] Bruce D. Berkowitz, "Realignment in International Treaty Organizations," *International Studies Quarterly* 27 (1983); Michael T. Altfeld, "The Decision to Ally," *Western Political Quarterly* 37 (December 1984); and David Lalman and David Newman, "Alliance Formation and National Security," *International Interactions* 16 (1991). I lay out my criticisms of the security-as-utility-for-war model in Chapter 3.

[34] Altfeld, "Decision to Ally," and Lalman and Newman, "Alliance Formation and National Security."

[35] Lalman and Newman, "Alliance Formation and National Security."

explanation is preferred to the distribution of power explanation, given that learning correctly predicts both this general tendency after each formative event and the individual choices of states for neutrality or alliances based on their individual experiences. Also, individual learning outperforms the global distribution of power explanation in a critical experiment: when the global distribution of power explanation and the individual learning hypothesis make different predictions, the individual learning hypothesis is correct 80 percent of the time.[36] Further support for the causal explanation that formative experiences determined alliance choices is offered in the case studies in the following chapter.

The results of the quantitative analysis are quite striking. For small power behavior in the twentieth century, the evidence clearly points to learning, especially from individual experience, as the dominant explanation of why small powers choose alliance with great powers or neutrality in peacetime. This relationship holds across five decades and remains strong even as the temporal distance between the formative event and time of observation increases to as great as twenty-two years. The conventional realist explanation of why states prefer alliance as a reaction to external threat has only marginal effects on the propensity of small powers to prefer alliance, and the evidence indicates that even this very limited relationship is in the direction opposite to the predictions of realist theory. These findings hold up if some of the specifications of the model are altered, further increasing confidence in the robustness of these findings. One interesting finding outside of the hypotheses tested here is that that sometimes militarized crises between great powers can serve as formative events.

The effects of past, individual experiences on alliance choices are lesser for great powers than for small powers. The admittedly brief survey of great power alliance behavior conducted in this chapter demonstrated the difficulty in applying the small power hypotheses; virtually each great power faced a different set of circumstances and therefore a different set of possible lessons. Additionally, the learning theory did not apply very well at all to some of the great powers, such as the Axis powers after World War II, because their foreign policy goals had changed between the experience of the event and the appli-

[36] The global distribution of power and systemic learning hypotheses make essentially similar predictions for the interwar and post–World War II periods, so I have applied the previously presented analysis comparing the individual and systemic learning hypotheses to the comparison of the global distribution of power and individual learning hypotheses.

cation of the lesson. This preliminary examination indicates some important limits of learning theory, in particular, it is likely to be less applicable or at least more difficult to apply to decisions that are more complicated.

[6]

Case Studies:
Lessons Heeded

The previous chapter presented powerful statistical evidence demonstrating the importance of learning for the alliance choices of small powers. The limitation of this and most other quantitative work is that it demonstrates only by correlation, leaving the black box of decision largely unexplored. With the goal of providing a richer description and illustration of the statistical findings, in this and the following chapter I explore in greater detail several cases taken from the data set. These two chapters have different empirical tasks: for the cases in this chapter, the individual learning hypothesis accurately predicted behavior; and for those in the following chapter, the individual learning hypothesis made incorrect predictions.

This chapter has two primary goals. The first is to explore the question of causation—do the processes laid out in learning theory accurately describe the factors that determined the actual decisions, or are these outcomes better attributable to other explanations? The second is to assess whether and how states learn in ways different from those envisioned in the learning hypotheses. The hypotheses express fairly broad, simple conceptualizations of how states draw lessons from formative experiences, and the simple observation of whether a state preferred alliance is unlikely to tell the whole story. By examining the details of a number of cases, this chapter conducts an open search for evidence of different kinds of learning. A fuller empirical description of how states learn ought to facilitate an improved understanding of the role of learning in international politics.

These two goals motivated the selection of cases for analysis. The criterion for case selection for this chapter is that the individual learning hypothesis made an accurate prediction for the case. This reflects the primary purpose of this chapter: to assess the causal validity of the main correlative finding of Chapter 5, that a nation's individual learning experience in a world war drives its alliance choices after the war. Of course, choosing only cases for which the favored theory made accurate predictions prevents this chapter from being considered a valid scientific test of the hypotheses. This is not the goal of this or the following chapter—the results of appropriate tests for validity were presented in Chapter 5.

An important part of assessing the causal validity of the individual learning hypothesis is the comparison of predictions made by the competing theory, balance of threat, with the predictions of learning. This comparison is accomplished by selecting clusters of cases within which there are divergences between the predictions of learning and balance of threat. The geostrategic similarity of the countries in each cluster means that they faced roughly similar threats from potentially revisionist third parties and therefore, according to balance of threat theory, ought to have made similar alliance choices. Also, the nations within each cluster had different wartime experiences, so that the individual learning hypothesis predicts that within each cluster there ought to have been different alliance choices that reflected these different experiences. This cluster technique is a most-similar method, in the sense that the cases within each cluster are generally similar (most important, the level of external threat is similar) except for differences in individual experiences, and ought to provide a means of exploring whether and how different experiences motivate states to react differently to the same set of external circumstances. Two such clusters are analyzed: Belgium/Netherlands/Switzerland, with a heavier emphasis on Belgium, and Sweden/Norway, with an even treatment of both cases. For all five cases, the analysis will cover important alliance decisions from the end of World War I up to the emergence of the cold war in the late 1940s.

Analysis of each case will approximate Alexander George's method of congruence tracing.[1] George's method fits particularly well into the purposes of this book, for it was designed specifically for testing a theory that decision makers act on the basis of their beliefs. This method endeavors to answer two questions: Is consistency between predicted and observed outcomes genuine or spurious? And what is the relative explanatory power of the hypotheses? An important part of the test for causation in this procedure is the determination of what

---

[1] Alexander L. George, "The Causal Nexus between Cognitive Beliefs and Decision-Making Behavior: The 'Operational Code' Belief System," in *Psychological Models in International Politics*, ed. Lawrence S. Falkowski (Boulder, Colo.: Westview, 1979), 95–124.

actions and beliefs would be consistent with the predictions of the competing theories. Such determinations, in terms of analyzing both real events and counterfactuals, constitute the majority of the historical analysis and argumentation in this chapter.

BELGIUM, THE NETHERLANDS, AND SWITZERLAND

After the Napoleonic Wars, the great powers in Europe saw the need to impose more control on the way in which power was distributed and political disputes were resolved. One example of such control was the creation of the neutral state of Belgium. In 1830, the great powers immediately intervened diplomatically after a group of rebels revolted from Dutch rule to declare the emergence of the Belgian nation. Over the next decade, the perpetual neutrality of Belgium was hammered out in treaties, in which the great powers agreed both to respect and to guarantee Belgian neutrality, while Belgium agreed to maintain its status as a neutral.

This framework yielded for Belgium a rather unique mix of benefits and disadvantages. In conventional thinking about alliances, neutrality is assigned the benefit of enhanced freedom in making policy choices, at the cost of forgoing the promise of external military assistance in the event of war. The 1839 treaties, though, provided for Belgium a stance of neutrality which guaranteed them assistance in the event of war and restricted their foreign policy autonomy by foreclosing the option of entering into international alliances, a mix of costs and benefits opposite to that which neutrality is supposed to provide. Confidence in imposed neutrality was solidified by Belgium's escape from involvement in the Franco-Prussian War of 1870, from which Belgians drew the lesson that neutrality could save them from destruction if great power war did break out.[2]

World War I

Through the end of the nineteenth century, the great powers of Europe kept their parts of this bargain in Belgian neutrality. The storm clouds of war which began to roll across Europe in the first decade of the twentieth century did not discourage the Belgian commitment to neutrality. In January 1904, Kaiser Wilhelm invited King Albert of

[2] André Roussel Le Roy, *L'Abrogation de la neutralité de la Belgique* (Paris: Presses Universitaires de France, 1923), 134.

Belgium to Berlin, and when his offer of an alliance with Germany was refused, he threatened that Belgian neutrality would be violated in the next war, that Belgium must make a choice, "For us or against us!" That same year, French intelligence showed the Belgians a captured copy of German war plans, which called for a German sweep through Belgium to strike at France from the north.[3] When Albert made another royal visit to Berlin in November 1913, the Kaiser greeted him with a tirade against France, warning that not only was war with France inevitable but also that "the Day," as the Germans referred to it, was fast approaching. Also discussed was the question of the Belgian response to a foreign invader, as the tactlessly curious Germans were eager to know if the Belgian government would permit the German Army unhindered passage en route to Paris. To this, the Belgians responded that any invading force would meet resistance. This portentous visit came just a few months after Belgium had passed a law substantially expanding the army; after the visit, Albert commissioned a study of the question of Belgian military response to a German invasion. In the several months before the war, Belgium adhered to its stance of political neutrality; government officials remained in opposition to signing alliances with great powers on the grounds that to do so would compromise the guarantees of neutrality given by other nations. During the crisis of 1914, Belgium appropriately distributed its military forces to all frontiers, ready to defend its neutrality against any invader, showing favor to no nation. Even as late as July, as bridges back to peace were being burned by all sides in the escalating crisis between Serbia and Austria and as the tide of war gathered greater and greater momentum, the great majority of Belgians believed that the treaties of 1839 would ensure their safety. Not even the invasion of the adjacent, neutral duchy of Luxembourg on August 1 could dislodge this belief.[4]

To the surprise of the Germans, Albert and the Belgians kept their promise and resisted the German invasion of August 1914. The German attack was a great shock to Belgium, as well as to the rest of the world; Germany, after all, had declared its adherence to the treaties respecting and guaranteeing Belgian neutrality. On hearing the news of the Ger-

[3] Gerhard Ritter, *The Schlieffen Plan: Critique of a Myth*, trans. Andrew Wilson and Eva Wilson (Westport, Conn.: Greenwood, 1979), 93–94; Jane Kathryn Miller, *Belgian Foreign Policy between Two Wars, 1919–1940* (New York: Bookman Associates, 1951); William E. Lingelbach, "Belgian Neutrality: Its Origin and Interpretation," *American Historical Review* 39 (October 1933): 48–72.

[4] Barbara W. Tuchman, *The Guns of August* (New York: Bantam, 1962), 128–130; Henri Pirenne, *Histoire de Belgique des origines à nos jours* (Brussels: La Renaissance du Livre, 1952), 4:241–242; Miller, *Belgian Foreign Policy*, 23; Michael Francis Palo, "The Diplomacy of Belgian War Aims during the First World War," Ph.D. diss., University of Illinois, 1978.

man invasion, Belgian foreign minister Paul Hymans felt "as if I had been punched in the chest, and I felt myself go pale."[5] The destruction visited on Belgium by the German invasion and occupation in the years that followed exhibited the nature of total war in the twentieth century. The western front ran through Belgium through much of the war, ensuring horrific destruction in this small industrial nation. Large portions of the population hovered on the brink of starvation for periods during the war, saved only by massive external aid. The physical devastation in the country was deepened in the latter years of the war by the German policy of dismantling and physically removing entire industries from Belgium to Germany. By the end of the war, 85 percent of Belgium's industry had been wrecked, and the unemployment level had risen to 75 percent. The level of human suffering in Belgium was as great as that of virtually any other participant in World War I, and the industrial damage it suffered was undoubtedly the most extensive.[6]

The invasion clearly represented a failure for the Belgian policy of imposed neutrality. Learning theory predicts that this experience would stimulate a search for new alternatives, as the old policy would be assigned blame for the failure. Predicting the content of the new policy, then, requires understanding the nature of the old policy. Again, Belgian foreign policy was unlike the conventional neutrality stance, as its neutrality entailed constraints on its foreign policy choices but provided for security guarantees for its defense. For the old policy to be blamed, one or more aspects of the old policy must be declared responsible for the disaster of 1914, aspects from which the new policy would differ. One possible conclusion from the experience would be that the external guarantees *attracted* the German invasion, but the illogic of this lesson seems insurmountable: Belgium had no reciprocal commitment to go to the aid of its guarantors, besides which Germany was one of Belgium's guarantors, which further strained the argument that the system of guarantees put Belgium in the British and French camp. A somewhat different but more reasonable conclusion would be that external guarantees are insufficient to deter an aggressor and perhaps that Britain and France in particular are undesirable guarantors. Another possible conclusion is that the restrictions on Belgian foreign policy imposed by the treaty of 1839 were to blame, and that without these restrictions, Belgium would have been able to take effective measures against a German attack, either avoiding it or defending against it.

[5] Paul Hymans, *Mémoires* (Brussels: Institut de Sociologie Solvay, 1958), 1:85.
[6] Sally Marks, *Innocent Abroad* (Chapel Hill: University of North Carolina Press, 1981), 170–177.

Most Belgians drew the last of these lessons. The immediate result of the 1914 invasion was a strong and widespread reaction against the old system of imposed neutrality. By the spring of 1915, a number of voices in the Belgian government were expressing dissatisfaction with the treaties of 1839, calling strongly for independence of action in Belgian foreign policy.[7] In August 1915 the decision was made at the highest levels of the Belgian government that the 1839 structure of imposed neutrality was unacceptable. The emphasis of this initial reaction was on the imperative of lifting these fetters from Belgian foreign policy, allowing it to enjoy real independence. In a confidential memo, a high-level Belgian official unequivocally described the extent of the new opposition to imposed neutrality: "A nearly complete unanimity has been established on this point amongst Belgians at home and abroad. Everyone demands the abandonment of this political servitude, this diminution of national sovereignty, this illusory means of protection in which the Belgian people had put their faith for too long. *The rejection of permanent neutrality is one of the fundamental articles of a program to which all members of the Government have rallied.*"[8]

Opposition to the old system of imposed neutrality developed as the war progressed. In 1916, the Belgian foreign ministry conducted an opinion survey of forty members of the Belgian elite. The sample included individuals from different political parties and from a variety of professions, both political and nonpolitical. Part of the survey asked what the status of Belgian neutrality ought to be after the war. The majority opinion, cutting across party lines, was that the system of imposed neutrality must be reformed. Further, a number of the individuals couched their arguments for abandonment of imposed neutrality in terms of the experience of the 1914 invasion. For example, one individual remarked, "The past has made impossible the reestablishment after the war of the situation imposed on our country by the treaties of 15 November 1831 and 19 April 1839." Another agreed: "The regime of permanent and guaranteed neutrality *imposed* on Belgium by the treaties of 1839 has been condemned by experience."[9] The path to a change from the old policy of imposed neutrality was assured by 1918, when one of the last well-known defenders of the old system of imposed neutrality, former foreign minister baron de

[7] Ministère des Affaires Étrangères, Classement B, Brussels [hereafter MAE], dossier no. 383, "Révision Traités 1839," 12 March, 15 April, and 3 June 1915. For an extensive discussion of the development of Belgian debates about neutrality during World War I, see Palo, "Diplomacy of Belgian War Aims."

[8] Hymans, *Mémoires*, 1:168–169.

[9] MAE, dossier no. 377, "Enquête auprès de personnalités politiques, financiers, scientifiques, etc., sur l'avenir de la Belgique."

Beyens, publicly switched to agreement with those arguing for abandonment of the old system. In his speech following the signing of the armistice, King Albert of Belgium declared the nation free of its imposed neutrality and called for the search for new safeguards of Belgian security, a stance that was supported and publicly defended by foreign minister Paul Hymans before the Parliament the following month. Belgium formally requested the full revision of the 1839 treaties with the aim of elimination of imposed neutrality at the Paris Peace Conference in January 1919, acting with the general support of Belgians from across the political spectrum; even the opposition Socialist Party supported the revision.[10]

One interesting dynamic in the discourse on neutrality was the connection of imposed neutrality with the relatively low level of preparedness of the Belgian armed forces. A number of Belgians, both inside and outside government, attributed the low level of prewar preparedness directly to the system of imposed neutrality, arguing that the system of imposed neutrality inhibited Belgian preparation for its own defense by undermining the national commitment to provide for its own defense, thus acting like a narcotic.[11] In this way, blame for a decision that appears to have rested in the hands of the Belgians themselves, insufficient domestic armament, could be laid at the doorstep of factors outside of the control of Belgium, the 1839 treaties, a self-serving inference. The tendency for individuals to make self-serving attributions has been widely observed in experimental work and cross-culturally.[12]

As the debate developed in governmental and public circles during the war, discourse revolved around three postwar policy options. The first possibility was a return to the old system of imposed neutrality. As described above, this option had very few defenders, and by the end of the war a very broad consensus in favor of change had developed in the country. The second was what might be called a move to voluntary neutrality, in which Belgium would remain out of political alliances, would not be bound by treaty to remain neutral, and would probably have some form of external guarantee, hopefully from Britain and

---

[10] *Bulletin Périodique de la Presse Belge* (hereafter *BPP*), no. 16, 7 October 1918: *Le Peuple*, 23 November 1918, and 12 December 1918; Marks, *Innocent Abroad*, 255. On the Socialist Party, see *Le Peuple*, 28 December 1918, 4 February 1919, and 10 March 1919.

[11] This argument was made both within the government and in public discourse. See, for example, *Documents diplomatiques belge* (Brussels: Palais des Académies, 1964) [hereafter *DDB*], 1:92; *Documents on British Foreign Policy, 1919–1939*, 1st ser., vol. 5 (London: Her Majesty's Stationery Office, 1954) [hereafter *DBFP*], 883, 967; *La Libre Belgique*, 28 November 1918, 14 March and 8 June 1920; *L'Indépendance Belge*, 10 April 1920; Le Roy, *L'Abrogation de la neutralité*, 143.

[12] For a review of the relevant literature, see Shelley E. Taylor and Susan T. Fiske, *Social Cognition*, 2d ed. (New York: McGraw-Hill, 1991), 78–82.

France. This would allow Belgium the greatest freedom of action in foreign policy by minimizing its actual commitments but still providing it some external guarantees. The third option would be to enter political alliances, though under the assumption that Belgium would be able to choose its allies. Toward the end of the war, Prime Minister Paul Hymans framed the Belgian choice in these terms, thinking that Belgium could not return to the policy of imposed neutrality and that the choice for postwar foreign policy was between "voluntary neutrality and a policy of alliance."[13]

The effect of World War I as a formative event, then, was to eliminate one option (imposed neutrality) and leave two other options as possible choices. Of the two alternatives, the experience seemed to favor alliance moderately, as the disaster of 1914 was seen to be due partly to insufficient military preparation and planning, a problem remedied (at least somewhat) by military coordination within the framework of an alliance. A benefit of alliance, as one editorial pointed out, would be that peacetime military planning and coordination of military forces would be possible: "[An alliance with Britain and France] is precisely that which could not be done if it was desired under the Treaty of 1839 and the regime of imposed neutrality. With this regime, we were paralyzed, and we could not conclude, in peacetime, with foresight, the ententes which, meanwhile, were imposed during the war. In the absence of such preparation, we were caught unawares in 1914. Besides, the regime did not prevent Germany from declaring that we had concluded alliances in order to give some semblance of justification for its crime."[14] Further, the emerging and as yet untested League of Nations was seen as inadequate protection of Belgian security, heightening the need for formal guarantees from specific nations.[15]

External political issues were strong determinants of the eventual outcome of military alliance with France. Belgium actively sought the participation of Britain as well as France in the construction of a three-way security framework. But the deadly destruction of the war had renewed Britain's hesitancy toward Continental commitments. In the negotiations immediately following the war, the best Britain could offer Belgium was a five-year security guarantee for Belgium in exchange for Belgium's assurance that it would remain neutral.[16] This offer of virtual renewal of imposed neutrality met with a vehemently

---

[13] Hymans, *Mémoires*, 1:179.

[14] *L'Indépendance Belge*, 12 June 1920.

[15] de Gaiffier to Hymans, *DDB*, 1:89.

[16] *DBFP*, 393; and *DDB*, 1:64, 335–337. On the attempts of Belgium to protect its interests in the postwar peace negotiations, see Marks, *Innocent Abroad*; and *DBFP*.

negative response, as the Belgian delegates informed the British that such an arrangement would cause "an upheaval in the country and would be regarded as an invitation by His Majesty's Government to Belgium to renew friendly relations with Germany."[17] Significantly, the Belgians were not satisfied with one-way external commitments to national security from other countries—they sought mutual alliances with Britain and France as the best means of constructing a sound security framework. Explaining the government's rejection of a renewal of neutrality to the Belgian parliament, Paul Hymans argued that "neutrality is the policy of a state which abstains from taking part in war between two or more third parties. Belgium would have a vital interest not to observe neutrality in the case of a new war between Germany and France or Britain."[18] But British participation in an alliance was not politically feasible in the interwar period, in large part because of the lessons it drew from its World War I experience. The offer of assured neutrality was the only one made by the British, as British domestic politics would not permit the consideration of an Anglo-Belgian or Anglo-Franco-Belgian security alliance. One historian has argued that Hymans was slow to grasp that domestic political constraints in Britain prevented a commitment to Belgium because of Hymans's 1914 experience, in which he saw Britain rush to Belgium's rescue.[19]

With Britain eliminated as a potential ally or guarantor, Belgium turned to France. France was very interested in a military alliance with Belgium, particularly one that would allow for joint military planning. The creation of an anti-German security structure, however, was only one of a number of postwar issues in the process of being resolved. One particular issue on which the Belgians and French were at loggerheads was the control of railroads in Luxembourg. Though the French had conceded to Belgium economic control of most of Luxembourg through economic union, the French had insisted in 1919 on control of Luxembourg's railroads, as this would afford them certain economic benefits from the control of the movement of iron ore. The Belgians, of course, opposed this concession, as this economic gain for the French would come at their own expense. The Belgians were not shy about linking the settlement of the two issues in quid pro quo fashion, implicitly offering Belgian agreement on some sort of military alliance in exchange for French concessions on the railways. The French initially showed little interest in such a deal. But the prospects improved in April 1920 when

[17] Crowe to Curzon, 4 December 1919, *DBFP*, 885.
[18] Hymans to de Gaiffier, *DDB*, 1:78.
[19] See Marks, *Innocent Abroad*, 269, 272.

the Belgians gave political support to the French by sending Belgian troops to join French forces that were quelling political instability in Germany. The French were quite grateful to the Belgians, especially since the British had initially strongly opposed the dispatch of French forces and Belgian political support had prevented a French political defeat at the hands of the British. They rewarded Belgian help in the German matter by speeding along the Luxembourgian economic negotiations to the Belgians' favor, to which the Belgians responded by permitting the negotiations on a military accord to continue. These negotiations culminated in a military agreement in September 1920.[20]

The Belgian leadership often defended this accord on the basis of lessons learned from World War I.[21] Such public defenses are either genuine reflections of the beliefs of the government's leadership, or if they did not learn these lessons from World War I, these references to the Great War were made to attract public support. If the latter interpretation is correct, then the leadership's arguments might be viewed as instrumental, but we still would say that Belgian foreign policies reflected learning, as the group with real political power in Belgium (the public) had genuinely learned the lesson that neutrality was undesirable, and Belgian policy reflected these preferences. Certainly, the Franco-Belgian agreement was met with general approval in Belgium; one lesson drawn from the previous experience seems to have been that French and Belgian security was interlinked, requiring military cooperation and ties to provide a strong defense. The primary argument in favor of neutrality—that it enabled the sidestepping of future conflict—had lost credibility. One editorial noted: "And if, in the future, [Germany] attacks France, if she achieves victory without passing through our country, then without any doubt she will then seize our country. There is no German aggression that would not put us in danger. Since 1914, we can't doubt it. Therefore, if Germany again becomes bellicose,

---

[20] On the role of Belgium in the peace treaty negotiations, see Marks, *Innocent Abroad*. On the negotiations between France and Belgium for the treaty, see Jonathan E. Helmreich, "The Negotiation of the Franco-Belgian Military Accord of 1920," *French Historical Studies* 3 (Spring 1964): 360–378, and Helmreich, "Convention politique ou accord militaire? La Négociation de l'accord franco-belge de 1920," *Guerres Mondiales et Conflits Contemporains*, no. 159 (1990): 21–36; Jean-Marie d'Hoop, "Le Maréchal Foch et la négociation de l'Accord Militaire Franco-Belge de 1920," in *Mélanges Pierre Renouvin Études d'histoire des relations internationales* (Paris: Presses Universitaires de France, 1966), 191–198; Jean Stengers, "L'Accord Militaire Franco-Belge de 1920 et le Luxembourg," in *Les Relations franco-luxembourgeoises de Louis XIV à Robert Schuman*, ed. Raymond Poidevin and Gilbert Trausch (Metz: Centre de Recherches Relations Internationales de l'Université de Metz, 1978), 227–243.

[21] For example, Interior Minister Rankin made this argument at the 1920 Catholic Congress. *La Libre Belgique*, 31 May 1920.

we must, inevitably, defend ourselves in cooperation with France, together."[22]

The formation of the Franco-Belgian alliance provides confirmation that learning theory accurately describes the thought processes of Belgian decision makers. Most Belgians learned from the German invasion and occupation during World War I that the prewar policy of imposed neutrality had failed—their response was to junk the old policy and fashion a new foreign policy, a significant component of which was a military alliance with France. An important remaining question, however, is whether realism's balance of threat predictions also correctly predict the outcome. From the balance of threat perspective, the alliance is a clear example of Belgium and France balancing against Germany. But what was the Belgian perception of the nature of the German threat in the years just following the war? This balance of threat prediction assumes that a serious German threat was perceived at that time.

Contrary to the balance of threat prediction, examination of German foreign policy after the war and Belgian perceptions of German foreign policy reveal no serious German threat in the early 1920s, either real or perceived. German demilitarization after the war was quite extensive, with caps on the size of the military reducing it to a fraction of prewar strength, bans on certain kinds of weapons (such as aircraft and submarines), the demilitarization and allied occupation of the Rhineland, and limits on the production of war materiel. British historian E. H. Carr wrote in 1937 that "by 1924, Germany had been subjected to a measure of disarmament more rigorous and complete than any recorded in modern history."[23] Aside from Germany's demilitarization, the political conditions permitting military aggression were absent in the years immediately following the war. Wilhelmine Germany had been succeeded by the democratic Weimar regime, which had tremendous domestic problems to deal with, including starvation, mass influenza, hyperinflation, French demands to make the crushing Versailles reparations, as well as serious—and occasionally revolutionary—threats to political stability.[24] Renewed international adventures in the aftermath of the war were certainly far from the minds of German leaders. ·

[22] *L'Indépendance Belge*, 4 September 1920. See also *L'Indépendance Belge*, 17 April, 16 June, and 2 May 1920; *La Libre Belgique*, 29 August 1920, and 23 June 1920; and *BPP*, no. 28, 18 February 1920, no. 25, 26 November 1919, and no. 26, 28 December 1919. The accord attracted minor opposition from Francophobic Flemish extremists and some socialists and communists, the last because of the right-wing tendencies of the Poincaré cabinets in France. J. A. Wullus-Rudiger, *La Défense de la Belgique en 1940* (Villeneuve sur Lot: Alfred Bador, 1940), 98; and *Bulletin Presse Belge*, no. 33, 7 November 1920, 3.

[23] E. H. Carr, *International Relations since the Peace Treaties* (London: Macmillan, 1937), 49.

[24] See Gordon A. Craig, *Germany, 1866–1945* (New York: Oxford University Press, 1978); and Sally Marks, *The Illusion of Peace: International Relations in Europe, 1918–1933* (New York: St. Martin's 1976).

Belgian thinking about German foreign policy and the German threat took two forms in the years just following World War I. One attitude was that Germany posed no real threat because of the extremely severe terms of the Versailles Treaty and the commitment of Britain and France to combat German militarism should it reemerge. In the spring of 1920, then foreign minister Hymans wrote in a publicly distributed article: "Without doubt [Belgium] is not menaced by an imminent peril. German military power is shattered and for 15 years the allied occupation of the Rhineland will cover the nation's eastern frontier."[25] As a leading proponent of Belgian abandonment of neutrality, Hymans would have had strong political motivation to exaggerate publicly the presence of a German threat so as to garner support for his policies, especially the alliance with France. Therefore, we may view his public denial of a present German threat as an accurate reflection of his thinking and indication that his preference for alliance with France was motivated by his experiences in World War I rather than by a reaction to the international environment.

Others in Belgium thought it possible for a new threat to emerge in the international arena with no notice, such that preparatory measures should be taken as a long-term measure. A Belgian newspaper editorial expressed this view, arguing that Belgium must "consider not only a hypothesis determined by danger, but to embrace if possible all contingencies which could arise in the long run. The world is complex and changing. The current balance of power, international rapport, and grouping of interests in Europe may not exist in ten, or even five years."[26] A strict adherent of balance of threat theory might argue that this position represents a balance of threat view, as an alliance with France is seen as necessary to cope with a long-term menace. Such a view implicitly adopts an extremely broad view of threat, however, one in which a state can feel endangered even if it cannot currently identify the source of threat. This would make balance of threat theory close to unfalsifiable, since threat could be always coded as present, at least in the form of a potential, as yet unknown threat emerging in the future. Aside from the falsifiability problem, it is reasonable to inquire how individuals come to be so hypersensitive to threat; such a paranoid attitude certainly does not characterize all states at all times, as one need only compare Belgium's attitude in 1920 to its attitude in 1914, when the government played down the possibility of a German invasion even as the July crisis began to unfold. One answer to this question of understanding where these beliefs come from is that they emerge

[25] *L'Indépendance Belge*, 10 April 1920.
[26] *La Libre Belgique*, 10 June 1920.

from experiences, that a nation is likely to be more concerned about its security after it has been invaded and overrun. In this way, Belgium seems to have learned about threat as well as about alliance and neutrality. The notion of learning about threat demonstrates the importance of beliefs for understanding realist concepts like threat.

An important illustration of the failure of balance of threat theory to explain the 1920 Franco-Belgian agreement is the comparison of the postwar behavior of two other small powers, the Netherlands and Switzerland. These two countries and Belgium faced roughly similar geopolitical circumstances in 1914: all three were neutral small powers situated on possible invasion routes between Germany and France. But only Belgium was invaded, and only Belgium abandoned its neutrality after the war. For the Netherlands, Belgium's northerly neighbor, the World War I experience confirmed the wisdom of neutrality: "In the aftermath of World War I each country was, diplomatically speaking, refighting that war in the light of its own experience. Thus, France and Belgium, motivated by fear, wanted every possible guarantee of assistance against renewed German attack. Holland, whose good fortune it had been to escape involvement, was absolutely determined to maintain her neutrality and to commit herself to nobody, in hopes that this policy would protect her as well in the future as in the past."[27]

Interestingly, the Dutch drew the lesson from Belgium's experience not that neutrality was ineffective but that Belgium brought disaster on itself by not being neutral enough, that is, the nation was ruined because Belgium threw in its lot with one side after being invaded by the other. In the later years of the war, the Dutch declared that they would avoid this mistake by maintaining a strict neutrality, namely, by resisting *all* aggressors, even the entry of assisting British or French forces into the Netherlands following a German invasion.[28] This odd inference is evidence in favor of the individual learning hypothesis (Hypothesis 1) and against the systemic learning hypothesis (Hypothesis 2), for it demonstrates that it was the Dutch's own experience that drove their thinking about neutrality and that they interpreted the Belgian experience selectively to reinforce rather than question their strong belief in the value of neutrality.

The Swiss experience was similar. Before and during the war, neutrality was held in doubt by many; as late as 1912, the Swiss government seriously considered alliance with one of the belligerents in the

---

[27] Marks, *Innocent Abroad*, 273. See also S. I. P. Van Campen, *The Quest for Security* (The Hague: Martinus Nijhoff, 1958), 7–9.
[28] E. H. Kossmann, *The Low Countries, 1780–1940* (Oxford: Clarendon, 1978), 547–548.

European war that they saw coming.[29] After the attack on Belgium in 1914, there was great division in the country: as the French-speaking Swiss were horrified by the attack and advocated joining the Allies, whereas the German-speaking Swiss, heavily influenced by German culture and politics, advocated joining the Central Powers. These were not academic conflicts limited to the cafés of Geneva or the beer gardens of Zurich: serious social tensions bubbled to the surface, leading to strikes and even a revolutionary climate in 1917 and 1918.[30] Ultimately, the Swiss did not join either coalition, and their successful experience with neutrality removed a number of doubts about the belief that neutrality was the best means to safeguard territorial integrity. The Swiss hesitantly entered the League of Nations, though its entry was conditioned on being excused from mandatory participation in league military sanctions. The Swiss commitment to neutrality was demonstrated in 1921, when they refused to let international contingents of troops pass through Swiss territory on their way to execute a league-sanctioned operation in Vilna.[31]

The diverse postwar policies of these countries constitute a powerful empirical blow to balance of threat theory. If there was no German threat in the early postwar years, then the Franco-Belgian alliance remains unexplained. If, however, one has a very broad definition of threat, thereby coding the existence of a long-term German threat, Dutch and Swiss neutralities after World War I are unexplained. The individual learning theory, on the other hand, explains both Belgian alliance and Dutch and Swiss neutrality as emerging from individual wartime experiences.

Interwar Years

The Franco-Belgian alliance was fated to founder on the rocks of Belgian domestic politics. The terms of the 1920 agreement were kept secret, which enabled its opponents to concoct wild and inaccurate extrapolations of its contents and the responsibilities it placed on Bel-

---

[29] Hans-Ulrich Jost, "Menace et Repliement, 1914–1945," in *Nouvelle histoire de la Suisse et des Suisses*, vol. 3 (Lausanne: Payot, 1983), 94.

[30] Edgar Bonjour, *Histoire de la neutralité suisse*, trans. Balise Briad (Neuchatel: La Baconnière, 1946), 317; Yves Beigbeder, "La Neutralité suisse en question: Isolement ou solidarité internationale," *Revue Belge de Droit International* 24 (1991): 29; Jost, "Menace et Repliement," 123.

[31] Beigbeder, "Neutralité suisse en question"; Bernard Dutoit, *La Neutralité suisse à l'heure européenne* (Paris: Librairie Générale de Droit et de Jurisprudence, 1962), 30–31. See also the message dated 4 August 1919, delivered to the Swiss Federal Assembly by the Swiss president and chancellor, in *Feuille Fédérale Suisse*, 3 September 1919, 4:567–681.

gium. In particular, the agreement served as a flash point for the Francophobic Flemish population in Belgium, who feared French political hegemony and control of the Belgian military via the agreement. By the 1930s, however, opposition to the agreement began spreading across political and cultural lines, even to the French-speaking Walloon population of Belgium. This eventually culminated in the Belgian withdrawal from the 1920 alliance with France and declaration of an "independent" foreign policy in 1936. Some historians have proposed that the collapse of the Franco-Belgian agreement was due to the feeble French response to the German remilitarization of the Rhineland in 1936,[32] but this argument has a fatal flaw: the 1920 agreement broke down *before* the Germans actually moved into the Rhineland in March. A more accurate portrayal of the causes of the breakdown points to a number of other factors. Not insignificant was the general unpopularity in Belgium of France; French trade tariffs on Belgian products and the mistreatment of Belgian laborers who worked in French factories, for example, were issues that cut across ethnic and political lines in Belgium. Another concern that was magnified by the secrecy of the Franco-Belgian agreement was the 1935 Franco-Soviet Pact. While most Belgians may have been willing to join France in a fight against Germany in the West, they were made nervous by the prospect of having to join France in the assistance of the (to most Belgians) ideologically distasteful Bolshevik Soviet Union. Finally, it became evident that the expansion of the military—particularly the extension of the term of mandatory service—would be politically acceptable to Parliament and the public only if it was assured that Belgian foreign policy was independent and that the Belgian army was not committed to being merely the left wing of the French army. In 1937, Britain and France declared that they would guarantee Belgian neutrality and independence against attack.[33]

The Belgian exit from the alliance with France raises an important question: How does this shift in Belgian policy in the late 1930s from alliance to neutrality fit in with the theories under examination in this study? This case is not correctly predicted by the balance of threat hypothesis, as the threat of European war increased rather than decreased as the 1930s progressed. Belgium should have been tightening

[32] See, for example, Robert L. Rothstein, *Alliance and Small Powers* (New York: Columbia University Press, 1968); and Craig, *Germany, 1866–1945*, 691.

[33] The definitive secondary work on the breakup of the Franco-Belgian alliance and shift in Belgian foreign policy in the mid-1930s is David Owen Kieft, *Belgium's Return to Neutrality* (Oxford: Clarendon, 1972). Kieft's work is superior in depth of analysis to that of Rothstein, and it enjoys access to more archival materials than did Miller when she wrote *Belgian Foreign Policy between Two Wars*.

its ties to France rather than abrogating them; they seem to have been adhering at least somewhat to buck-passing logic, though the primary reason for the break lay in domestic politics. This was not due to inadequate information about the German threat. In January 1940, four months after war between Germany and the Allies had broken out, Belgium intercepted from a crashed German airplane secret German plans for an invasion of France through Belgium. Not only did Belgium retain its neutrality in the face of such irrefutable evidence of a German threat, it even declined an invitation to hold official staff conversations with Britain to discuss operational plans in the event of a German attack.[34]

The individual learning hypothesis does no better, however, because the failed neutrality experience of World War I should have encouraged Belgium to seek great power alliance throughout the 1930s. Yet, although the leading historical interpretation of the 1936 break points to domestic factors as crucial, Belgium's experience in 1914 did set parameters for Belgian foreign policy which were respected in the 1936 shift of foreign policy. The experience in World War I had led most Belgians to conclude that imposed neutrality was at fault and that postwar foreign policy must provide for the respect of Belgian sovereignty and independence of Belgian foreign policy. In the wake of the failure of Belgian neutrality in 1914, Hymans saw Belgium as having two choices: voluntary neutrality and political alliance. By the 1930s, exogenous factors precluded the latter as an option, leaving only voluntary neutrality as a viable foreign policy, which was the course chosen.

The inability of either the balance of threat or learning hypothesis to explain this shift back to neutrality points to a shortcoming in the specification of the model, namely that its exclusion of domestic politics and relatively crude formulation of states' foreign policy choices is a simplification—in some cases (such as this one), a simplification that comes at the expense of predictive accuracy. The misprediction of a handful of cases is an acceptable shortcoming, however, given the generally high performance of such a parsimonious model. Of course, it would be possible to specify the model further to attempt to explain the dozen or so cases that are not predicted accurately, but the problem with that approach is the need to add variables to accommodate the idiosyncrasies of different cases. If only one additional case was correctly predicted per additional variable, the explanatory power of the model is not truly enhanced, and the generalizability of the results

---

[34] Brian Bond, *Britain, France, and Belgium, 1939–1940* (London: Brassey's, 1990), 35–42.

becomes more dubious. I prefer to accept a very parsimonious model that has a high (though not perfect) level of predictive performance as demonstration of the significance of learning in foreign policy formation.

Whereas Belgium's reconsideration of neutrality in the late 1930s is a failure of learning theory, the learning hypothesis successfully predicts the neutrality of both the Netherlands and Switzerland, although balance of threat theory predicts that both should have sought alliance in the face of the rising Nazi menace. Switzerland's reaction to the increasing likelihood of war was not to balance against or bandwagon with Nazi Germany, as balance of threat theory would predict; rather, the abject failure of the League of Nations in controlling Italian aggression in Ethiopia caused it to become more neutral, backing away from even the limited commitments for collective security it had given the league in 1920.[35] Switzerland in 1938 and 1939 is a particularly powerful refutation of balance of threat theory, with Nazi Germany taking military actions against two nearby central European states, Austria and Czechoslovakia, and thus heightening Switzerland's perceived threat. Bringing Switzerland as well as Austria and Czechoslovakia into the German fold was part of the Nazi pan-Germanic design of uniting nations of allegedly pure Aryan blood, as evidenced at the time by German collusion with Swiss Nazis and later by Nazi documents. Remarkably, the increasing Nazi aggression did not at first stimulate Swiss efforts to increase its *own* defensive preparations to balance against the threat: as late as August 1939, the Swiss did not have an organized military doctrine or plan for the deployment of the army in case of invasion. When the army was mobilized on 28 August 1939, its low state of preparedness could be described as almost criminal: there were no military gasoline reserves, no tire reserves, no spare parts, and no military meteorological service; the frontier troops could not be equipped for several days; weaponry was old and insufficient (some artillery pieces dated to the nineteenth century), 54 percent of the rifle cartridge and 77 percent of the machine gun allotments were lacking; and there were general shortages in explosives, doctors, and medical personnel.[36] This was not a realist leadership carefully balancing against the rising Nazi threat but more a nation that had clung to the

---

[35] *Feuille Fédérale*, 8 June 1938, 849–854; Dutoit, *Neutralité suisse à l'heure européenne*, 32–33.

[36] Daniel Bourgeois, *Le Troisième Reich et la Suisse, 1933–1941* (Neuchatel: La Baconnière, 1974); Jost, "Menace et Repliement," 150; Jon Kimche, *Spying for Peace* (London: Weinfeld and Nicolson, 1961), 11–13; Werner Rings, *La Suisse et la guerre, 1933–1945*, trans. Charles Oser (Lausanne: Éditions Ex Libris, 1975), 153–156.

life preserver of neutrality for too long, putting off precautionary measures until the very last moment. This stubborn hold on neutrality was based on the lesson of World War I, that neutrality is the best way to protect the national security.[37] With the appointment of Henri Guisan as commander of the Swiss armed forces in 1939, the World War I belief that armament was not necessary for security was overcome, though the Swiss retained the belief that avoiding alliances was best.

The Netherlands also clung to its traditional policy of neutrality, even as war approached. Signs of the rising Nazi menace in Europe only fortified the Dutch hold on neutrality, their devotion to neutrality fortified by memories of their successful neutral stand in World War I. The Dutch saw their stance of neutrality as a virtual political duty to the international order, to set an example as an island of peace in an ocean swept by the storms of belligerence and militarist passions. This is not to say, however, that they perceived neutrality as a sacrifice of the national interest: rather, they viewed neutrality as the best hope for protecting the national security, resting their hopes on the possibility that neutrality would allow them to skirt conflict. When war broke out in September 1939, the Netherlands refused to abandon its neutrality. Contrary to the predictions of balance of threat theory, as evidence mounted in the next eight months that Germany would not spare the Netherlands in its campaign against France, the Dutch refused to deviate from their stance. Indeed, their dogmatic adherence to neutrality hindered military cooperation with France and Britain during the Phony War, cooperation that might at least have made the May 1940 German invasion more of a military contest and less of a walkover.[38]

World War II and After

Unfortunately, Belgium's renewal of neutrality in the late 1930s did not save it from the same fate it suffered in World War I. Up to the German invasion and conquest in the spring of 1940, Belgium held onto its neutrality as its only hope for avoiding a second German invasion in a quarter century, making its primary foreign policy objective avoiding

[37] Jacques Freymond, *Pas d'Armée pas de guerre?* (Lausanne: Le Matin, 1989), 12.
[38] Hans Daalder, "The Netherlands and the World: 1940–1945," in *The Foreign Policy of the Netherlands*, ed. J. H. Leurdijk (Alphen aan den Rijn: Sijthoff & Noordhoff, 1978), 50–53; Janet Eisen, *Anglo-Dutch Relations and European Unity, 1940–1948* (Hull: University of Hull Publications, 1980), iii–iv; Frederic S. Pearson, *The Weak State in International Crisis: The Case of the Netherlands in the German Invasion Crisis of 1939–40* (Washington: University Press of America, 1981); Henry L. Mason, "War Comes to the Netherlands: September 1939–May 1940," *Political Science Quarterly* 78 (December 1963): 548–580.

the provocation of a German invasion.[39] After the invasion, leaders of the Belgian government (though not King Leopold) fled Belgium to establish a government-in-exile in London. It was there that a reconsideration of Belgian foreign policy began. The secretary general for foreign affairs, Fernand Van Langenhove, drew up a lengthy and incisive memo in March 1941 which was aimed at drawing lessons about the usefulness of collective security and neutrality and at trying to construct a robust system of security for Belgium and the rest of Western Europe.[40] This reconsideration soon led to a shift back to pre-1936 policies, favoring Belgian participation in a collective security regime for Western Europe. At a meeting of the Allies in St. James Palace in June 1941, the Belgian representative declared the Belgian desire to participate in a collective security arrangement under British initiative, in which it was understood that "Belgium will assume for its part necessary sacrifices."[41]

The belief that the prewar Belgian policy of neutrality demanded revision was widely held among the Belgian leadership. Foreign Minister Paul-Henri Spaak was in agreement with the St. James declaration, favoring the need for extensive military and political cooperation in Europe after the war and arguing that the post-1936 policy of "independence" did not safeguard Belgian security any better than the 1914 policy of "neutrality."[42] As early as 1942, Spaak was making contacts with the governments-in-exile of two other occupied nations, the Netherlands and Norway, about the possibility of a postwar military alliance with Great Britain and the United States.[43] In a wartime memorandum, Spaak laid out the position of the foreign ministry. The experience of the 1940 invasion had shown unambiguously the folly of neutrality, illustrating the need for greater international cooperation: "The 18 day campaign, or rather the entire military campaign of 1940, demonstrated to us that before the German danger the isolated defense of the peoples of Western Europe was an illusion. . . . The foreign policy of Belgium will be based in the future on as tight an entente as possible with Luxembourg, Holland, France, and Great Britain."[44]

[39] Birdsall S. Viault, "La Belgique et la Hollande à la recherche d'une paix négociée (1939–1940)," *Revue d'Histoire de la Deuxième Guerre Mondiale* 32 (April 1982): 37–46; Paul-Henri Spaak, *Combats Inachevés* (Brussels: Fayard, 1969), 1:68.

[40] Fernand Van Langenhove, "Note succinte sur le problème de la securité," 16 March 1941, in *La Securité de la Belgique: Contribution à l'histoire de la période, 1940–1950* (Brussels: Éditions de l'Universitaire de Bruxelles, 1971), 21.

[41] Ibid., 30. Van Langenhove supported this policy (43).

[42] *La Pensée européene et atlantique de Paul-Henri Spaak (1942–1972)*, ed. Paul-F. Smets (Brussels: J. Goemere, 1980), 1:3–6.

[43] *Pensée*, 11.

[44] MAE, dossier no. 11.754, "Charte d'Atlantique et Nations Unies," 2 March 1943.

The ghosts of past errors continued to dominate Spaak's thinking about Belgium's postwar foreign policy. In 1944, Spaak told the Belgian parliament in the first public debate on foreign policy since the 1940 invasion that "it is necessary this time, at all cost, to avoid the return of the double tragedy that we suffered in 1914 and in 1940. It is for us, in the strict sense of the word, a question of life or death."[45] Jean Stengers, a leading Belgian historian, attributed Spaak's strong advocacy of postwar cooperation in large part to the shock he experienced in seeing the policy of independence that he had supported fail so utterly in 1940:

> Spaak was haunted—the word is not too strong—by the loss of Belgian independence and neutrality, of which he had been in 1940 one of the most vigorous champions. This policy, he said, "has become bankrupt because it did not prevent war in Belgium." . . . Struck after the committing of what he considered to be a grave error, he wanted at all costs for his country—and other countries of Western Europe—to avoid the risk of again surrendering to the temptations of independence and neutrality. He wanted to drive off the sirens once and for all. For this, there was only one way: tie the five countries together solidly this time with economic and military links.[46]

Scholar Rik Coolsaet went even farther, arguing that Spaak felt that if he had acted to support the system of collective security in the late 1930s, the whole war might have been avoided.[47]

The shock of the 1940 invasion had not crippled Spaak's keen political sensibilities, however. He knew that a new structure of international cooperation must be politically stable over the long term. The conclusion that Spaak had drawn from the interwar experience was that military cooperation must be joined by economic and political cooperation. Without a balanced and complete network of cooperation, Spaak believed, military cooperation would eventually be undermined in a drift to independence and neutrality, as he felt happened to the Franco-Belgian alliance in 1936. In this way, Spaak synthesized the lessons from three experiences—the 1914 and 1940 invasions and the 1936 breakup of the Franco-Belgian alliance—to arrive at his policy prescription: 1914 and 1940 advocated alliance, and 1936 argued for economic as well as military cooperation.[48]

[45] *Pensée*, 52.

[46] Jean Stengers, "Paul-Henri Spaak et le Traité de Bruxelles de 1948," in *Histoire des débuts de la construction européenne (Mars 1948–Mai 1950)*, ed. Raymond Poidevin (Brussels: Bruyant, 1984), 127–128.

[47] Rik Coolsaet, *Histoire de la politique étrangère belge*, French ed. trans. from the Dutch by Jan Van Kerkhoven and Claudine Leleux (Brussels: Vie Ouvrière, 1988), 115.

[48] See, for example, René Massigli, *Une Comedie des erreurs, 1943–1956* (Paris: Plon, 1978), 29, 109–110; and Stengers, "Paul-Henri Spaak," 130. See also the Benelux

Spaak's commitment to international cooperation in Western Europe continued after Germany surrendered in 1945. After Britain and France signed a mutual defense agreement, Spaak began to lobby for a similar agreement that would include Belgium and its large neighbors, proposing at first an Anglo-Belgian military agreement, which other countries would be able to join. Significantly, Spaak wanted an agreement that would unreservedly call for mutual military assistance; he considered the World War II experience as having invalidated lesser agreements, such as the one-way guarantees offered by Britain and France to Belgium in 1937.[49] Spaak was certainly not alone in his support of mutual security pacts with Great Britain and France—even the Belgian Communist Party advocated the maintenance of strong ties with France and the USSR after war's end.[50] In January 1948, the British and French proposed a military alliance between themselves and Belgium, the Netherlands, and Luxembourg to be based on the Anglo-French Dunkirk Pact. Though this was essentially what Spaak had previously proposed, he held out for an agreement that included economic as well as military cooperation.[51]

Significantly, Spaak's lobbying efforts for the new agreement were couched in terms of repairing past errors. This must be considered strong evidence in favor of the learning hypothesis, because, as foreign minister in 1940, Spaak had been a supporter of Belgian neutrality; he would have himself had a strong incentive for distancing himself publicly from that policy after the war so that he would not be attached to the earlier failure. We might expect him to argue that the invasion and conquest was inevitable and unavoidable, with the neutrality policy enabling Belgium at least to maintain its independence and sovereignty of foreign policy. Instead, Spaak made specific and repeated references

---

governments' reaction to the January 1948 proposal for a five-way security pact, in MAE, dossier no. 12.237, "Direction générale de la politique."

[49] Collsaet, *Histoire de la politique étrangère belge*, 116–117; MAE, dossier no. 10.957, "Examen de la question des pactes d'assistance," 3 June 1947.

[50] For other high-level Belgian endorsements of such agreements, see the comments of the Secretary General of Foreign Affairs Baron de Gruben, MAE, dossier no. 12.237, "Conclusion de traités de assistance par le Belgique," 21 March 1947 and 3 July 1947; and Van Langenhove, *Sécurité de la Belgique*, 176, 180. On the Communist Party, see the report of the Belgian News Agency, INBEL, 6 February 1945, in MAE, dossier no. 15.074/1. Spaak occupied a dominant position on foreign policy questions both within the Belgian government and within the Benelux community, so much so that the Benelux contries were occasionally referred to jokingly as "Spaakistan." See Stengers, "Paul-Henri Spaak," 124–125; and Coolsaet, *Histoire de la politique étrangère belge*, 115–116.

[51] MAE, dossier no. 10.957, 20 March 1947, 19 June 1947, and 30 December 1947; and Stengers, "Paul-Henri Spaak," 127. The gist of the British and French offer, formalized international cooperation within Western Europe, was met with enthusiasm. See MAE, dossier no. 12.237, 28 January 1948.

to the need to avoid repeating past mistakes, though he was in no small way associated with these mistakes. A good example is a speech Spaak gave to the Association of the Socialist Journalists of Belgium in January 1948: "The question is to discern whether we are taking a position like the one we adopted in 1935, which appeared to be erroneous. Since 1935, we have adopted between Britain and France on the one hand and Germany on the other hand a position which inspired the policy of independence, or neutrality, and which failed, because it did not prevent Belgium from being involved in the war."[52] The negotiations eventually culminated with the signing of the Brussels Pact in March 1948, an agreement that included provisions for economic and military cooperation and met with general approval in Belgium.[53]

Learning offers a strong explanation of Belgian alliance choices after World War II, but how does the balance of threat explanation perform? Unlike the years just after World War I, Belgium after World War II faced a clear systemic threat—the Soviet Union. At that point, it was unclear whether there were limits to Soviet political ambitions in Europe, and Western Europe in general saw Soviet foreign policy as one of its primary concerns in the postwar world. Spaak was no exception; in February 1948, Spaak spoke to the American ambassador to Belgium of the need for the formulation of a Western bloc (hopefully with American participation) to check the "USSR and her aggressive westward designs."[54] Spaak's personal worries about Soviet expansionism were clearly demonstrated in a speech he gave at the United Nations seven months later, in which he pointed to a number of recent Soviet foreign policy actions that, he argued, painted a picture of an aggressive and expansionist power.[55] Certainly, the Soviet threat was part of the motivation behind the formation of the Brussels Pact and the emergence generally of international cooperation in Western Europe. The possibility of the reemergence of the German threat did not seem to worry Spaak greatly. By 1947, he no longer supported the dismemberment of Germany as he had during the war, and in a meeting in July of that year, he advocated reviving the German economy.[56]

[52] Paul-Henri Spaak, "L'Organisation de l'Occident," *Chronique de Politique Étrangère* 1 (February 1948): 41.

[53] See, for example, *Le Soir*, 5 March 1948, and *Le Peuple*, 11 February 1948.

[54] *Foreign Relations of the United States* [hereafter *FRUS*], 3:18, 3 February 1948; and Stengers, "Paul-Henri Spaak," 130.

[55] For a full text of the speech, see *Pensèe*, 148–160. The speech has since been referred in the title of "We Are Afraid."

[56] Germany was explicitly mentioned in the Brussels Pact to avoid provoking the USSR, but the primary concern of the Western Europeans was on the Soviet rather than the German threat. See MAE, dossier no. 12.237, "Memorandum britannique," 19 February

Both learning theory and balance of threat theory successfully predict the preference for alliance of Belgium, the Netherlands, and Luxembourg. Learning theory points to the failed neutrality policies of each, while balance of threat theory points to the presence of a Soviet threat. Significantly, though, the discourse in the Benelux countries focused on the lessons offered by past experience. Trying to persuade his country's leadership of the necessity of the Brussels Treaty, for example, Luxembourg's Foreign Minister Bech wrote: "Two invasions have proven that we cannot depend on remaining neutral and that we cannot remain outside of conflict if war eventually breaks out in Europe."[57] In the Netherlands, the traditional Dutch faith in neutrality had been shaken by wartime experience. For the Dutch, the failure of neutrality in 1940 pointed to the necessity of military and economic cooperation. During the war, the Dutch government-in-exile began to see its place in a scheme of military and economic cooperation with the other Western European democracies after the war. The Dutch foreign minister gave a speech at the end of 1943 in which he foresaw a postwar structure of cooperation involving the United States and Western Europe very similar to what was eventually to become NATO. After the war, the Dutch sought alliance with the United States and Western Europe—they held grave doubts about the efficacy of the United Nations, in light of the failure of the League of Nations. Though its break with neutrality was slower than Belgium's (perhaps because the 1940 German attack was the first breach of Dutch neutrality, whereas Belgium had been burned twice by a policy of neutrality), it eventually came to embrace the idea of regional military cooperation, culminating with its signing of the Brussels Pact in 1948 and, soon after, the North Atlantic Treaty.[58]

Significantly, balance of threat theory offers the wrong prediction for Switzerland, a nation that is geopolitically similar to the Benelux countries. Indeed, although Switzerland had participated in the League of Nations experiment after World War I, the failure of that organization to enforce collective security in the 1930s, coupled with the success of

1948; MAE, dossier no. 12.071, Guillaume to Spaak, 12 February 1948, 17 February 1948, and 2 March 1948; and Coolsaet, *Histoire de la politique étrangère belge*, 119–120.

[57] 'L'Organisation politique de l'Europe Occidentale," *Chronique d Politique Étrangère* 1 (May 1948): 16.

[58] Van Campen, *Quest for Security*, 13–14; H. A. Schaper, "The Security Policy of the Netherlands, 1945–1948," in Leurdijk, *Foreign Policy of the Netherlands*, 90; Eisen, *Anglo-Dutch Relations*; Steven Smith, *Foreign Policy Adaptation* (New York: Nichols Publishing, 1981), 79; L. G. M. Jaquet, "The Role of a Small State within Alliance Systems," in *Small States in International Relations*, ed. August Schon and Arne Olav Brundtland (New York: John Wiley & Sons, 1971), 61.

Swiss neutrality in World War II, impelled Switzerland not only to maintain its neutrality after World War II but also to decline member-ship in the United Nations.[59] The Swiss retention of neutrality was driven by their own successful experiences with neutrality. Edgar Bonjour, perhaps the leading Swiss historian in modern times, wrote during World War II: "For the experience of Swiss history yields one perfectly unambiguous result—without neutrality, no national sover-eignty. But without neutrality also, no Swiss freedom, which must be taken to cover the manifold institutions of liberty which are regarded by the world as being of the very essence of Swiss policy. Only under the shield of neutrality could they thrive and bloom."[60] This checkerboard pattern of alliance and neutrality, with the Benelux coun-tries joining NATO while Switzerland remained neutral, offers support for the individual learning hypothesis over the systemic learning hy-pothesis. Interestingly, the Benelux countries discounted the successful Swiss experience in World War II by attributing it to military consid-erations rather than Swiss neutrality, thus enabling them to believe that only their own experiences were relevant.[61]

In summary, individual learning explains well the alliance choices of Belgium, the Netherlands, and Switzerland since World War I. If Bel-gium had three foreign policy options before World War I—imposed neutrality, voluntary neutrality, and political alliance—the lesson of the German invasion of 1914 eliminated imposed neutrality as a possi-bility. Belgium opted for alliance during most of the interwar period, but domestic politics forced it to shift to voluntary neutrality in 1936, still remaining within the parameters of the lesson set by the 1914 experience. The lesson of the 1940 German invasion eliminated volun-tary neutrality as a possibility, steering Belgian foreign policy to politi-cal alliance after World War II. Further, the 1936 breakup of the Franco-Belgian alliance itself provided an important lesson for Spaak: that economic cooperation must accompany military cooperation if an entente is to remain politically viable in the long run. This has proven to be a farsighted and successful foreign policy: economic cooperation in Western Europe strengthened and stabilized the military coopera-

[59] Jacques Freymond, "The Foreign Policy of Switzerland," in *Foreign Policies in a World of Change*, ed. Joseph E. Black and Kenneth W. Thompson (New York: Harper & Row, 1963), 149–169; and "Rapport de Conseil Fédéral à l'Assemblée fédérale sur les relations de la Suisse avec les Nations Unies," Geneva, 16 June 1969.

[60] Edgar Bonjour, *Swiss Neutrality: Its History and Meaning*, trans. Mary Hottinger (London: George Allen & Unwin, 1946), 119.

[61] F. A. M. Alting von Geusau, "Between Lost Illusions and Apocalyptic Fears: Benelux Views on the European Neutrality," in *The European Neutrals in International Affairs*, ed. Hanspeter Neuhold and Hans Thalberg (Boulder, Colo.: Westview, 1984), 62.

tion laid out in the Brussels Pact and North Atlantic Treaty, contributed to the general prosperity of Western Europe and the eventual inclusion of Germany in these networks of cooperation, and facilitated the entrance of Germany into the community of Western democracies, thereby preventing the reemergence of German militarism. One might say, then, that the best policies emerge from the effective integration of a number of historical lessons, and Spaak's ability to do this marks him as an exceptional statesman.

Learning theory also helps us understand why nations facing the same level of international threat make different alliance choices. The individual national experiences of the Low Countries and Switzerland are the key factors explaining why the Netherlands and Switzerland chose neutrality after World War I, whereas Belgium switched to a preference for alliance, and why after World War II only Switzerland preferred neutrality. Balance of threat theory, on the other hand, fails to predict this checkerboard pattern of alliance choices, because it maintains the assumption that all states react to threat in the same manner, an assumption that in these cases does not hold.

SCANDINAVIA

Norway and Sweden provide a good opportunity for most-similar case analysis. These countries share similar cultural traditions and are governed by comparable political systems. Further, the rough geostrategic similarity of these nations facilitates the comparison of balance of threat predictions regarding how they might ally in response to a systemic threat. Yet the different experiences of Norway and Sweden in World War II offer varying learning predictions as to what lessons they should have learned about the desirability of alliance and neutrality. In this section I will explore and compare the experiences, threats, and alliance choices of Norway and Sweden, paying special attention to the relative significance of external threat and experiences in driving these nations' alliance decisions after World War II.

Norway

Norway was politically united with Sweden throughout most of the nineteenth century, in which a policy of neutrality successfully protected the national security of the union. Norway maintained a policy of neutrality when it declared its independence in 1905, holding fast to it when war broke out in Europe in 1914. An important part of this

Norwegian belief in neutrality was the conviction that it was in Britain's interest to prevent the occupation of the Norwegian coast and that Britain would take actions to guard against such a development even without a mutual alliance, just as it and France had guaranteed Norway against possible Russian aggression during the Crimean War. This confidence in Britain as protector of Norwegian neutrality would last until the British failed to prevent Norway's conquest in 1940.[62]

World War I can safely be viewed as a success for Norway's stance of neutrality. Norway not only managed to stay out of the war but was also awarded the island of Spitsbergen in the settlement that followed the armistice. This success reinforced the belief that Norway could avoid being involved should war come again; in 1920, a former foreign minister told the Norwegian parliament that "neutrality has been seen as so to speak an unwritten part of the Constitution of the Kingdom of Norway, a state maxim, a principle of the state, independent of changing cabinets and Parliaments."[63] Similar to many other World War I neutrals, Norway believed in general neutrality because of its successful experience with it but was willing to deviate from the strictest interpretation of neutrality to participate in the League of Nations (Norway claimed itself to be exempt from obligatory military sanctions that the league might impose, thereby retaining its essential neutrality). Norway had extremely high confidence in the effectiveness of a stance of neutrality as well as the general resurgence of international idealism as embodied in the League of Nations, the Locarno Pact, and the Kellogg Pact. This confidence, coupled with the desire to channel economic resources to domestic ends and long-standing pacifist sentiments, encouraged Norway to slash its military forces in the mid-1920s and early 1930s. As late as 1933, a bill was passed that set the number of active officers in the Norwegian armed forces at 470, with 1100 in reserve.[64]

[62] Gerald Aalders, "The Failure of the Scandinavian Defence Union, 1948–1949," *Scandinavian Journal of History* 15 (1990): 134.

[63] Quoted in Olav Riste, "Was 1949 a Turning Point? Norway and the Western Powers, 1947–1950," in *Western Security: The Formative Years*, ed. Riste (New York: Columbia University Press, 1985), 129. See also Olav Riste, "The Historical Determinants of Norwegian Foreign Policy," in *Norwegian Foreign Policy in the 1980s*, ed. Johan Jørgen Holst (Oslo: Norwegian University Press, 1985), 15; and F. A. Abadie-Maumert, "Le Pacifisme norvégien entre 1919 et 1940 et ses conséquences," *Guerres Mondiales et Conflits Contemporains* 40 (October 1990): 9.

[64] Riste, "Was 1949 a Turning Point?" 129; Martin Wight, "Switzerland, the Low Countries, and Scandinavia," in *Survey of International Affairs, 1939–1946: The World in March 1939*, ed. Arnold Toynbee and Frank T. Ashton-Gwatkin (London: Oxford University Press, 1952), 161; Annette Baker Fox, *The Power of Small States: Diplomacy in World War II* (Chicago: University of Chicago Press, 1959), 81; T. K. Derry, *A History of Modern Norway, 1814–1972* (Oxford: Clarendon, 1973), 336–347; Magne Skodvin, "Norwegian Neutrality

Norway also believed that political cooperation among the Scandinavian neutrals would ensure its security. In December 1930, Norway, Sweden, and Denmark signed the Oslo Convention, which laid a formal groundwork for greater political and potentially even military cooperation. The failure of the League of Nations to take effective action against either the Japanese invasion of Manchuria or the Italian invasion of Ethiopia eroded Norwegian confidence in the league. The Oslo Pact provided a basis for Norway and the other signatories to back away from their minimal commitments to collective security toward unconditional neutrality. Contrary to balance of threat theory, these growing tensions and instabilities in Europe did not encourage substantial Norwegian rearmament; a 1933 plan called for a "small but good" defensive force, oriented toward responding to unintentional or limited violations of neutrality, as opposed to a military prepared for defense against a full invasion. It was assumed that only a small force was necessary given the traditional factors favoring Norwegian defense, including the generally forbidding geography and long lines of supply an attacker would face. The ruling Labour Party gradually revised its strongly pro-disarmament attitude in the late 1930s, though the additional defense allocations were relatively slow in coming as compared with the rapidly escalating threat.[65]

After the outbreak of war in September 1939, Norway endeavored to maintain its neutrality. Respect for the legalistic aspect of neutrality remained strong, and the Norwegians attempted to act at least generally within the international guidelines for the proper behavior of a neutral.[66] When war broke out, both Britain and Germany saw the strategic importance of Norway. Germany relied on Sweden for the lion's share of its iron ore, and the only way that this ore could be moved to Germany in the winter months was through the ice-free Norwegian port of Narvik. The British deemed the interdiction of the flow of iron ore to be so important a strategic mission that they considered taking military action against German maritime traffic in Norwegian waters, a violation of declared neutrality.[67] The Germans beat them to the punch, however, invading Norway in April 1940 to ensure

---

and the Question of Credibility," *Scandinavian Journal of History* 2 (1977): 126; Abadie-Maumert, "Pacifisme norvégian," 11–16; and Nils Örvik, *The Decline of Neutrality, 1914–1941* (Oslo: Johan Grundt Tanum Forlag, 1953), 226–227.

[65] Derry, *Modern Norway*, 359–360; Skodvin, "Norwegian Neutrality," 127–130; Fox, *Power of Small States*, 81–82.

[66] Skodvin, "Norwegian Neutrality," 133–139.

[67] See Patrick Salmon, "Churchill, the Admiralty, and the Narvik Traffic, September–November 1939," *Scandinavian Journal of History* 4 (1979): 305–326.

year-round access to Swedish iron ore, completing its conquest of the country in two months. Historian Olav Riste noted that although Great Britain and Germany learned Norway's strategic importance from World War I, Norway itself was blind: "History does not repeat itself, however, for some try to learn from the past and others do not. In 1940 Germany was determined not to let her naval resources go to waste in passivity, whereas Great Britain was planning a blockade of Germany which would be effective from the outset. . . . A victim of the proverbial tendency to prepare for the previous war, Norway watched the gathering storm in an almost fatalistic commitment to the neutrality of the past."[68]

The Norwegian government fled to London, where it established a government-in-exile. It was there that the major break with Norway's tradition of political neutrality was made. The British were skeptical that the Norwegians had actually broken with their neutral past, so the task of building Anglo-Norwegian ties lay with the Norwegians. From the outset of the German occupation, the Norwegians were committed to cooperation with Great Britain. In the summer and autumn of 1940, the Norwegians debated how much they should cooperate with the British, eventually settling for more extensive collaboration within the context of an Anglo-Norwegian alliance. The replacement of the prewar, neutralist foreign minister, Halvdan Koht, with the pro-cooperation Trygve Lie in November 1940 marked an institutional shift from neutrality to alliance in the Norwegian leadership. As early as January 1941, Lie began high-level discussions on the nature of a postwar defense structure that would include the United States, Great Britain, and Norway. A formal alliance laying out the terms for Anglo-Norwegian military cooperation was signed on 28 May 1941. A year later, the cabinet approved a document entitled *The Principle Features of Norway's Foreign Policy*, which foresaw participation in a global, collective security organization as well as Norwegian entry into an Atlantic security defense system (which would exclude Soviet participation) after the war.[69] After the USSR entered the war on the side of the Allies, though,

---

[68] Olav Riste, *The Neutral Ally: Norway's Relations with Belligerent Powers in the First World War* (Oslo: Universitetsforlaget, 1965), 229. On Germany's learning of Norway's strategic importance from World War I for naval operations in World War II, see Hans-Dietrich Loock, "Weserübung—A Step towards the Greater Germanic Reich," *Scandinavian Journal of History* 2 (1977): 67–88.

[69] Olav Riste, "Norway in Exile, 1940–45: The Formation of an Alliance Relationship," *Scandinavian Journal of History* 12 (1987): 317–329; Philip M. Burgess, *Elite Images and Foreign Policy Outcomes: A Study of Norway* (Columbus: Ohio State University Press, 1968), 48–53; Sven G. Holtsmark, *Between "Russophobia" and "Bridge-Building": The Norwegian Government and the Soviet Union* (Oslo: Institutt for forsvarsstudier, 1988), 41–42.

the leadership slowly began to shift its position, toward publicly emphasizing Norway's role as a builder of bridges between the Western powers and the USSR in a postwar security system. It also began to de-emphasize its Atlantic orientation, though Norway's leanings to the West were never fully erased. Norway's commitment to placing itself in the Western camp was evidenced by its cool response to the Polish proposal to construct a postwar alliance of small European states and its rejection of Swedish initiatives for a postwar Scandinavian federation.[70]

During the bridge-building phase of 1945 and 1946, Norway found itself hesitant on the question of joining alliances, though neutrality had definitely been given a bad name by the 1940 experience. The goals of bridge building were somewhat in conflict with an alliance with Britain and the United States, as the latter would infringe on the credibility of Norway as an impartial link between East and West, though bridge building reflected the lesson from World War II that Norway must participate in international politics. Norway saw the importance of maintaining a balance between East and West, such that it did not unnecessarily provoke the Russians by placing it too firmly in the Western camp.[71]

These years are best described as an interim period, before the Norwegians had laid down the real foundations of their postwar foreign policy. Even in these transitional years of indecision, however, it was clear that a cornerstone of postwar policy would be the rejection of the prewar policy of neutrality. Foreign Minister Lie, in a speech given to the Norwegian parliament on 19 June 1945, explained that the experience of the just-ended war spoke against continuing a policy of neutrality. He argued that the war had shown both that Norway itself could not defend its long coastline and that the important strategic position of Norway would make it difficult to avoid participation in a future conflict. Beyond that, though, Lie was rather vague as to specific guidelines for action. He proposed that cooperation with the Atlantic great powers and the USSR would be important in safeguarding Norwegian

---

[70] Sven G. Holtsmark, "Atlantic Orientation or Regional Groupings: Elements of Norwegian Foreign Policy Discussions during the Second World War," *Scandinavian Journal of History* 14 (1989): 312; and Holtsmark, *Between "Russophobia" and "Bridge-Building"*, 62. Some Norwegians living in Stockholm during the war supported Swedish proposals for Nordic cooperation after the war, with the ultimate goal of federating or uniting all Europe. Holtsmark, "Atlantic Orientation," 318–322.

[71] Geir Lundestad, "The Evolution of Norwegian Security Policy: Alliance with the West and Reassurance in the East," *Scandinavian Journal of History* 17 (1992): 229; Lundestad, *America, Scandinavia, and the Cold War, 1945–1949* (New York: Columbia University Press, 1980), 47–48; Burgess, *Elite Images*, 80–81; Nils Morten Udgaard, *Great Power Politics and Norwegian Foreign Policy* (Oslo: Universitetsforlaget, 1973), 91–94.

security and that Norway should support and seek protection from a global collective security organization.[72] Lie's vagueness was not a diplomatic gambit disguising a sophisticated master plan of bridge building: in practice, bridge building amounted to more of a negative policy in the sense of avoiding issues that might involve the great powers, rather than a positive effort to resolve great power conflicts or take real initiatives.[73]

Norway began to lay the foundations of its postwar foreign policy in 1947. In May of that year, George Marshall made his now famous speech proposing a program of massive economic aid from America to war-torn Europe. While many European nations jumped for this economic life preserver, Norway viewed it more cautiously. The main concern at the outset was that joining this American-sponsored organization would endanger Norway's policy of bridge building. At first, the Norwegian government preferred to avoid joining if economically feasible. A study by the Norwegian Ministry of Finance was generally upbeat on Norway's economic prospects absent participation in the Marshall Plan; it noted that Norway would not need credits from the United States to finance imports for at least eighteen months. It was generally thought that Norway could benefit economically in the long run from participation in the Marshall Plan, but economic considerations did not make participation imperative. Two factors eventually encouraged Norwegian willingness to participate. First, the decision of Sweden and Denmark to join turned the Marshall Plan question into an issue of Scandinavian unity, and Norway did not wish for its nonparticipation to threaten such unity. Second, it soon became apparent that a decision not to participate would make Norway appear a virtual de facto member of the Eastern bloc, thereby threatening bridge building. Ultimately, the lesser of two evils was to participate, "as not joining would constitute a greater break with the established policy than joining."[74] Norway, then, was not forced into the Marshall Plan by dire economic necessity, nor did participation in the Marshall Plan irrevocably commit Norway to joining Western military arrangements.

The summer of 1947 saw the beginnings of the breakdown of political support for the Norwegian policy of bridge building. Influential Norwegian newspapers began to question the validity of the bridge-

[72] Udgaard, *Great Power Politics*, 125–126. A new government took over soon after Lie made his speech, though they pledged to stay the previous course in foreign policy.

[73] Helge Ø. Pharo, "Bridgebuilding and Reconstruction: Norway Faces the Marshall Plan," *Scandinavian Journal of History* 1 (1976): 128.

[74] Pharo, "Bridgebuilding and Reconstruction," 134–136.

building policy, motivated in part by increasing international tensions in Europe between East and West.[75] In January 1948, the Norwegian parliament held its first postwar debate on foreign policy, and some of the opposition parties attacked the bridge-building policy. Two days later, British foreign secretary Ernest Bevin made a speech proposing political and military cooperation in Western Europe. This set the stage for a turning point in Norwegian foreign policy, as it was becoming increasingly clear that a real rift between the Soviet Union and the Western great powers might emerge, with Norway having to choose a side or to try and keep up its balancing act between them. In a speech in mid-February, Norwegian foreign minister Halvard Lange declared his general support for the Bevin proposals, stating that in the event of a split between East and West, Norway would be in the Western camp. Also in February, the leaders of the Scandinavian Social Democratic Parties met in Stockholm. Here, the leaders of the ruling Norwegian Labor Party expressed their leanings toward alignment with the West, motivated largely by their World War II experiences:

> Fears for a Quisling-like coup by the communists and concern for the merchant fleet—Norway's most important foreign policy instrument during the war—point to the pervasive influence which the recent war-experiences had on Norwegian thinking at this juncture. The whole Labour Party leadership had been active in the war, Gerhardsen and Lange having suffered physically in concentration camps, and in this very period the inquiry commission published reports which revealed the short-comings of their predecessors—over-optimism, miscalculation of the time needed for rearmament, lack of arrangements with foreign powers. Almost every speech on foreign policy and defense now contained a reference to 1940. . . . To Haakon Lie, the lesson was of a more practical nature: in 1940 Norway had had to improvise her defence, and that would not have been necessary if she had had military co-operation with Britain. . . . Again referring to 1940, the Norwegians present at the meeting described neutrality as an illusion—a voice from the grave—and Nordahl threw in the bridgebuilding policy as well.[76]

Leading Norwegian newspapers were becoming increasingly critical at this time of the bridge-building policy, encouraging the serious consideration of the proposals in the Bevin speech. One article drew the lesson from World War II experience that Hitler was able to attack a number of neutral nations successfully because they did not

[75] Udgaard, *Great Power Politics*, 224–228.
[76] Ibid., 244–245.

cooperate, which meant that collaboration is the best guarantee of security.[77]

Soviet foreign policy in early 1948, particularly its pressure on Finland to sign a defense agreement and its support of the Communist coup in Czechoslovakia, demonstrated that the rift between the great powers that bridge building was designed to prevent had arrived. The action against Czechoslovakia was especially significant for Norway, as Czechoslovakia had also attempted to carry off a bridge-building policy. The rapidly shrinking bloc of independent states in 1948 demonstrated to Norway that bridge building could no longer be the basis of Norwegian foreign policy if it wanted to avoid falling into the cracks of world politics and that the best option was alliance with the West. By March, Norway had begun to give stronger signals of its interest in entering the Western bloc: Oslo, claiming to be trying to maneuver Sweden and Denmark into the Western bloc, asked Washington directly what assistance it might expect in case of attack. Additionally, the Norwegian defense budget was increased through emergency legislation by 50 percent, and Norwegian communists were ostracized and declared unpatriotic in the aftermath of the actions taken by the USSR in Czechoslovakia. The cold war had come to Norway.[78]

As the discussions about entrance into the Western bloc proceeded in 1948, the Norwegians were also making requests for American military aid under the Vandenberg Resolution. This resolution outlined the provision of military aid, with priority given to countries with whom the United States had alliance responsibilities. Since the American capacity for providing military aid did not match the requests it received, the question arose of whether Norwegian entrance into the Western bloc would be necessary to ensure timely delivery of military aid. The National Security Council of the United States produced a policy paper dated 3 September 1948 which recommended a leverage policy in Scandinavia, giving Norway and Denmark limited military aid with the promise of more if they agreed to participate in some sort of Western collective defense arrangement.[79] The U.S. ambassador in Oslo was instructed to convey to the Norwegian government that priority for

---

[77] See the comments of the Belgian minister to Norway to Spaak, MAE, dossier no. 12.237, 3 February and 17 February 1948.

[78] Udgaard, *Great Power Politics*, 246–247, Pharo, "Bridgebuilding and Reconstruction," 153; Grethe Værnø, "The United States, Norway, and the Atlantic Pact, 1948–1949," *Scandinavian Studies* 50 (Spring 1978): 157–158; Tom Hetland, "The Soviet View of the Nordic Countries and NATO, 1948–1952," *Scandinavian Journal of History* 11 (1986): 152.

[79] *FRUS*, 1948, 3:233.

arms transfers would be given to those nations who had joined regional or collective self-defense arrangements.[80]

An interesting question, then, is whether the American carrot of military aid was necessary to encourage Norwegian involvement in what was to become NATO. If true, it would cast doubt on the importance of learned lessons in motivating Norway's entrance into NATO, as this action would have been taken in order to receive American military aid, not because Norway acted on the lesson that alliances are desirable. One problem with this argument is that Norway's interest in alliance with the West predates the U.S. policy of linking aid to alliance membership. As discussed above, the attitudes of Norwegian leaders and the public were clearly shifting toward favoring alliance with the West by late 1947 and early 1948. Further, from the start of the negotiations for a Scandinavian Defense Union (SDU) in May 1948, Norway rejected the option of a neutral SDU and demanded close ties to the West, a stance motivated both by the World War II lesson that neutrality endangers national security and by Norway's experience of union with Sweden in the nineteenth century, which left it with a deep distrust of Swedish political domination.[81] Additionally, if the Norwegians were being maneuvered against their will into a Western alliance, their actions did not reflect it. On 8 September, Foreign Minister Lange asked the American ambassador in Oslo if there was such linkage and actually suggested that the United States make the linkage known to improve his negotiating position with Sweden on the issue of Scandinavian defense cooperation, remarking that his "position in Foreign Ministers meeting [between Norway and Sweden] might be fortified should answer suggest restriction of aid under these conditions."[82] Two months later a member of the Norwegian Foreign Office made the same point to the U.S. ambassador to Sweden, expressing his hope that the Swedes understood that "the terms of the Vandenberg Resolution precluded unilateral support by the US of a Scandinavian Defense Pact. . . . He said that the Norwegian Government clearly understood the point but that, should it arise in future discussions between Sweden and Norway, the Norwegian position would be strengthened if they knew, and the Swedish Government knew that they knew, that we had informed the Swedes of our governments [*sic*] interpretation of the Vandenberg Resolution in this re-

---

[80] Værnø, "United States, Norway, and the Atlantic Pact," 168.

[81] Nikolaj Petersen, "Danish and Norwegian Alliance Policies, 1948–49: A Comparative Analysis," *Cooperation and Conflict* 14 (1979): 198–199; Aalders, "Failure of the Scandinavian Defence Union," 134.

[82] *FRUS*, 1948, 3:236.

spect."[83] The picture that emerges, then, is not one in which military weakness forced Norway, against its will, to enter NATO to secure military aid. Rather, the Norwegians desired some form of defense alliance with the West even before the United States devised its pressure strategy, and Lange may have even manipulated the American carrot-and-stick strategy to undermine the Swedish proposal for a neutralist SDU.[84]

The experience of invasion and conquest in the context of declared neutrality served to engender a tremendous reversal in Norwegian thinking about the usefulness of neutrality and alliance. Historian Sven Holtsmark commented: "The experience of participation as a belligerent in the Second World War—and the trauma of 9 April 1940—was pivotal in shaping the strategic outlook of many influential Norwegians. Contrary to Sweden's experience, Norway came out of the war with a strong belief in the need for military co-operation and alliances between small *and* great powers to prevent new aggression and war."[85] For example, Foreign Minister Lange was deeply scarred by his experience in World War II and often mentioned having been arrested by German occupation authorities and sent to a concentration camp. This experience motivated the Norwegians to doubt the desirability of nonaligned Nordic cooperation, as they equated that with neutrality and saw alliance with a great power as the only definite way to ensure their security. The Norwegians learned from their World War II experience that Norway's strategic importance and vulnerability meant that they would not be able to avoid a future great power war. The war also substantially eroded the strong elements of pacifism in Norwegian political culture, as the folly of disarmed neutrality was aptly demonstrated. In the years following the war, Norway's defense spending was three to four times higher in real terms than prewar spending.[86]

Of course, Norway's willingness to enter into cooperation with the Atlantic powers is consistent both with individual learning theory and with balance of threat theory. It is certainly true that the emerging Soviet threat played a substantial role in the Norwegian decision to

[83] Ibid., 277–278.

[84] This argument is made by Grethe Værnø and Karl Molin, "Winning the Peace: Vision and Disappointment in Nordic Security Policy, 1945–49," in *Scandinavia during the Second World War*, trans. Thomas Munch-Petersen, ed. Henrik S. Nissen (Minneapolis: University of Minnesota Press, 1983), 364.

[85] Holtsmark, "Atlantic Orientation," 311.

[86] Aalders, "Failure of the Scandinavian Defence Union," 134; ibid., 319–320; Abadie-Maumert, "Pacifisme norvégian"; Lundestad, "Evolution of Norwegian Security Policy," 228; Burgess, *Elite Images*, 132 n, 146.

enter NATO, and it could be argued that this decision is powerful proof of the balance of threat theory over learning theory, as the Norwegians seemed to be drifting back to some version of prewar neutrality after World War II and shifted back to choosing alliance only after the Soviet threat was undeniably displayed in its actions against Finland and Czechoslovakia in February 1948.[87]

It should be noted, though, that even when Norwegian doubts about alliance with the West were at their greatest, the focus was on bridge building and not a return to prewar neutrality. Bridge building was based on the idea that Norwegian security is best served if tension between the superpowers is low and that Norway can reduce this tension, which is quite different from the extreme isolationism verging on the absence of foreign policy that was characteristic of Norway in the interwar period. Further, the whole notion that bridge building is necessary emerges from the World War II experience, from which Norway recognized for the first time that its security would be threatened in the event of great power war.

More important, though, the way in which Norway recognized and framed the Soviet threat was strongly motivated by the lessons drawn from wartime experiences. Just before the events of early 1948, a commission established to examine the events that led to the 1940 invasion had presented findings that the prewar foreign minister Halvdan Koht had failed to take sufficient heed of warnings of imminent German attack. With this in mind, the Norwegian Foreign Ministry wanted to avoid a repeat of the 1940 experience by taking seriously the signs of the rising Soviet threat. The lesson of the 1940 invasion, then, had sensitized the Norwegians to external threats: without that lesson, they probably would have reacted as they did in 1940, paying little attention to the growing international tension and not seeking to form protective alliances.[88] Additionally, the World War II experience eroded the Norwegians' belief in their geostrategic safety. Before World War II, they believed that their northerly location and rough terrain would be enough to dissuade attackers. The war, however, powerfully demonstrated that Norway contained a good deal of strategically important territory; thus Norway's chances of avoiding conflict in a future great power war would be very low. Indeed, as historian Nils Morten Udgaard noted, this was the one lesson from World War II that nearly

[87] Burgess argues that the appearance of threat in early 1948 was crucial in forming the Norwegian strategic image, although he also argues that Norway's World War II experiences demonstrated the strategic vulnerability of Norway and the unacceptability of traditional neutrality. Burgess, *Elite Images*, 102–104.

[88] Hetland, "Soviet View of the Nordic Countries and NATO," 153.

all Norwegians agreed on: "In post-war Norway there was practically complete agreement on one particular lesson to be drawn from the war-time experience, namely that Norway—in contrast to the belief gener-ally held before the war—had to consider herself as occupying a territory of significant strategic importance to the Great Powers."[89] Therefore, the World War II experience sensitized the Norwegians to international threat by making them aware of their geostrategic vulner-ability, and it also indicated that the best solution to an increase in threat was alliance with a great power.

Sweden

Once a great power in Europe, Sweden had by the end of the Napo-leonic Wars slipped decidedly to middle rank. In the aftermath of these wars, neutrality began to develop as a component of Swedish foreign policy. The Swedish government remained neutral during World War I in the face of some domestic opposition that favored joining the Allies, and Sweden was spared the horrors of modern warfare and the indig-nities of conquest and occupation. In a bitter debate following the war, Sweden agreed to join the League of Nations. The strong current of opinion favoring armed neutrality was satisfied when the league recog-nized in 1921 that Sweden could opt out of obligatory military sanc-tions imposed by the league.[90]

Sweden retained its confidence in the League of Nations as an instru-ment of collective security for several years after World War I. When Italy invaded Ethiopia in 1935, Sweden was determined to support league sanctions against Italy, partly because it wished to avoid repeat-ing the league's failure to take effective action in the 1923 Corfu inci-dent or the 1931 Japanese invasion of Manchuria, partly because of Swedish concern over the European balance of power, and partly be-cause of general Swedish opposition to Italian fascism. Dissatisfaction with the eventual inability of the league to check Italian aggression was coupled with a recognition that Sweden's active interest in collective security had threatened traditional Swedish neutrality. The result, in the late 1930s, was a shift back toward traditional neutrality and away

[89] Udgaard, *Great Power Politics*, 185. Udgaard goes on to note that "otherwise the interpretations of the war-time lessons differed, much in accordance with views held before the war." See also Lundestad, "Evolution of Norwegian Security Policy," 228.
[90] Elis Håstad, "Sweden's Attitude toward the United Nations," in *Sweden and the United Nations* (New York: Manhattan Publishing, 1956), 16; Herbert Tingsten, *The Debate on the Foreign Policy of Sweden, 1918–1939*, trans. Joan Bulman (London: Oxford University Press, 1949); Samuel Abrahamsen, *Sweden's Foreign Policy* (Washington, D.C.: Public Affairs Press, 1957), 14–15.

from support of the league. Sweden recognized that the League of Nations could not ensure its security, so it looked to fortifying its stance of armed neutrality. Defense spending began to increase with the Defense Act of 1936, and by the autumn of 1939 Swedish industry had begun to convert to war production. In reality, though, the Swedish armed forces were prepared at that stage to defend against only unintentional violations of neutrality (such as minor border incidents) rather than a full-scale campaign, as the provisions of the 1936 act had been just partly implemented.[91]

The Swedish government saw neutrality as its best option for the coming European war. The fairly unanimous support of neutrality in Sweden at this time differed from the environment in 1914, when opinion was divided between neutrality and entry into the war on the side of the Allies.[92] The Swedes hoped that neutrality would permit a repeat of their successful World War I experience, not recognizing the important political and military changes of the last two decades: "The [Swedish] Foreign Ministry's assessment was thus that the expected struggle between the Great Powers would in essentials follow the same pattern as in 1914–18, even if weapons now had a longer range and were more effective, and even if less regard for the rule of international law could be expected. Sweden—and other Northern lands—should have the prospect of again staying out of a major war."[93]

The Russian invasion of Finland that year presented a considerable challenge to the Swedish policy of neutrality. Swedish public opinion— as well as Foreign Minister Sandler—was solidly pro-Finnish in the negotiations leading up to the invasion; the Finns may have not unreasonably surmised that the Swedes would come to their defense in the event of Russian military action. Faced with the reality of a Russo-Finnish war, however, Sweden balked at direct military assistance to the Finns, and Sandler found so little support for his pro-Finnish line that he offered his resignation on 2 December. With his departure, the four main political parties in Sweden converged on a common foreign

---

[91] John F. L. Ross, *Neutrality and International Sanctions: Sweden, Switzerland, and Collective Security* (New York: Praeger, 1989), 61–86; Abrahamsen, *Sweden's Foreign Policy*, 22–26; Stig Ekman, "La Politique de défense de la Suède durant la Seconde Guerre Mondiale," *Revue d'Histoire de la Deuxième Guerre Mondiale* 32 (January 1982): 13–15; Erik Lönnroth, "Sweden's Ambiguous Neutrality," *Scandinavian Journal of History* 2 (1977): 96–97; Jerry Wilson Ralston, "The Defense of Small States in the Nuclear Age: The Case of Sweden and Switzerland," Ph.D. diss., Université de Genève (Neuchatel: La Baconnière, 1969), 63.

[92] Lönnroth, "Sweden's Ambiguous Neutrality," 96; Ralston, "Defense of Small States," 64.

[93] W. M. Carlgren, *Swedish Foreign Policy during the Second World War*, trans. Arthur Spencer (New York: St. Martin's, 1977), 14.

policy line: not to declare neutrality regarding the Russo-Finnish conflict, though greater military involvement was not recommended, and to retain neutrality regarding the conflict between Germany and the Western powers. The change of government engendered by Sandler's departure allowed for a renewal of Swedish neutrality, avoiding a shift to greater involvement which Sandler might have encouraged. This renewal of Swedish neutrality came despite the burgeoning realization of the imminent danger posed to Sweden by the USSR, as evidenced by the Soviet action against Finland. A further test of Swedish commitment to neutrality came on 9 April 1940, when Germany occupied Denmark and attacked Norway. The Swedes responded by quadrupling the number of troops they had under arms (to 320,000) and confirming their neutral status with Britain and Germany, which included the statement that Sweden would resist any border incursion. By mid-April, reports of an imminent German attack began to flow into Stockholm; on 24 April, Prime Minister Günther commented that he expected German troops had already entered Swedish territory. These fears were renewed in May when Germany demanded that Sweden permit the transit of military supplies en route to the campaign in Norway, a request that Sweden mostly refused in order to maintain its status of neutrality. Great power ambition in the region was highlighted in the following months by the Soviet invasions of the Baltic states.[94]

Sweden perceived a very high external threat in 1940. The German war effort was dependent on Swedish iron ore, which consequently made the continuous flow of trade from Sweden of vital interest to Germany (indeed, Germany invaded Norway in large part to maintain winter access to Swedish iron ore) and therefore made the cessation of Swedish iron ore exports to Germany a strategic priority for Britain.[95] Further, two separate, major military operations occurred that year in nations adjacent to Sweden, Norway and Finland. Yet, in spite of this tremendous threat, Sweden did not seek alliance with any of the three threatening great powers, seeking instead to fortify its traditional and proven policy of neutrality. This behavior is in strong contrast to the predictions of balance of threat theory, namely, that Sweden would choose an alliance partner, bandwagoning with it and simultaneously balancing against the others.

Sweden successfully avoided military participation in World War II,

---

[94] Ibid., 22–27, 54–70; Lönnroth, "Sweden's Ambiguous Neutrality," 99.

[95] Patrick Salmon, "British Plans for Economic Warfare against Germany, 1937–1939: The Problem of Swedish Iron Ore," *Journal of Contemporary History* 16 (January 1981): 53–71.

though it kept up substantial trade relations with Germany throughout the war. On 31 July 1945, the wartime coalition government in Sweden was replaced by a new government, with Östen Undén taking Günther's place as the new foreign minister. The new government was still strongly opposed to joining one of the emerging blocs, but it did put faith in the United Nations as an instrument of collective security. Significantly, Sweden recognized that the UN could not force its members to participate in economic or military sanctions, which thereby left the essential core of its neutrality intact. This departure from the isolationism of the late 1930s did not extend to a desire to enter one of the emerging great power blocs, however. Sweden rejected overtures to join the Brussels Pact, stating that it would not belong to any political bloc. Undén, with the nearly unanimous support of all Swedish political parties, strongly favored neutrality; the only group that advocated greater ties with the West was the military, who wanted to ensure Swedish access to Western military aid.[96]

As did Norway, by 1948 Sweden perceived higher levels of external threat. After the Czech coup in February 1948, the Swedish reaction was anything but indifferent. The Swedish prime minister, Tage Erlander, gave a speech on 18 March 1948 in which he very clearly stated his opposition to the recent events in Czechoslovakia and the threat that Sweden felt from Communism:

> One need not any longer be in doubt as to where Communism stands. It has placed itself outside the democratic community. The fight against communism is hardening. . . . We have experienced events which have thrust themselves upon us with violent, dramatic force. Above all the recent events in Czechoslovakia have made a strong and profound impression on our people. Our minds have been deeply disturbed by the fact that an apparently sound clear-cut democratic institution has been trampled under foot. Practically the whole of our nation reacts violently against this action.[97]

Significantly, while these events also brought fear to Norway and encouraged its movement toward alliance with the West, they sparked a different reaction from Sweden. Growing Swedish concern about the Soviet threat and rising East-West tensions did not dislodge Swedish confidence in neutrality—a few Swedish newspapers broached the idea of Swedish entry into the Western bloc, but this suggestion attracted no

---

[96] Abrahamsen, *Sweden's Foreign Policy*, 58–66, 68; Nils Andrén, *Power-Balance and Non-Alignment* (Stockholm: Almquist and Wiksell, 1967), 38–39, 73; Aalders, "Failure of the Scandinavian Defence Union," 125–131.

[97] Quoted in Abrahamsen, *Sweden's Foreign Policy*, 87.

support from the political parties. In June 1948, the Swedish foreign minister reaffirmed the Swedish commitment to neutrality in a parliamentary debate.[98] Balance of threat theory, therefore, poorly predicts Swedish behavior, as the Swedes preferred neutrality in the face of perceived external threat. Alternatively, if one argued that Sweden preferred neutrality in 1948 because it did not face a real threat, then this makes predictions for Norwegian behavior problematic, for it implies that they preferred alliance without worrying about an external threat. Only learning theory successfully predicts the decision of Norway (and Denmark) to join NATO and of Sweden to remain neutral.

One might argue that Norway's eventual participation in NATO was due to American manipulation of the stick of military aid. It ought to be mentioned that the Americans tried much harder to pressure the Swedes into forgoing their neutrality, to no avail. The American ambassador in Stockholm waged a virtual "private war" against Swedish neutrality, using a number of weapons to try to bring the Swedes into the Western alliance, including diplomatic isolation and promising to withhold military and economic aid if Sweden remained neutral. His tactics occasionally strayed to the more heavy-handed, as he once mentioned that the United States would bomb Sweden if national security required it.[99] Swedish resistance to these tactics was encouraged both by its firm commitment to neutrality and by its belief that the threat to cut off military aid was not credible.[99] Sweden's resistance to American pressure tactics is important evidence against the argument that small powers are nothing more than puppets of the great powers, indirectly increasing our confidence that Norway's entrance into NATO was not due to American pressure, which was far more intense and overt for Sweden than Norway.

Sweden's postwar adherence to neutrality was supported nearly unanimously by all the political parties and was strongly driven by its successful experience with neutrality in World War II.[100] The main lesson it drew was that neutrality backed by strong armed forces best guaranteed Swedish security. In a 1948 memorandum, Foreign Minister Undén remarked that "the experience of the two past world wars cannot simply be denied as being meaningless. On the contrary, this experience is of great weight."[101] Even when negotiations collapsed

---

[98] Andrén, *Power-Balance and Non-Alignment*, 56; ibid., 87.

[99] Aalder, "Failure of the Scandinavian Defence Union," 139–148; Lundestad, *America, Scandinavia, and the Cold War*, 220–222.

[100] Aalders, "Failure of the Scandinavian Defence Union," 125–126; Abrahamsen, *Sweden's Foreign Policy*, 80; Burgess, *Elite Images*, 106.

[101] Quoted in Aalders, "Failure of the Scandinavian Defence Union," 153.

for the Swedes' alternative to great power alliance, the SDU, they did not accept the alternative balancing option of joining NATO. In a message to Parliament on 9 February 1949, the Swedish government defended its adherence to neutrality by pointing to the lessons offered by Swedish history:

> For Sweden the stranding of the negotiations means that we retain the attitude which we have so far assumed. The Swedish people remains [*sic*] as little disposed as before to assume a position marking that we engage ourselves in the present "cold war." The fact that Sweden has been able to maintain peace for 135 years has without doubt a great psychological effect on the attitude of the Swedish public to the security problem. During this period Europe has been shaken by tremendous wars in which our country has not been involved. Whatever the explanation of our escape from wars our people can in any case not be easily convinced that their security now would demand that we throw away neutrality as a wrong and obsolete policy.[102]

Interestingly, the experiences of failed neutrality of Denmark and Norway did not introduce doubt into Swedish confidence in neutrality. The Swedes attributed Norway's conquest to its military unpreparedness, not its neutrality. As early as 1941, the Swedish foreign minister argued:

> Nothing has been more clearly shown in this war than that the greatest danger for a small country, which is in close relation to rival great powers, is a military vacuum or emptiness. It is not that the great power will always throw themselves upon the weaker just to conquer, but rather that small countries who do not want to defend themselves against an attack are looked upon as a danger by the former. Each of them fears that its rival will conquer such a defenseless area and thereby increase its power, improve its position for an attack, and obtain an improved area for deployment of its forces. It is therefore necessary to prevent attack rather than be attacked.[103]

This lesson, that neutrality must be backed by a strong military to be successful, permitted the Swedes to use the Danish and Norwegian experiences of failed neutrality to justify their own armed neutrality:

> Again, this rejection was neither due to any doctrinaire belief in neutrality, nor to a lack of sympathy with the West, but was based on historical experience and on evaluation of the situation prevailing with the country

---

[102] Message reprinted in Andrén, *Power-Balance and Non-Alignment*, 71.
[103] Quoted in Ralston, "Defence of Small States," 81.

at the time. . . . When it was pointed out that Germany's treatment of Norway and Denmark during the war showed that neutrality was no longer a viable policy, Sweden rebutted by arguing that hers was an armed neutrality, and that if the other Scandinavian countries had been well enough armed their fates might have been different—i.e. similar to Sweden's. . . . Whether or not her neutrality was the sole reason Sweden was spared during two world wars or was merely incidental, it has nevertheless exerted a powerful influence on the Swedish people. Public opinion and all the country's democratic parties regard it as self-evident that this historically proven concept should continue as a fundamental national policy.[104]

In sum, balance of threat theory fails to explain Sweden's decisions to remain neutral in the late 1930s and again in the late 1940s. In contrast, learning theory correctly predicts both. Further, learning theory correctly predicts the pattern of alliance preferences in Scandinavia as a whole during both periods: Norway, Denmark, and Sweden preferring neutrality even in the face of the German threat in the late 1930s, whereas after World War II, only Norway and Denmark preferred membership in NATO. It was the individual, formative experiences of each state which determined their preferences:

> Divergent wartime experiences played a significant role in the SDU negotiations and clearly affected the outcome of the negotiations between Sweden and Denmark. For Sweden there was little reason to change a successful foreign policy that had served her well since the Napoleonic wars. Danish and Norwegian neutrality, however, was shattered by the German attack on 9 April 1940, and the event raised serious doubts as to the desirability of continuing the old policy. Oslo and Copenhagen feared a repetition of April 1940, this time with the Soviet Union as aggressor. The Swedish political scientist Krister Wahlbäck addresses much attention to what he calls the 9 April syndrome.[105]

The cases of the traditional neutrals in Western Europe powerfully demonstrate the significance of learning as an explanation of whether states choose alliance or neutrality. Examination of the details of these cases reveals that the experiences in the formative events played decisive roles in determining the attitudes of the decision makers toward

[104] Ibid., 70, 209.
[105] Aalders, "Failure of the Scandinavian Defence Union," 133–134. Foreign Minister Lange made a similar point in a speech on 4 June 1948, observing that "the different experiences of our three countries during the war have created a different atmosphere regarding the attitude toward the main contemporary foreign policy questions in Norway, Sweden, and Denmark." Quoted in Burgess, *Elite Images*, 104. See also Andrén, *Power-Balance and Non-Alignment*, 58–59.

alliance and neutrality. Though the specifics of the cases sometimes revealed the narrowness of the learning hypotheses used for the quantitative tests, the choices that were made were ultimately explicable through the application of the principles of learning theory. Further, the alliance checkerboards observed in Western Europe and Scandinavia are explained well by learning theory but are not explained by balance of threat theory. Admittedly, threat is a difficult concept to measure but the checkerboard alliance/neutrality patterns in these two clusters demonstrate the robustness of the learning predictions across different operationalizations of the threat variable. If one assumes that the German threat was completely dormant in the 1920s, then balance of threat theory cannot explain the Belgian preference for alliance; conversely, if one assumes that the German threat was latently present in the 1920s, then balance of threat theory cannot explain the neutrality of the Netherlands, Switzerland, and, to a lesser extent, Norway and Sweden. Similarly, if one assumes that there was a real Soviet threat in the late 1940s, then balance of threat theory cannot explain the Swedish and Swiss preferences for neutrality, whereas if one assumes that there was no real Soviet threat, then balance of threat theory cannot explain the signing of the Brussels Pact and the formation of NATO. The empirical finding in support of learning and against balance of threat theory, then, is very robust, in that it would appear to hold in the face of very diverse codings of the presence of external threat.

What the cases reveal is that experiences often determine how alliance decisions are made by shaping how decision makers think about threat. Formative experiences shape beliefs as to how vulnerable the nation is to external threats. After World War I, all Europe was theoretically at risk from the long-term renewal of German militarism. Yet of all the six nations discussed in this chapter, just Belgium—the only one of this group to be invaded during the war—felt that alliance was required to safeguard its long-term security. The experience of World War I sensitized the Belgians to the possible renewal of the German threat. The other nations felt that neutrality had passed the test of fire and that the best response to a new German threat would be to cling to neutrality. One might argue that only the Belgians were truly threatened because Germany would attack only Belgium, but this begs the question, How did this group of states come to that conclusion? The answer is that one of the lessons learned from World War I is that in the event of great power conflict, only Belgium would be a target of German attack. The fact that three of these post–World War I neutrals—the Netherlands, Denmark, and Norway—were attacked by Germany in World War II highlights the power and perseverance of this lesson of the safety of neutrality even in the face of rapidly changing political and military conditions.

These cases also indicated that the learning involves more than just the choice between alliance and neutrality. From formative experiences states also draw lessons about other aspects of their security policies, particularly their level of domestic armaments. Sweden and Switzerland, for example, drew the lesson from World War II that neutrality would be effective only if it was backed by a strong army. Norway drew the lesson from its World War II experience that domestic armament is necessary to safeguard the country, though it also drew the lesson that alliance is necessary. These examples illustrate learning about high versus low levels of armament, as well as about alliance versus neutrality. This is an important expansion on some expected utility models of alliance formation, which argue that both alliances and arms can provide security and that other considerations, such as economic welfare and foreign policy autonomy, often determine which means a state will choose to improve its security.[106] This chapter demonstrates, however, that perceptions of the marginal impacts of arms and neutrality to security and autonomy are not logical certainties but beliefs that are strongly determined by past experiences rather than structural factors. In mathematical terms, this chapter indicates that experiences teach states about the relative sizes of the coefficients for arms or alliances for increasing security, answering the question of whether adding arms or allies contributes great or small amounts to the state's security. Experiences also teach states whether the sign of the coefficient is positive or negative, as a state believing that neutrality is best is likely to believe that adding allies would decrease the state's security. Therefore, the sort of formative learning discussed in this book can be used to understand how states come to comprehend the relative contributions of arms and alliances to their security.

---

[106] See, for example, James D. Morrow, "Alliances and Asymmetry: An Alternative to the Capability Aggregation Model of Alliances," *American Journal of Political Science* 35 (November 1991): 904–933; and Gerald L. Sorokin, "Arms, Alliances, and Security Tradeoffs in Enduring Rivalries," *International Studies Quarterly* 38 (September 1994): 421–446.

[7]

Case Studies:
Lessons Not Learned?

The previous chapter laid out cases for which the individual learning hypothesis made accurate predictions, illustrating the accuracy of the theory's description of the decision-making process. Results in Chapter 5, however, indicate that out of 127 cases, 16 were not predicted correctly. This chapter explores these cases, examining the sources of particular alliance decisions. In searching for alternative explanations to the individual learning hypothesis, discussion of each case revolves around three specific questions: Does the balance of threat hypothesis best explain the outcome? Does the learning theory explain the outcome, but is the individual learning hypothesis ill-suited to the specific historical circumstances of the case? Do factors outside the purview of learning and balance of threat theories best explain the alliance decision?

This chapter contains short descriptions and discussions of all sixteen cases from the data set (where a single case is a country's alliance choice in one of the observation years) which were not correctly predicted by the individual learning hypothesis. These cases are Albania in the early 1920s, Romania in the early 1920s and late 1930s, Yugoslavia after World War II, Iraq in the late 1940s and early 1950s, Egypt in the late 1940s, Spain after World War II, and Belgium and Turkey in the late 1930s. After reviewing individual cases, a few underlying patterns in the outliers are discussed. Chapter 8 is devoted to the discussion of one pattern, that democracies are more likely to act in accordance with the lessons of history than are nondemocracies.

Albania attained its independence from the Ottoman Empire in 1912, establishing internationally recognized frontiers in 1913. Albania attempted to remain out of World War I, but at various times Austrian, Italian, and Greek forces moved through Albanian territory, which indicates a failed attempt at neutrality by the coding rules outlined in Chapter 4. Individual learning theory predicts that Albania should have learned that neutrality is undesirable and would therefore pursue alliances in the interwar period. In the first part of this period, however, Albania preferred neutrality. In 1920, Italy withdrew its remaining forces from Albanian territory, giving up on the idea of imposing a mandate over Albania. These matters were settled in an accord signed with the Albanian government on 2 August 1920; Albania's 1913 borders were reconfirmed fifteen months later at the Declaration of the Conference of Ambassadors. Under the declaration, Great Britain, France, Japan, and Italy agreed that they would advise the League of Nations to sponsor military intervention under Italian command if Albanian independence was threatened; the declaration was not, however, a binding military alliance. The declaration also ordered Yugoslavia to remove its troops from the country. Nevertheless, both Yugoslavia and Greece retained territorial ambitions over portions of Albania.[1]

Balance of threat theory seems to explain Albanian neutrality best. The main threat to Albanian independence, namely, Italian desires for some form of political control, appeared to abate following certain Italian statements and actions. Lesser threats remained from Greece and Yugoslavia, but Albania also enjoyed verbal commitments to defend its independence from a number of great powers. Hence, there was a low external threat, which was effectively countered by the great powers' commitments, leaving the Albanians with a low incentive to enter an alliance. Individual learning theory predicts that the infringement of Albanian sovereignty and violation of its neutrality during the war would encourage it to seek a great power protector, either bandwagoning with Italy or enlisting British or French assistance; instead, Albania avoided alliances. Though one could argue that Albania

---

[1] Malcolm Muggeridge, ed., *Ciano's Diplomatic Papers* (London: Odhams Press, 1948), 205 n; Hugh Seton-Watson, *Eastern Europe between the Wars, 1918–1941* (Hamden, Conn.: Archon Books, 1962), 369–371; Maxwell H. H. Macartney and Paul Cremona, *Italy's Foreign and Colonial Policy, 1914–1937* (London: Oxford University Press, 1938), 101–102; Réné Albrecht-Carrié, *A Diplomatic History of Europe since the Congress of Vienna*, rev. ed. (New York: Harper & Row, 1973), 432–433; Barbara Jelavich, *History of the Balkans*, vol. 2 (London: Cambridge University Press, 1983), 212.

probably would have preferred an alliance but could not find a willing great power ally at that time, the historical record does not definitively indicate whether this was the case or whether Albania was in fact genuinely uninterested in alliance. In the interest of strengthening the test of the learning hypotheses, Albania was coded as preferring neutrality, in opposition to the prediction of the individual learning hypothesis. Realistically, Albania's postwar experience was probably similar to the environment in Europe after the Napoleonic Wars. The unavoidable political reality was that Albania was a new, very weak state resting within what was recognized as the Italian sphere of influence. More than that of other small powers, its fate was under the control of the great powers, and its sovereignty was correspondingly limited, as was that of most small powers under the Concert of Europe.

ROMANIA

Romania joined the Allied forces during World War I, mainly for reasons of territorial ambition rather than to balance against the Central Powers. Though Romania suffered military losses during the war, it made considerable acquisitions in the postwar settlements, more than doubling both its prewar territory and its population.[2] Strictly speaking, the individual learning hypothesis would predict that Romania would learn that alliance pays and seek alliance in the interwar period. Interesting, however, is that unlike for most of the other small powers, Romania's wartime alliance decisions were driven by expansionist rather than security motives. Therefore, Romania would draw lessons from the experience oriented around the question of how alliances advance expansionist goals rather than how alliances protect against threats to national security. But Romania so completely attained its offensive aims in the postwar settlement that in the interwar period its foreign policy shifted toward establishing legitimacy for and maintaining the defense of its new frontiers. Therefore Romania could not use its World War I lesson that alliance facilitates territorial acquisitions to inform its postwar foreign policy because it no longer sought territorial expansion, having become a status quo power.

---

[2] The Romanian acquisition of Southern Dobruja, Bukovina, Bessarabia, and Transylvania from its neighbors gave it a population of 15,541,424 and a territory of 295,049 square kilometers compared with a 1912 population of 7,160,682 and a territory of 130,177 square kilometers. Joseph Rothschild, *East Central Europe between the Two World Wars* (Seattle: University of Washington Press, 1974), 281.

In the early 1920s, Romania was not faced with serious external threats. Russia was preoccupied by internal reconstruction and, because of the failure of revolution to sweep Europe, generally too disillusioned with foreign policy to consider an attempt to reclaim Bessarabia, which had been transferred to Romania from Russia in the post–World War I settlement.[3] Hungary did not challenge the Romanian annexation of Transylvania, expressing its acceptance of the desires of Romanian Transylvanians to be under a Romanian flag. Hungary's action was expected in part because it had no great power sponsor for actions against Romania, so it focused its efforts toward revisionism against Czechoslovakia.[4] The third country from which Romania had acquired territory was Bulgaria, which was unlikely to attempt to recapture its lost territory. Interestingly, a primary reason for this was because of its formative experience of failure in World War I. Like Romania, it had joined the war primarily for offensive reasons, but unlike Romania, it had experienced failure. The lesson learned by the Bulgarians was that revisionism did not pay and that it was more fruitful to pursue peaceful policies with its neighbors than to be aggressive; this lesson was reflected in the foreign policies of both the Agrarian Party, which held power after war's end, and the bourgeois government that took power after the revolution of 1923.[5]

At the time, however, Romania declared itself to be the target of a number of threats. In 1920 and 1921, Romania concluded defense agreements with Yugoslavia and Czechoslovakia regarding possible actions by Hungary or Bulgaria and a similar agreement with Poland regarding possible military action by Russia, claiming the need to defend against external threats.[6] Creating an external threat served a number of domestic political purposes of the Romanian government:

> The conclusion of a complex "antirevisionist" system of alliances in 1921, supported by France and comprising the Little Entente of Yugoslavia, Czechoslovakia, and Rumania and the anti-Russian alignment with Poland, was allegedly based on the threat posed to Rumania's territorial integrity by bitter and hostile neighbors. In fact, these threats were minimal. But it was convenient for internal political purposes for Bucharest to

[3] Seton-Watson, *Eastern Europe between the Wars*, 363.

[4] Rothschild, *East Central Europe between the Two World Wars*, 164–165; Arnold J. Toynbee, *Survey of International Affairs, 1926* (London: Oxford University Press, 1928), 145; Stephen Fischer-Galati, *Twentieth Century Rumania*, 2d ed. (New York: Columbia University Press, 1991), 32.

[5] Arnold J. Toynbee, *Survey of International Affairs, 1920–1923* (London: Oxford University Press, 1928), 333–335.

[6] Seton-Watson, *Eastern Europe between the Wars*, 363–364.

brand the Hungarians potential aggressors and inveterate enemies of the Rumanian people in order to discredit the moderate Transylvanian political parties advocating adherence to the spirit and the letter of the treaties regulating Hungarian-Rumanian relations. It was also deemed desirable by Averescu to fan popular fears of Russia and to inflame Rumanian anti-Semitism and anticommunism by waving the red danger flag and dramatizing Russia's demands for reconsideration of the "illegal seizure" of Bessarabia.[7]

The Romanians allied with other small powers to inflate the public perception of external threat. The historical record does not definitively settle the question of whether the absence of a Romanian alliance with a great power in the early 1920s was due to Romanian rejection of the idea of an alliance or the lack of a willing partner for Romania, though the Romanian rejection of a French overture for an alliance in January 1924 is the clearest sign of their disinterest in a great power alliance.[8] Though at least one historian has argued that Romania wanted an alliance with France in the early 1920s, I coded Romania as preferring not to ally with a great power in the early 1920s, thus strengthening the test of the individual learning hypothesis, which predicts that Romania should have favored alliance with a great power throughout the interwar period.[9] Still, Romania did prefer alliance with a number of small powers, even without any real external threat. This is in opposition to what balance of threat theory would predict. It seems that domestic political factors were chiefly responsible for Romania's alliance policy, as domestic conditions encouraged the government to create an external threat in order to solidify its political control. This explanation seems to fit well with the internal balancing model proposed by a handful of international relations scholars, which suggests that alliance policy is driven by the need to balance against internal as well as external threats.[10]

The breakdown of negotiations between the Soviet Union and Romania over the Bessarabian question in April 1924 encouraged Romania to

[7] Fischer-Galati, *Twentieth Century Rumania*, 37–38.

[8] Arnold J. Toynbee, *Survey of International Affairs, 1924* (London: Oxford University Press, 1926), 441.

[9] Dov B. Lungu, *Romania and the Great Powers, 1933–1940* (Durham: Duke University Press, 1989), 190.

[10] Michael N. Barnett and Jack S. Levy, "Domestic Sources of Alliances and Alignments: The Case of Egypt, 1962–1973," *International Organization* 41 (Summer 1991): 369–395; Jack S. Levy and Michael N. Barnett, "Alliance Formation, Domestic Political Economy, and Third World Security," *Jerusalem Journal of International Relations* 14 (December 1992): 19–40; Stephen R. David, "Explaining Third World Alignment," *World Politics* 40 (January 1991): 233–256.

reconsider French overtures for an alliance. Romanian insecurities were heightened by an armed raid on a Bessarabian town, presumably launched from Soviet territory, and the Soviet declaration of the Moldavian Autonomous Republic on the left bank of the Dniestr River. In 1926, Romania and France signed a treaty of friendship, which fell short of constituting a mutual defense pact, though not because of Romanian hesitancy; rather, the French feared provoking the Soviet Union and committing themselves to involvement in a possible Russo-Romanian military conflict over Bessarabia.[11] This prediction is a successful one for balance of threat theory.

The Soviet threat appeared to abate in 1933, when an agreement was signed between the USSR and Romania recognizing the status of Bessarabia as part of Romania. Though the Soviets had not given up on reacquisition of Bessarabia through unilateral military action, the Romanians believed that the agreement represented a genuine removal of the Russian military threat. They did not find the arrangement with the French obsolete, however: in 1934, King Carol stressed to French military representatives Romanian loyalty to France and its need for continued French support, especially in terms of military equipment. Romanian loyalty to France and the West was not to last, however. The conciliatory policy of France and Britain to Germany and Italy in the late 1930s eventually made the Franco-Romanian alliance a dead letter, and the Romanians felt their best option was to try to steer between Nazi Germany and the West. In March 1939, two months after brushing off a German invitation to join the anti-Comintern Pact, King Carol and his prime minister and foreign ministers decided against entering mutual defense pacts with Britain or France because of the unavoidable risks of provoking Germany. This avoidance of mutual defense pacts ought to be considered a failure of balance of threat theory, especially given the emerging Hungarian threat to Romania, a threat highlighted by Hungarian mobilizations and troop movements in 1939. Romania was not completely isolated, however: in April 1939, Great Britain made a unilateral commitment to come to Romania's aid if attacked. Though this guarantee might appear to mitigate the empirical blow to balance of threat theory because the external threats to Romania are somewhat balanced by the British commitment, remember that the British guarantee was made *after* the Romanians decided to steer be-

---

[11] Toynbee, *International Affairs, 1924,* 263–265, 441; Lungu, *Romania and the Great Powers,* 7–9; Robert L. Rothstein, *Alliances and Small Powers* (New York: Columbia University Press, 1968), 146. The treaty called for neither side to attack the other and for military consultations in the event of war. For a full text of the treaty, see Toynbee, *International Affairs, 1926,* 485–487.

tween Germany and the West, and the British commitment did not prevent Romania from making economic concessions to the Germans in an attempt to keep them appeased.[12]

Yugoslavia's attempt at neutrality in World War II failed when Nazi Germany invaded in 1941. At war's end, Yugoslavia was the only Eastern European country unoccupied by Soviet troops. Its conversion to Communism under Tito transpired with relatively little interference from the Soviet Union, as opposed to the situations faced by the other Eastern European nations. As individual learning theory predicts, Yugoslavia followed the lesson of its World War II experience of failed neutrality by entering an alliance with a great power, the Soviet Union. In 1948, however, Stalin shunned Tito and Yugoslavia, probably because of Tito's evident political ambitions in the Balkans. The eventual result was the ejection of Yugoslavia from the Soviet bloc and a full-scale pressure campaign against it, including a number of border incidents and the probable preparation for a concerted Eastern European and Soviet invasion of Yugoslavia in 1950.[13]

The interesting theoretical question is what predictions learning and balance of threat theory would make for Yugoslavia's alliance behavior following the Tito-Stalin split. The historical record does not reveal whether Tito preferred to enter NATO after the split with Stalin, though Yugoslavia did eventually begin to receive American military aid. In the interest of strengthening the test of the individual learning

[12] Lungu, *Romania and the Great Powers*, 24–29, 41–43, 157, 235; Sidney Aster, *1939: The Making of the Second World War* (London: Andre Deutsch, 1973), 138; A. Chanady and J. Jensen, "Germany, Rumania, and the British Guarantees of March–April 1939," *Australian Journal of Politics and History* 16 (August 1970): 205, 211–216; Simon Newman, *March 1939: The British Guarantee to Poland* (Oxford: Clarendon, 1976), 141; Arnold J. Toynbee, *Survey of International Affairs: The Eve of War, 1939* (London: Oxford University Press, 1958), 68–72, and 107–110. Romania entered into a security agreement with Turkey, Greece, and Yugoslavia in 1934, but this agreement was rigged so that its signatories were not committed to entering a conflict involving a great power. Jelavich, *History of the Balkans*, 213.

[13] S. Victor Papacosma, "Yugoslavia," in *Europe's Neutral and Nonaligned States*, ed. Papacosma and Mark R. Rubin (Wilmington, Del.: Scholarly Resources, 1989), 184–185; R. Barry Farrell, *Jugoslavia and the Soviet Union, 1948–1956* (Hamden, Conn.: Shoe String Press, 1956), 10; Hélène Carrère d'Encausse, *Big Brother*, trans. George Holoch (New York: Holmes & Meier, 1987), 126; Rothschild, *East Central Europe*, 132; Bela Kiraly, "The Aborted Soviet Military Plans against Tito's Yugoslavia," in *At the Brink of War and Peace: The Tito-Stalin Split in a Historic Perspective*, vol. 10, ed. Wayne S. Vucinich (New York: Social Science Monographs, Brooklyn College Press, 1982), 273–288.

hypothesis, Yugoslavia from 1949 on was coded as preferring neutrality, contrary to the predictions of the individual learning hypothesis. Despite this coding, one could make the argument that Yugoslavia did act in accordance with its World War II experience when the Soviet Union was an available ally, thus validating the learning hypothesis, but its ejection from the Soviet bloc, which itself might be considered a formative event for Tito's attitudes toward alliance, caused it to change that policy.

Balance of threat theory might predict that Yugoslavia would join the Soviet bloc in the later 1940s, depending on whether one coded a Soviet threat to Yugoslavia at that time. A high threat to Yugoslavia certainly exists after the Tito-Stalin break, but at that stage, bandwagoning with the Soviet Union was not a feasible option; Yugoslavia's attempts at diplomatic reconciliation after the first break were ignored. Balancing by joining NATO was not pursued: Yugoslavia did not prefer it and/or NATO would not have accepted Yugoslav membership. Yugoslav preference to go it alone would be an empirical defeat for balance of threat theory, which would predict that facing a threat and absent a bandwagoning option, Yugoslavia should have tried to join NATO or form a regional, anti-Soviet security pact.[14] Curiously, such a regional pact with Yugoslavia, Turkey, and Greece as signatories appeared briefly in 1955. But this pact came after the Soviet threat was reduced when Khrushchev took the crow-eating steps of visiting Belgrade and apologizing for the Cominform break with Yugoslavia, indicating a Soviet desire for at least limited rapprochement with Yugoslavia.[15]

IRAQ

Iraq and Britain signed a treaty in 1930 which committed Britain to defend Iraq if it came under attack and ensured Britain access to all necessary facilities on Iraqi soil in the event of war to protect British interests in the region. This treaty was coded as a defense pact. An Iraqi commitment to defend the British Isles would not have made sense, given the geographical distance and weakness of the Iraqi military. In short, Britain gave Iraq what it wanted in the way of military commitment, and vice versa. This agreement was in force through World War II, so Iraq was coded as attempting alliance in the war. In 1941, there

[14] Yugoslavia's acceptance of American military aid might be considered balancing behavior, though I view military aid as itself closer to neutrality than balancing because the aid had no important strings attached (as would an alliance).

[15] Papacosma, "Yugoslavia," 187.

was a successful, pro-Axis coup in Baghdad, which was followed by British military intervention. Some Iraqi resistance sprang up but was crushed.[16] Since Iraq was not compensated postwar for its losses in the British intervention, its World War II experience is coded as a failed policy of alliance, with the prediction that it should prefer neutrality in the postwar period.

During the first years after World War II, Iraq did not act in accord with this lesson of neutrality. Iraq was coded as preferring alliance because its treaty with Britain remained intact. An attempt to sign an additional defense pact between Britain and Iraq, the Treaty of Portsmouth, foundered in January 1948 when public pressure and protest in Iraq forced the Baghdad government to back away from such an agreement. But the negative reaction in response to the Treaty of Portsmouth, an agreement that was arguably in Iraq's strategic interest because it gave Iraq more influence over defense planning than did the previous treaty, is evidence of the depth of hatred of the British at all levels of Iraqi society, a hatred that demanded the abrogation of the 1930 treaty, not just its revision. Iraqi nationalists were still bitterly resentful over the British actions to squelch the 1941 uprising.[17] The Soviet Union was coded as not threatening Iraq, given the absence of verbal threats or military actions taken against Iraq.[18] Iraqi desires for great power alliance continued through the 1950s, though: in the first months of 1955, the Iraqi government expressed interest in a regional defense agreement that would include the United States and the United Kingdom as members, a desire eventually met with the signing of the Baghdad Pact. This was a deviation from the public preferences expressed in the backlash to the Treaty of Portsmouth, however, and part of a general anti-Western trend in Iraq. In 1958, this nationalist, anti-Western trend culminated in a coup that removed the old regime from power, a change that inspired a shift in Iraqi foreign policy, including a formal exit from the Baghdad Pact.[19]

Both learning and balance of threat theory fail to predict correctly Iraq's neutrality stance through the middle 1950s, and both correctly

---

[16] Howard M. Sachar, *Europe Leaves the Middle East, 1936–1954* (London: Allen Lane, 1974), 18; George Lenczowski, *The Middle East in World Affairs*, 4th ed. (Ithaca: Cornell University Press, 1980), 273–274.

[17] Sachar, *Europe Leaves the Middle East*, 429–431; Phebe Marr, *The Modern History of Iraq* (Boulder, Colo.: Westview, 1985), 103.

[18] For an argument that Iraq did face a Soviet threat, especially in the late 1940s, see Sachar, *Europe Leaves the Middle East*, 428.

[19] *Foreign Relations of the United States*, vol. 12 (Washington, D.C.: U.S. Government Printing Office, 1955–1957), 12, 19 n, 36, 966; Marion Farouk-Sluglett and Peter Sluglett, *Iraq since 1958: From Revolution to Dictatorship* (London: KPI, 1987), 50.

predict Iraq's neutrality from the late 1950s onward. It seems, however, that the pre-coup Iraqi government's desire for alliance with the West was out of step with the more independence-minded currents in Iraqi society. Further, these anti-Western feelings can be traced to years of British control of Iraq, exemplified by the 1941 invasion. In this way, the formative experience of the British invasion did teach a number of lessons to Iraqis, including that the West could not be trusted and that independence was the best route. These lessons could be implemented as policy, however, only upon the change of government in 1958.

EGYPT

Egypt had a long history of domination by Britain before achieving its independence in the twentieth century. A 1936 treaty between Egypt and Britain served a similar function to the 1930 agreement between Iraq and Britain in that it committed Britain to assist in the defense of Egypt in exchange for permitting Britain to use Egyptian territory and facilities for military purposes. This arrangement did not prevent General Erwin Rommel's Afrika Korps from reaching as far inside Egyptian territory as El Alamein in 1942, however. The individual learning hypothesis views this as is an experience of failed alliance: Egypt was invaded in World War II but did not receive adequate compensatory postwar settlements and so should prefer neutrality in the postwar period. As in Iraq, though, the traditional government adhered to a pro-alliance posture up to the early 1950s. In Egypt, though, the change to a radical, anti-Western regime came faster, as a military dictatorship replaced King Farouk in the Free Officers' coup of 1952. This had followed attempts by Farouk's government to distance itself from Britain. As early as December 1945, the Egyptians formally requested the revision of the 1936 treaty, with special attention to the issue of the peacetime placement of British troops on Egyptian soil. Expectedly, the treaty was revoked in 1951. Though Egypt eventually acted in accordance with predictions by choosing neutrality, this shift actually had more to do with anti-Western feelings in Egypt that had been simmering for at least decades.[20] In other words, the social change overdue in Egypt by the late 1940s was necessarily going to carry a considerable

[20] John Marlowe, *A History of Modern Egypt and Anglo-Egyptian Relations, 1800–1956* (Hamden: Archon, 1965), 335–336; Lenczowski, *Middle East in World Affairs*, 518; Stephen M .Walt, *The Origins of Alliances* (Ithaca: Cornell University Press, 1987), 53–62. Marlowe (354) compares 1947 Egypt with prerevolutionary France.

anti-Western flavor with it, and the neutrality accompanying this anti-Western backlash probably had little to do with the Egyptian experience of World War II.

Determining the accuracy of balance of threat predictions is a bit tricky. The Soviet threat to Egypt seems to be low throughout the post–World War II period. Starting in the middle 1950s, a real threat from Israel appears which does not abate until the Camp David Accords are signed in 1979. Yet, in opposition to balance of threat predictions, Egypt did not seek alliance with a great power to balance against this threat. Egypt did court the Soviet Union through most of these years as a great power sponsor, acquiring the payoff of substantial arms transfers, but this is not an alliance. After the Six-Day War, however, Soviet military support began to increase substantially, including the provision of air defense support against Israeli air strikes. This is stronger evidence of balancing behavior on Egypt's part; the intensification of the Israeli threat after 1967 motivated a greater desire by Egypt to acquire Soviet support. After the October War in 1973, the Egyptians abandoned their Soviet patron and began to court the United States. American interest in maintaining Egyptian friendship eventually stimulated the Egyptian-Israeli peace process, culminating in the return of the Sinai to Egypt and substantial reduction of the Israeli threat.

Throughout the period of intense conflict with Israel (1950s to 1970s), the Egyptians balanced against Israel primarily by securing arms transfers and other military assistance from the USSR. This behavior is in line with the basic principles of balance of threat theory in that Egyptian foreign policy took actions to counter the Israeli threat. Once the old regime was overthrown and the new, ardently nationalist government was installed under Abdel Nasser, however, the strong desire of this new government to maintain its sovereignty and minimize commitments to foreign powers put limits around foreign policy actions, such that arms transfers from the USSR were acceptable but entrance into an alliance was not. In this way, balance of threat theory as an explanation of alliance behavior does poorly. This case is strong evidence for the model that views alliances as providing security, but at the cost of foreign policy independence, for after the coup, Egypt put a high enough value on its sovereignty to outweigh the benefits of security from an alliance with the USSR.[21]

[21] See James D. Morrow, "Alliances and Asymmetry: An Alternative to the Capability Aggregation Model of Alliances," *American Journal of Political Science* 35 (November 1991): 904–933; and James D. Morrow, "Arms versus Alliances: Trade-Offs in the Search for Security," *International Organization* 47 (Spring 1993): 207–233.

Though Spain leaned at times towards the Axis during World War II, it remained a mostly nonparticipating neutral.[22] The individual learning hypothesis predicts that Spain ought to remain neutral during the post–World War II period as it avoided invasion during the war. A cursory analysis reveals this to be the case, as Spain did not join NATO for several decades, perhaps until after the neutrality lesson from World War II had faded with time. But I coded Spain as preferring alliance after the war, because compelling evidence indicates that Spanish dictator Francisco Franco would have jumped at the chance to join NATO if given the opportunity. The government-controlled press in Spain made no secret of the Spanish eagerness to join NATO, and Franco himself stated his desire for Spanish participation in an anti-Soviet alliance with other Western nations as early as November 1948. Franco's interest in joining NATO grew from a larger need for Spain to join the Western family of nations. He thought such a policy change necessary to establish the trade and foreign aid ties critical to reviving the Spanish economy, which in the late 1940s hovered on the brink of collapse. Spain remained cast out from the Western and even much of the world community because of its pro-Axis neutrality during the war and its own rather distasteful brand of fascism. Indeed, Spain was not permitted to join the United Nations until 1955.[23]

Eventually, with the signing of the 1953 Pact of Madrid with the United States, Franco did enter the Western alliance as a junior partner. This agreement allowed the United States to make use of military bases in Spain in exchange for American military assistance. The reaction in Spain to this policy, though muted because of political repression, was highly negative: opposition to the agreement reached across political lines, including both supporters of and opponents to the Franco regime. An important part of this opposition grew from the traditional Spanish adherence to neutrality.[24] Although Franco himself did not

[22] On Spanish neutrality during World War II, see Raymond L. Proctor, *Agony of a Neutral: Spanish-German Wartime Relations and the "Blue Division"* (Moscow, Idaho: Idaho Research Foundation, 1974).

[23] Arthur P. Whitaker, *Spain and Defense of the West* (New York: Harper & Brothers, 1961), 36, 312 n; J. Lee Shneidman, *Spain and Franco, 1949–59* (New York: Facts on File, 1973); Benny Pollack, *The Paradox of Spanish Foreign Policy: Spain's International Relations from Franco to Democracy* (London: Pinter Publishers, 1987), 15.

[24] Whitaker, *Spain and Defense of the West*, 41; Eusebio Mujal-Leon, "Spain: Generational Perspectives on Foreign Policy," in *The Successor Generation: International Perspectives of Postwar Europeans*, ed. Stephen F. Szabo (London: Butterworths, 1983), 128; Anthony Gooch, "The Foreign Relations and Foreign Policy of Spain," pt. 3, "Spain, the United States, and NATO," *Contemporary Review* 260 (May 1992): 240.

follow the lesson of neutrality from World War II, a substantial part of the Spanish public did believe in this lesson. The proclivity of the Spanish public for neutrality has lasted for several decades. On the eve of Spanish entry into NATO in 1981, public opinion polls revealed a majority opposing this action: one poll indicated that 52 percent opposed Spanish entry into NATO while only 18 percent supported it. Traditional Spanish opposition to foreign interference persisted after 1981, as evidenced by the fierce, anti-NATO political battle in 1986, which led the government to declare limits to its involvement in NATO, and the popular demand in 1987 for the removal of American F-16s from the base at Torrejón.[25]

Balance of threat theory would predict that the Spanish interest in joining NATO was motivated by a perceived external threat. Yet the one foreign policy problem that Spain did not face after World War II was an external threat. A potential flash point with de Gaulle's France was defused soon after the end of the war, and Spain maintained good relations with its other neighbors. As far as the Soviet Union was concerned, Franco was certainly anti-Communist in ideology, but there was no imminent military danger to Spain from the Eastern bloc. If anything, Franco viewed the cold war opportunistically, perceiving (correctly) that the growing American concern about the Soviet Union would make it more willing to improve its relations with Spain. Further, Franco's interest in joining NATO persisted, in years of both high and low tension between the United States and USSR, in spite of the public perception that the Soviet threat to Spain was quite low.[26] Spanish behavior after World War II, then, is not accurately predicted by either the individual learning or the balance of threat hypothesis. Franco's desire to join NATO was motivated by a broader concern with becoming a member of the world community, mostly so Spain could acquire desperately needed economic assistance.

BELGIUM

Belgium's attempt at neutrality in World War I met with disastrous failure, and its lesson for alliance was realized in an alliance with

[25] Mujal-Leon, "Spain: Generational Perspectives," 131–135; Angel Viñas, "Spain and NATO: Internal Debate and External Challenges," in *NATO's Southern Allies: Internal and External Challenges*, ed. John Chipman (London: Routledge, 1988), 160–161; Gooch, "Foreign Policy of Spain," 241–243.

[26] Whitaker, *Spain and Defense of the West*; R. Richard Rubottom and J. Carter Murphy, *Spain and United States* (New York: Praeger, 1984), 13–18; Gooch, in "Foreign Policy of Spain," 240.

France in 1920, which it broke in 1936. This action is in opposition to the predictions of both learning and balance of threat theory, as Belgium had a very strong experience of failed neutrality in World War I and faced a growing threat from Nazi Germany in the 1930s. As described in the previous chapter, the break was driven by a number of primarily domestic factors, including rising Franco-Belgian tensions over economic issues; the inflammation of Flemish nationalism arising from the secrecy of the 1920 agreement; the need to forge a parliamentary coalition large enough to expand the Belgian military; and ideological distaste for the USSR, a French ally in the mid-1930s.[27] These factors are outside the purview of the model of this study, and the incorrect prediction of this case is a price of the parsimony of the model. But balance of threat does not correctly predict the Belgian return to neutrality, for Belgium broke its alliance with France as German power was increasing and Hitler's foreign policy was becoming increasingly aggressive.

TURKEY

Turkey's experience of defeat as one of the Central Powers in World War I points to the individual learning prediction that they would prefer neutrality in the interwar period. As expected, Turkey largely remained neutral. The growing threat from Nazi Germany in the late 1930s did not go unnoticed, however, and the March 1939 German invasion of Czechoslovakia and the April 1939 Italian invasion of Albania highlighted the threat to Eastern Europe and the Balkans. Initially, Turkey (as well as other Eastern European nations) hesitated at the suggestion of security cooperation with Britain and France, discouraged by what it saw as an anemic response to the invasion of Czechoslovakia. Turkey soon expressed interest in cooperation with Britain and France, eventually signing a defense pact with them in autumn 1939. The agreement called for Britain and France to defend Turkey if attacked and for Turkey to assist Britain and France if war came to the Mediterranean area.[28] These actions, then, are well explained by balance of threat theory. As the Italian and German threats grew and

[27] This is the argument of the definitive scholarly work on the subject of the break, David Owen Kieft, *Belgium's Ruturn to Neutrality* (London: Clarendon, 1972).

[28] For a text of the agreement, see J. C. Hurewitz, *Diplomacy in the Near and Middle East* (Princeton: D. Van Nostrand, 1956), 2:226–228. On the negotiation of the agreement, see Ludmila Zhivkova, *Anglo-Turkish Relations, 1933–1939* (London: Secker & Warburg, 1976); and Frank G. Weber, *The Evasive Neutral* (Columbia: University of Missouri Press, 1979).

became oriented on the Eastern Mediterranean, Turkey reacted by pursuing greater cooperation and eventually an alliance with two great powers, Britain and France. The individual learning hypothesis would incorrectly predict that Turkey's experience of failed alliance in World War I ought to have entrenched a lesson of neutrality which should have lasted through the 1930s.

One possible reason why Turkey did not apply a lesson of neutrality from World War I to its foreign policy in the late 1930s is that like Romania, it maintained fundamentally different aims during these two times. Turkey entered World War I with aggressive aims: the Ottoman Empire was not itself threatened by any of the Allies, but the Turks saw the possibility of expansion in the Balkans by joining the Central Powers. Therefore, alliance in World War I was meant to accomplish offensive goals. In the 1930s, on the other hand, Turkey was worried about threats to its national security from Germany and Italy, and alliance with Britain and France was intended to help achieve defensive goals. It is not surprising, then, that Turkey did not attempt to revive the Ottoman Empire after World War I, nor is it surprising that Turkey did not remain neutral in the late 1930s as a defensive solution to the emerging threats from Germany and Italy.

These outliers illuminate well the limits of learning theory. For some of these nations, their experiences were not formative in the way that they were for other members of the data set, so the inaccurate predictions of the individual learning hypothesis are not surprising. Turkey and Romania, for example, saw World War I as an opportunity for territorial expansion rather than as a threat to national security. When both states faced threats to their national security in the late 1930s, neither leaned on World War I experiences, as the decision problem then (protect national security) was fundamentally different from the one they faced in World War I (achieve territorial gains). Therefore, World War I was not formative of Turkish or Romanian beliefs as to what alliance policy best copes with external threats. In the absence of such formative experiences, realist explanations effectively explain their behaviors: Turkey balanced against the German and Italian threats by allying with Britain and France, and Romania exited its alliance with France and preferred no alliance with Britain because these two countries had lost credibility as allies.

It would be tempting to call the postwar Egyptian policy of neutrality a success for learning theory, dismissing the preference for alliance in the late 1940s as simply the lag in political change before the nationalist, anti-Western coup in 1952 adjusted Egyptian foreign policy in line with the lessons of World War II. This interpretation probably does not square well with history. Anti-British nationalism had been building in Egypt for several decades, driven mostly by basic concerns over political sovereignty and national identity rather than by foreign policy. The alliance with Britain which served to interfere with Egyptian sovereignty was certainly a lightning rod for Egyptian opposition, but this opposition would probably have been present regardless of Egypt's experience in World War II.[29]

Iraq's post–World War II experience can be classified in somewhat similar terms. The support for alliance in the Iraqi government that predominated in the late 1940s and 1950s was not reflective of the anti-Western desires of many Iraqis; that government had been installed by Britain in 1941 and held onto the reins of power for several years. In one sense, then, the support for alliance was more the reflection of a lag until the time of political change. Though it would be misplaced to describe the British intervention in 1941 (representing the experience of the failure of alliance) as exclusive motivation of the 1958 revolution, anger at the British for that specific intervention probably had a larger role in feeding the Iraqi nationalist backlash than did the Egyptian experience in World War II.

The Iraqi case points to a larger observation about the learning hypotheses of this study. The underlying logic of an alliance indicates that it is a success if it protects the nation from the powers in the opposite coalition. Iraq was invaded by its own ally, however, an action which was clearly antithetical to the desires of many Iraqis and which contributed at least in part to the eventual anti-British backlash. Being invaded by one's ally can be viewed as a failure of the alliance, of course, though the reasoning for the failure differs from that provided when invaded by a power from the other coalition. In the former case, alliance is viewed as a failure because it ties the small power too tightly to the great power and facilitates the interference by the great power on the small power's sovereignty; in the latter case, alliance is viewed as a failure because it does not provide adequate deterrence of the noncoalition members and perhaps even provokes an invasion.

More broadly, these cases indicate that an event must be of dominant political significance in relation to other factors for it to be formative. In a few situations, the World War experience was simply not as signifi-

---

[29] The British and Iraqi cases support the contention of Levy and Barnett that a complete explanation of alliance choices needs to include domestic and economic factors. Barnett and Levy, "Domestic Sources of Alliances and Alignments"; Levy and Barnett, "Alliance Formation, Domestic Political Economy, and Third World Security." See also David, "Explaining Third World Alignment."

cant as other political factors, such as the emergence of nationalism. This might lead to an argument that the data set is contaminated with cases for which World War II is not significant, introducing bias into the results. But such bias would skew the results toward playing down the importance of a state's individual experience, and the quantitative results from Chapter 5 clearly indicate strong support for the individual learning hypothesis anyway. Cases in this chapter indicate some support for the hypothesis that for developing nations, nonmilitary factors such as domestic politics and economic considerations are especially likely to dominate alliance decisions.

The cases also illustrate that an event is sometimes formative only in regard to a certain aspect of alliance policy. For Turkey and Romania, for example, World War I experiences were formative of beliefs as to how alliance policy helped meet goals of territorial expansion, but these experiences were not formative of beliefs regarding how alliance policy can best be used to defend against an external threat. Lastly, the outliers seem to indicate that in the absence of a formative experience or domestic factors, realist factors can emerge as important in determining alliance choices. Significantly, though, realism does not predict whether threats cause alliances to form or break apart. For example, the rising German and Italian threat in the late 1930s drove Turkey into an alliance with Britain and France—realist thinking drove it to a balancing strategy. At the same time, though, realist thinking drove Romania to doubt the credibility of the British and French guarantees because of their ineffectual responses to the Nazis in the previous crises. This offers more support to the broader theoretical argument that realism is insufficiently specified to make falsifiable hypotheses.

[8]

Political Structure
and Learning

The learning theory presented in Chapter 2 is relatively simple politically: it assumes that states act on the basis of these lessons as if they were unitary actors. Of course, like all types of public policy, foreign policy is often strongly determined by domestic politics. More broadly, the learning theory presented here is really about how preferences get formed, not about how policy gets made. A more complete view of the role of learning in making foreign policy requires the construction of a model of the foreign policy–making process, within which one part discusses learning as a means of preference formation and another part analyzes how preferences get transformed into policy.[1]

This chapter is a preliminary, admittedly rough attempt to build just such a model. The aim is to provide a few assumptions about how domestic political forces affect foreign policy and then to ask the question, When would we expect policy to reflect the lessons of a formative event? The basic argument is that political structure can affect whether lessons are translated into policy. The analysis here focuses on the question of whether a country's political structure is democratic, and the chapter lays out one set of assumptions that predict that democracies ought to be more likely to act on the basis of the lessons of formative events and a second set of assumptions that predict that democracies ought to be less likely to act on the basis of the lessons of formative events. These predictions are then tested on the small power alliances data as well on two other data sets. I hope to contribute toward the construction of a more systematic insight

[1] Jack S. Levy, "Learning and Foreign Policy: Sweeping a Conceptual Minefield," *International Organization* 48 (Spring 1994): 312.

into why some states act on the lessons of history whereas others do not.

At least one other scholar has analyzed the links between political structure and learning. Thomas Risse-Kappen tried to predict the impact of ideas (again, one can think of a lesson from history as a particular kind of idea) on foreign policy based on domestic political structure. In analyzing the influence of ideas about common security on Soviet, West German, and American foreign policies in the late 1980s, he argued that the political structure of each country had important effects on how and whether these ideas came to affect policy. Specifically, he posited that in the statist, centralized Soviet system, ideas of common security could not penetrate society until a receptive leadership had come to power, but once this had occurred, the ideas affected policy relatively quickly. In the United States, what Risse-Kappen calls a society-dominated polity, the ideas entered relatively easily but had little effect on policy because of the difficulties of forming a coalition in such a structure. In the Federal Republic of Germany, described as a democratic corporatist structure, entry of ideas was more difficult than in a society-dominated structure though easier than in a statist structure, and policy impact was more incremental though longer-lasting because changes were institutionalized.[2] Unfortunately, this model's application to areas outside of common security seems to be limited. Additionally, it does not explain why some ideas prosper at the expense of others. For example, the inability of the idea of common security to gain ground in the United States in the late 1980s was probably not due to the difficulty for any idea to establish a foothold in the American political environment: the American foreign policy elites held to the idea of peace through strength as they rejected the idea of common security.

The political structure model proposed here attempts to go beyond what is offered by Risse-Kappen's model, predicting across issues when a certain kind of idea (a lesson from a formative event) is likely to affect policy, based on differences in domestic political structure. Here, a relatively simple framework of the foreign policy process is used as a context for the learning process. The assumptions of this framework are as follows: (1) political leaders seek both to stay in office and to protect

[2] Thomas Risse-Kappen, "Ideas Do Not Float Freely: Transnational Coalitions, Domestic Structures, and the End of the Cold War," *International Organization* 48 (Spring 1994): 185–214. See also Matthew Evangelista, "The Paradox of State Strength: Transnational Relations, Domestic Structures, and Security Policy in Russia and the Soviet Union," *International Organization* 49 (Winter 1995): 1–38.

the interests of the nation; (2) foreign policy is a tool that can serve or subvert either end; (3) political structures can make leaders more or less accountable to the opinions of nonleadership groups, such as the public; and (4) foreign policy can be guided by the lessons of history. Therefore, if political structure gives the preferences of different groups (such as the elite leadership versus the mass public) more or less weight in the formation of foreign policy and if we suspect that the probability of a group's preferences reflecting the lessons of a formative event differs between groups, then political structure ought to play a role in determining whether the lessons of formative events affect policy. The reader may have noticed that the dependent variable under discussion is whether "policy reflected the lessons of history," not whether "learning occurred." This distinction is intentional, as the point is to assess whether a certain set of preferences determines policy.

As a first rough cut at the question of how political structure affects whether lessons from formative events are translated into policy, I will compare two ideal types of political structure, democracy and nondemocracy. Democracy is conceptualized here as a political system in which the governmental leadership is relatively more accountable to the mass public, whereas a nondemocracy is a political system in which the governmental leadership is relatively less accountable to the mass public.[3]

One key difference between democracies and nondemocracies is that democratic political institutions (such as regular elections) encourage leaderships to be more responsive to public opinion. This implies that democratic leaders are more likely to make policy in harmony with the interests of the public at large than are nondemocratic leaders. The proposition that public policy follows public opinion in democracies has attracted empirical support for the case of the United States, especially in matters of foreign policy.[4] Ideal types of these two political systems might be described as follows: democratic policies reflect the majority opinion of the public, whereas nondemocratic policies reflect the opinion of a single person or a small group of persons. Here, this

[3] On democratic theory, see Robert A. Dahl, *A Preface to Democratic Theory* (Chicago: University of Chicago Press, 1956). For a discussion of defining democracy in the context of the democratic peace argument, see James Lee Ray, *Democracy and International Conflict* (Columbia: University of South Carolina Press, 1995); and Bruce Russett, *Grasping the Democratic Peace: Principles for a Post-Cold War World* (Princeton: Princeton University Press, 1993).

[4] See, for example, Alan D. Monroe, "Consistency between Public Preferences and National Policy Decisions," *American Politics Quarterly* 7 (January 1979): 3–19. For a review of the literature on the linkages between public opinion and foreign policy in democracies, see Bruce Russett, *Controlling the Sword: The Democratic Governance of National Security* (Cambridge: Harvard University Press, 1990).

distinction begs the question. Are democratic policies more likely to reflect learning from formative events than nondemocratic policies?

The Condorcet Jury Theorem, a proposition in democratic theory, suggests that the answer to this question is yes. The theorem assumes that a choice needs to be made between two possible options, P and Q. If the probability of an individual choosing P is p and if p is greater than 0.5, the theorem makes the following proposition: If a group of people all vote for either P or Q, then the probability that a simple majority will be for P is higher than p (again, p is the probability that any individual will choose P). Further, as the number of people who vote increases, the probability that a simple majority will choose P increases and eventually converges to 1.[5] The Condorcet Jury Theorem has been applied to the issue of public opinion; Benjamin Page and Robert Shapiro have argued that public opinion in the United States tends to reflect the theorem's dynamics.[6]

The Condorcet Jury Theorem can be applied to the specific question at hand. Consider that the formative events theory is derived primarily from empirical propositions in two social sciences, social psychology and organization theory. As with all empirical propositions in the social sciences (and, strictly speaking, in the natural sciences, as well), these propositions are probabilistic, which means that the empirical support they attract from their respective fields encourages us to predict that behavior is *likely*, but not *certain*; to follow these lines for any given case. Therefore, we would expect cases in which the proposition does not make the right prediction and that such cases do not necessarily invalidate the proposition, given its probabilistic nature. At the individual level, the formative events theory predicts that an individual is likely to draw lessons from a high impact or vivid event. Since this hypothesis proposes that such is likely to happen (but not that it will always happen), there is some probability f that is greater than 0.5 but less than 1 (as the event is probable but not certain) that the individual will draw a lesson from this event.

Now, if a government's policy is made by a single individual, so that

---

[5] Bernard Grofman, "A Comment on 'Democratic Theory: A Preliminary Mathematical Model,' " *Public Choice* 21 (1975): 99–103; Nicholas Miller, "Information, Electorates, and Democracy: Some Extensions and Interpretations of the Condorcet Jury Theorem," in *Information Pooling and Group Decision Making: Proceedings of the Second University of California, Irvine, Conference on Political Economy*, ed. Bernard Grofman and Guillermo Owen (Greenwich, Conn.: JAI Press, 1986), 173–192; Bernard Grofman and Scott L. Feld, "Rousseau's General Will: A Condorcetian Perspective," *American Political Science Review* 82 (June 1988): 567–576.

[6] Benjamin I. Page and Robert Y. Shapiro, *The Rational Public: Fifty Years of Trends in Americans' Public Policy Preferences* (Chicago: University of Chicago Press, 1992), 388.

policy reflects that individual's beliefs, then we would predict, ceteris paribus, that the probability that the policy will reflect the lesson of the formative event will be f. In an ideal type of democratic system, policy is assumed to be a reflection of the will of the majority. Changes in policy are realized either because democratic leaders follow public opinion and adjust their policy stances to meet the preferences of the public in order to maintain office or because leaders who do not change their opinions are removed from office and replaced with politicians whose ideas are more in line with those of the public. If the probability that any single individual of the democratic public will prefer a policy that reflects the lesson from the formative event is this value f, then, drawing on the Condorcet Jury Theorem, the probability that a majority of the public—and therefore the policy—will reflect the lesson of the formative event ought to be greater than f. Therefore, the Condorcet Jury Theorem predicts that the probability that democratic foreign policy will reflect the lessons of a formative event is higher (probability higher than f) than the probability that the foreign policy of a non-democracy will reflect the lessons of a formative event (probability f).

The Condorcet Jury Theorem works especially well in analyzing the implications of the vividness effect. Recall from Chapter 2 that some experimental work in social psychology has uncovered an interesting permutation of the vividness effect, called the Carl Sagan Effect: an individual is especially likely to think that a vivid event is more likely to persuade *others* than are pallid events, even if the individual *himself* is not persuaded by the vivid event. Therefore, if a democratic leader does not herself draw lessons from a vivid event, social psychology predicts that she is likely to perceive that others (such as the public) have drawn lessons from the vivid event, which increases the likelihood that she will enact foreign policy that follows the lessons of the formative event. Because nondemocratic leaders are less concerned with public opinion than are democratic leaders, however, they are unlikely to be influenced by the Carl Sagan Effect and thus will be less likely to align their foreign policy with the lessons of formative events.

Of course, this discussion of the Condorcet Jury Theorem has used a very simple typology of political systems: democracy, in which the leadership is very accountable to the mass public, and a nondemocratic ideal type, in which the leader or leadership is virtually unaccountable to the mass public. Few real political systems are accurately described by these ideal types. The logic of the theorem can, however, be used for comparisons other than mass democracies versus single-leader dictatorships. The theorem states that as the number of people who vote increase, the probability increases that the outcome will be P (the choice that has a probability greater than 0.5). Therefore, a democracy is more likely to act on the basis of the lessons from formative events than is an authoritarian state, whether run by a small group of leaders or a single leader, for the mass public contains more people than does an authoritarian leadership cadre. Similarly, we would expect that the more accountable a political leadership is to its public, the more likely it is to act on the basis of the lessons from a formative event, given that the leadership is more likely to be sensitive to the beliefs of the public, beliefs that, in turn, are more apt to reflect the lessons of the formative event.[7]

Hypothesis 5: The foreign policies of democracies are more likely to reflect the lessons of formative events than are the foreign policies of nondemocracies.

It is important to note that this hypothesis is specific to formative events learning. It does not imply that nondemocracies are less likely to draw lessons from history in general. It may be that an authoritarian leader's thinking about policy is not determined by her nation's experience in the previous formative event; since she is unconstrained (or less constrained) by political structure, she is free to make policy on the basis of lessons from other kinds of events.

One possible criticism of this democracy/nondemocracy framework is that not all political systems fit neatly into this leadership accountability spectrum. One type of nondemocratic political structure that bears mention is the cartelized political system, described in Jack Snyder's study of great power overexpansion. In this system, various special interests, such as heavy industries and military services, can steer foreign policy by forming a logrolling political coalition. These groups pursue their own interests, such as maximizing industry profits or increasing military spending, which may differ from those in the national interest. This is significant, because such groups are unlikely to look to lessons from formative events to discern what kinds of policies best protect the national interest. Therefore, if a learning hypothesis

---

[7] Susan Peterson also argued that domestic political structure can affect whether cognitive explanations predict foreign policy actions, specifically crisis-bargaining behavior. However, she made the proposition that cognitive explanations are most likely to explain behavior when the foreign policy executive is unitary and autonomous from the legislature (a nondemocratic structure), and that behavior is more likely to reflect broader interests when executive power is more diffuse and less autonomous. She and I make opposite predictions, for I assume that because of the Condorcet Jury Theorem these broader interests are more apt to reflect a cognitive explanation (learning from formative events) than are the ideas of a single person. Susan Peterson, *Crisis Bargaining and the State* (Ann Arbor: University of Michigan Press, 1995).

predicts that a formative event provides a lesson about what kinds of policies best protect the national interest, then it is more likely that this hypothesis will correctly describe the actions of a democracy, in which foreign policy tends to serve the national interest, than a nondemocracy, in which foreign policy tends to serve the actions of special interests. These groups may draw lessons from the experience about what sorts of actions best advance the interests of the group, but such learning would produce outcomes different from the national interest–oriented learning of democracies. Of course, advocates for these special interest groups may use historical lessons as rhetorical strategy in political discourse, selectively pointing to lessons from past history which support the policies that are in the interests of the group.[8]

The literature on public opinion provides another way of thinking about how political structure determines the impact of the lessons of history. Some observers see public opinion as resembling a sleeping elephant: it pays no attention to small prods but roars to life in a fury if given a solid poke. Some scholars interpreted the American entry into World War II in this way: in the 1930s, the public ignored a number of smaller warning signs of the dangers of isolation until the attack on Pearl Harbor awakened the American public from its isolationist slumber. Once engaged in war with the Axis powers, the American public supported total war, accepting nothing less than unconditional surrender.[9] Michael Roskin found that American foreign policy has bounced back and forth between isolationism and internationalism in the twentieth century, as one lesson was followed until a crisis demonstrated that it had outlived its usefulness, creating a new lesson leading to a new policy, which also was adhered to for too long until the next crisis encouraged another major shift. In addition to the American emergence from isolation in the early 1940s, Roskin argued, the American rejection of active internationalism following the Vietnam experience was an example of a policy followed for too long and was changed when it led the United States into a foreign policy crisis, the Vietnam War.[10] Some analyses of survey data have supported this idea that a

[8] Jack Snyder, *Myths of Empire: Domestic Politics and International Ambition* (Ithaca: Cornell University Press, 1991).

[9] Walter Lippmann, *Essays in the Public Philosophy* (Boston: Little, Brown, 1955); and George F. Kennan, *American Diplomacy, 1900–1950* (Chicago: University of Chicago Press, 1951). See also Alexander L. George, "Domestic Constraints on Regime Change in U.S. Foreign Policy: The Need for Policy Legitimacy," in *Change in the International System*, ed. Ole R. Holsti, Randolph M. Siverson, and Alexander L. George (Boulder, Colo.: Westview, 1980), 233–259.

[10] Michael Roskin, "From Pearl Harbor to Vietnam: Shifting Generational Paradigms and Foreign Policy," *Political Science Quarterly* 89 (Fall 1974): 563–588. On the impact of

generation's foreign policy beliefs are defined by a single formative event, though other analyses have provided a more skeptical view of generations hypothesis.[11]

This point about the significance of formative events on public opinion was originally made by Walter Lippmann, George Kennan, and others as an argument for the inferiority of the foreign policy–making process in democracies. Their view was that the mass public was essentially ignorant about foreign policy matters and not equipped to interpret events in world politics properly. Interestingly, some recent work in political psychology may offer support for the view that the public is more likely than foreign policy elites to be steered by formative events. One study of public opinion found that foreign policy novices are more susceptible than experts to what is called the *priming effect*, the phenomenon by which media coverage of an event makes information more accessible, thereby making it more persuasive.[12] The media coverage variable in that study is quite similar to the vividness effect that underpins the formative events model. Just as novices are more likely to be persuaded by information made salient by media coverage, we would expect them to be more apt to draw lessons from events that are perceptually salient, that is, high-impact, formative events. This is in line with a body of literature from cognitive psychology which finds that expertise enables an individual to avoid some of the traps presented by cognitive heuristic shortcuts that ensnare novices performing

Pearl Harbor on American beliefs about foreign policy, see John Mueller, "Pearl Harbor: Military Inconvenience, Political Disaster," *International Security* 16 (Winter 1991/92): 172-203. Page and Shapiro (*Rational Public*) support the empirical proposition that public opinion tends to move after big events and is otherwise relatively stable, but they argue that the public is acting rationally.

[11] Research favoring the generations hypothesis includes Neil E. Cutler, "Generational Succession as a Source of Foreign Policy Attitudes: A Cohort Analysis of American Opinion, 1946–1966," *Journal of Peace Research* 7 (1970): 33–47; Graham T. Allison, "Cool It: The Foreign Policy of Young America," *Foreign Policy* 1 (Winter 1970/71): 144–160; Bruce Russett, "The Americans' Retreat from World Power," *Political Science Quarterly* 90 (Spring 1975): 1–21; Bruce Kuklick, "Tradition and Diplomatic Talent: The Case of the Cold Warriors," in *Recycling the Past*, ed. Leila Zenderland (Philadelphia: University of Pennsylvania Press, 1978), 116–131; Bruce Kuklick, "History as a Way of Learning," *American Quarterly* 22 (Fall 1970): 609–628. Research more skeptical of the generations hypothesis includes Ole R. Holsti, "Public Opinion and Containment," in *Containing the Soviet Union: A Critique of US Policy*, ed. Terry L. Deibel and John Lewis Gaddis (Washington, D.C.: Pergamon-Brassey, 1987), 20–58; Ole R. Holsti and James N. Rosenau, *American Leadership in World Affairs* (Boston: Allen & Unwin, 1984), 155–163; and Eugene Wittkopf, *Faces of Internationalism: Public Opinion and American Foreign Policy* (Durham: Duke University Press, 1990), 45–51.

[12] Jon A. Krosnick and Donald R. Kinder, "Altering the Foundations of Support for the President through Priming," *American Political Science Review* 84 (June 1990): 497–512.

unfamiliar tasks.[13] The formative events learning model proposes that individuals learn only from high-impact events because they rely on heuristic shortcuts like the vividness effect to cope with uncertainty. If we assume that the foreign policy elite is more likely to consist of experts, and the mass public to consist of foreign policy novices, then this encourages the conclusion that the public is more likely than are elites to draw lessons from only formative events. Therefore, foreign policy will probably follow the lessons of formative events in democracies, where leaders are more accountable to public opinion, than in nondemocracies, where leaders can afford to pay less attention to the beliefs of the public. This effect is termed the *Sleeping Elephant Syndrome* and is a second theoretical argument in support of Hypothesis 5. Like the Condorcet Jury Theorem, it implies only that nondemocracies are less likely to act on the lessons from formative events, not that they are less likely in general to act on lessons from history.

Of course, other models of foreign policy are worth considering as possibly providing a better insight into the relationship between domestic politics and learning than the set of assumptions presented above. Consider an alternative, bureaucratic model that proposes that the operations of governmental institutions play a central role in determining foreign policy behavior. As opposed to the formative events model, which posits that individuals look only at big events and do not pay attention to small events, this model assumes that individuals are rational in the classical sense: they weigh all information in drawing inferences. Bureaucratic structures can impede the ability of government to receive, process, and evaluate information efficiently and rationally, however, such that some types of bureaucracies are likely to learn differently from others. This alternative model makes the simple assumption that a state's foreign policy is the output of its foreign policy bureaucracy. Therefore, regarding the impact of learning on foreign policy, foreign policy behavior reflects lessons learned by the foreign policy bureaucracy.

The literature on bureaucratic decision making proposes that the foreign policy bureaucracies of nondemocracies should learn differ-

---

[13] For a summary of some of this literature in the context of analyzing the making of foreign policy, see Richard D. Anderson Jr., "Why Competitive Politics Inhibits Learning in Soviet Foreign Policy," in *Learning in U.S. and Soviet Foreign Policy*, ed. George W. Breslauer and Philip E. Tetlock (Boulder, Colo.: Westview, 1991), 111–118. One could also argue that the public is more likely to learn only from formative events because the information about formative events is readibly available, whereas the costs of acquiring additional information are relatively high. On the other hand, the cost of acquiring additional information is relatively cheap for the foreign policy elite, given their expertise and available resources, so they are less likely to look only to formative events.

ently from those of democracies. Specifically, it argues that nondemocratic bureaucracies ought to learn in the manner described by the formative events model, that is, from big events and not from smaller events, whereas democratic bureaucracies are more likely to learn incrementally, assessing experience from all events, not just high-impact ones. This distinction between democratic and nondemocratic bureaucracy has been made most pointedly in comparisons of the American and Soviet foreign policy bureaucracies. In the context of discussing the differences between Soviet and American nuclear learning, Vladislav Zubok, a Russian historian, indicated that the requirements of the Soviet Communist Party leadership for concentration of power and control of information precluded the formation of any effective governmental structures for the collection and analysis of information from foreign policy events, thereby generally impeding the Soviet nuclear learning process. Zubok commented that this characteristic of the policy-making structure "retarded the evolution of Soviet nuclear thinking. It made nuclear learning by the leadership slower than it could have been. . . . This factor also explains to a great extent why Soviet nuclear learning, more than U.S. learning, was probably a reaction to crises—not an outcome of doctrinal and strategic evolution dictated by domestic politics and technological developments."[14] Matthew Evangelista made an approximately parallel argument, proposing that Soviet weapons innovation was driven by directives from the top levels of political leadership, which in turn often required the stimulus of an international crisis, whereas American weapons innovation tended to be driven by the developments of the scientists themselves. Ted Hopf made a somewhat different argument with similar implications. He found that Soviet estimates of American resolve did not change after American geopolitical losses in the Third World, often because of rigidities in the Soviet belief system.[15] One could argue that these belief rigidities are due in large part to the ideological nature of Soviet policy making, which in turn is fostered by a one-party, authoritarian system.

It is possible to put Zubok's point in a broader context. His critique is really about how the political needs of an authoritarian leadership

[14] Vladislav Zubok, "Soviet Nuclear Learning—Peculiar Patterns," in *From Rivalry to Cooperation: Russian and American Perspectives on the Post-Cold War Era*, ed. Manus I. Midlarsky, John A. Vasquez, and Peter V. Gladkov (New York: HarperCollins, 1994), 49.

[15] Matthew Evangelista, *Innovation and the Arms Race: How the United States and the Soviet Union Develop New Military Technologies* (Ithaca: Cornell University Press, 1988); Ted Hopf, *Peripheral Visions: Deterrence Theory and American Foreign Policy in the Third World, 1965–1990* (Ann Arbor: University of Michigan Press, 1994).

place limits on information flows within the government, leading to suboptimal policy making. Analyzing the Soviet political system, Philip Roeder argued that the "forced departicipation" of Soviet society gave the bureaucrats monopolies over information within their respective realms, monopolies that could not be forcibly broken because of the dependency of the Soviet Communist Party on the bureaucrats. One means by which the party sought to control the bureaucrats was to establish multiple institutions that performed similar tasks, in the hopes that this interinstitutional competition would provide checks and balances. Unexpectedly, the competition that often resulted between agencies performing similar functions led to the withholding of information and suboptimal policy making. Both Roeder and David Holloway use examples from the making of foreign policy to illustrate this point about intragovernmental secrecy. Such secrecy and barriers to information flows generally impede policy performance, specifically hindering the learning process. A continual analysis of experience requires a steady flow of information, and without a reliable flow, learning generally happens only when a foreign policy crisis provides unmistakable evidence that policies need to be changed.[16]

Although both Zubok and Roeder discuss the Soviet case, they analyze phenomena that characterize many authoritarian regimes: the forced departicipation of society; the need of the ruling party or junta to maintain control over the governmental bureaucracy, which increases the need to control policy information; and so on. Generalized, their observations imply that nondemocracies tend to learn only infrequently (specifically, only after foreign policy crises), whereas the learning process in democracies tends to proceed at a smoother, more rapid pace. Therefore, the foreign policies of nondemocracies will likely reflect formative event learning (that is, infrequent learning that occurs only after foreign policy crises), whereas democratic foreign policies will probably reflect more gradual and frequent learning rather than a formative event learning pattern. Put another way, the foreign policy bureaucracy of an authoritarian regime is more apt to suffer the organizational rigidities envisioned by the formative events theory, thereby encouraging formative events learning, than is the foreign policy of a democratic regime. This argument is labeled the Bureaucratic Learning Model and implies the proposition opposite to that of Hypothesis 5.

[16] Philip G. Roeder, *Red Sunset: The Failure of Soviet Politics* (Princeton: Princeton University Press, 1993), 86–91; David Holloway, "Military Power and Political Purpose in Soviet Policy," *Daedalus* 109 (Fall 1980): 13–30.

Hypothesis 6: The foreign policies of nondemocracies are more likely to reflect the lessons of formative events than are the foreign policies of democracies.

What do these hypotheses have to say about whether democracies make *better* foreign policy than do nondemocracies? The Bureaucratic Learning Model implies that democracies are likely to make more effective foreign policy than nondemocracies, using information more efficiently than nondemocracies because institutions of democratic policy making function better. This vision of democracies is consonant with a broader idea from liberal democratic theory, namely, that democracies permit the functioning and flourishing of a marketplace of ideas, from which good ideas win out and bad ideas are dismissed. The importance of the free flow of information to the pursuit of truth was emphasized, in particular, by Thomas Jefferson and John Stuart Mill.[17] Some modern political scientists have made this argument in the context of foreign policy, arguing that the marketplace of ideas most often fostered by democracies, while not perfect, generally encourages prudent decision making more often than does the censorship usually characteristic of nondemocratic states.[18]

The Condorcet Jury Theorem and Sleeping Elephant Syndrome, however, do not see democratic foreign policy in such an optimistic light. Following the lessons of formative events does not guarantee enlightened foreign policy—indeed, the thrust of Lippmann's argument was that the institutional dependence on public opinion which democratic leaderships must accept puts serious constraints on the making of foreign policy, constraints that authoritarian leaders do not face. Ernest May, a leading scholar of American diplomatic history, has argued that American foreign policy–makers have drawn lessons from foreign policy crises but have not used history wisely.[19] Hypothetically, an enlightened nondemocratic leader might face a situation in which she could make the foreign policy choices that advance the national interest even though they may conflict with the "conventional wisdom" offered by the last foreign policy crisis. If she had to answer to public opinion, however she may have had to act in accordance with

[17] Frank L. Mott, *Jefferson and the Press* (Baton Rouge: Louisiana State University Press, 1943), 5; John Stuart Mill, *On Liberty* (1859; rpt., New York: F. S. Crofts, 1947), 19. See also Rodney A. Smolla, *Free Speech in an Open Society* (New York: Vintage, 1992).
[18] Jack Snyder, "Averting Anarchy in the New Europe," *International Security* 14 (Spring 1990): 19; Stephen Van Evera, "Primed for Peace: Europe after the Cold War," *International Security* 15 (Winter 1990/91), 27.
[19] Ernest R. May, *"Lessons" of the Past: The Use and Misuse of History in American Foreign Policy* (London: Oxford University Press, 1973).

the dictates of some long dead ghosts of history, such as Sarajevo, Munich, or Vietnam.

The empirical strategy here is to assess whether political structure was systematically correlated with the probability that a state would act on the lessons of formative events. Hypotheses 5 and 6 were tested on the alliance data set of this study as well as on two other quantitative studies of learning in international relations.[20] The battery of tests performed here, then, should offer a good assessment of the robustness of the democracy-learning propositions. No relationship between political structure and learning in any of the three data sets would be strong evidence against the propositions. A relationship in all three areas supporting one of the hypotheses would indicate robust support for that hypothesis. Finally, support for one of the hypotheses in only one or two tests of the hypothesis would indicate more limited support for that hypothesis.

The Condorcet Jury Theorem and the Sleeping Elephant Syndrome (Hypothesis 5) predict that democracies should be more likely to act on the basis of formative learning than nondemocracies. If this proposition is valid, then we would expect a higher proportion of democracies to act on the basis of formative learning than nondemocracies. The Bureaucratic Learning Model (Hypothesis 6) proposes that the foreign policies of nondemocracies are more likely to reflect the lessons of formative events than are the foreign policies of democracies. Table 11 lists all cases in the alliances data set, which include the population of postwar alliance choices of small powers located in major theaters of conflict during the two world wars, divided by whether the state followed the lesson from the formative event and whether it was democratic. Democracy codings were taken from Michael Doyle's data set.[21] The notes to the table give the counts of each cell.

Table 11 indicates that a higher proportion of democracies than nondemocracies made their alliance choices in line with the lesson of the formative event; in fact, only one democracy did not act in accordance with the lesson. Using a chi-squared test, the null hypothesis that

---

[20] A fourth quantitative study of learning in international relations could not be tested because it tracked the behavior across time of only one state, so there was no variance in the domestic structure variable. That study focused, however, on a democracy, the United States, and found that it did act in accordance with the lessions of a formative event, providing some support for Hypothesis 5. Edward Rhodes, "Do Bureaucratic Politics Matter? Some Disconfirming Findings from the Case of the U.S. Navy," *World Politics* 47 (October 1994): 1–41.

[21] Michael W. Doyle, "Liberalism and World Politics," *American Political Science Review* 80 (December 1986): 1151–1169.

Table 11. Political structure and acting in accordance with lessons about alliance and neutrality

	Acted in accordance with lesson		Did not act in accordance with lesson	
	Country	Years	Country	Year(s)
Democracies	Norway	1921, 1927, 1933, 1939 1949, 1955, 1961, 1967	Belgium	1939
	Denmark	1921, 1927, 1933, 1939, 1949, 1955, 1961, 1967		
	Sweden	1921, 1927, 1933, 1939, 1949, 1955, 1961, 1967		
	Belgium	1921, 1927, 1933, 1949, 1955, 1961, 1967		
	Finland	1949, 1955, 1961, 1967		
	Switzerland	1921, 1927, 1933, 1939, 1949, 1955, 1961, 1967		
	Netherlands	1921, 1927, 1933, 1939, 1949, 1955, 1961, 1967		
	Ireland	1949, 1955, 1961, 1967		
	Australia	1949, 1955, 1961, 1967		
	New Zealand	1949, 1955, 1961, 1967		
	Luxembourg	1949, 1955, 1961, 1967		
	Turkey	1955, 1967		
	Greece	1955, 1961, 1967		
Nondemocracies	Thailand	1949, 1955, 1961, 1967	Romania	1921, 1939
	Portugal	1921, 1927, 1933, 1939 1949, 1955, 1961, 1967	Yugoslavia	1949, 1955, 1961, 1967
	Spain	1949, 1955, 1961, 1967	Egypt	1949
	Romania	1927, 1933	Albania	1921
	Turkey	1921, 1927, 1933 1949, 1961	Iraq	1949, 1955
			Turkey	1939
	Albania	1927, 1933, 1939	Spain	1921, 1927,
	Bulgaria	1921, 1927, 1933, 1939		1933, 1939
	Iran	1949, 1955, 1961, 1967		
	Iraq	1961, 1967		
	Egypt	1955, 1961, 1967		

Notes:

	Followed lesson	Did not follow lesson	Proportion that followed lesson
Democracies	72	1	0.99
Nondemocracies	39	15	0.72
Total	111	16	0.87

whether a state is democratic is unrelated to whether it acted in accordance with the lesson of the previous world war can be rejected at the 0.001 level (chi-square = 19.66, with 1 degree of freedom). This is strong evidence that political structure does have an impact on a state's proclivity to act on the lessons of history, as envisioned by the formative events theory. Specifically, the data offers empirical support for Hypothesis 5 (the Condorcet Jury Theorem and Sleeping Elephant Syndrome propositions) and evidence against Hypothesis 6 (the Bureaucratic Learning proposition). One might wonder whether the balance of threat variables are more significant for nondemocracies, for which the learning variables seem to be less significant. However, in a logit regression of equation (1) on a data set of just nondemocracies (n = 54), none of the threat variables were statistically significant, and both the individual and systemic learning variables were substantively and statistically significant, though the estimated coefficient for individual learning was somewhat lower.

Closer analysis of a few of these cases indicates that the theoretical explanations for this relationship seem to have some validity. A good example of the Condorcet Jury Theorem, which predicts that a nondemocratic leader who does not learn the lesson in the predicted fashion can act against the lesson despite the opposition of the general population, is post–World War II Spain. From Spain's successful World War II experience, the formative learning theory would predict the lesson that neutrality best protects its national security, so that Spain would prefer to remain neutral as the rest of Europe divided itself into blocs in the late 1940s. Contrary to this prediction, however, the Spanish government preferred alliance with the West, though the Spanish public retained its preference for neutrality. More specifically, while Franco did not draw the neutrality lesson from the formative event of World War II, the Spanish public viewed the experience as confirming the wisdom of Spain's traditional neutrality. As predicted by the Condorcet Jury Theorem, Franco was able to ignore public opposition to his efforts to secure Spanish membership in NATO. Further, after Franco died and Spain became increasingly democratic in the 1980s, public demands for neutrality became increasingly louder, encouraging Spain to loosen its ties with NATO.

The Middle Eastern cases might also be considered to be illustrative of the Condorcet Jury Theorem. Both Egypt and Iraq had experiences of failed alliance in World War II, which admittedly probably played a bigger role in feeding anti-Western sentiment in these societies rather than in building a new consensus for neutrality. Yet the governments of these societies retained their pro-Western stances in the years following the war, in part because their political structures were undemocratic. Eventually, the pro-Western regimes in Egypt and Iraq were overthrown and replaced with anti-Western regimes that were more popular. An important part of the new foreign policies, then, was neutrality, the prediction of the individual learning hypothesis. Therefore, it is not unreasonable to propose that had Egypt and Iraq been more demo-cratic after World War II, the foreign policies of these states would have been more reflective of the preferences of the masses rather than the elites, so the shift to an anti-Western neutrality reflecting the lessons of the war might have come faster.

In contrast, democracies tend to follow the lessons offered by their wartime experiences. One example is Norway. After neutrality failed in 1940, Norway switched to a preference for alliance with the West. But the leading advocate of prewar neutrality, Foreign Minister Halvdan Koht, did not learn the lesson of failed neutrality and advocated that Norway still avoid associating itself too closely with Britain, even after the German invasion. His was by far the minority view, and Koht resigned in 1940 rather than preside over the foreign policy shift to alliance with Britain. This demonstrates well the Condorcet Jury Theo-rem. Koht was one of the minority unpersuaded by the experience of invasion, and his view did not guide post-1940 Norwegian foreign policy because Norway was a democracy. If the political structure had been autocratic, then Norwegian foreign policy would not have re-flected the lessons of 1940, because Koht as dictator would have main-tained Norway's neutrality even after the German invasion.

Belgium, another democratic political structure, also enacted the les-sons of a formative event as policy. During World War I, the Belgian government-in-exile was concerned enough about implementing popular policies that it conducted an opinion poll of leading Belgian elites during wartime to uncover majority opinions about postwar foreign policy. Additionally, Paul-Henri Spaak, a leading proponent of neutrality before World War II, was able to retain a strong command of Belgian foreign policy after the war because he himself came to believe in the importance of alliance with the West. Had he supported neutral-ity for Belgium after World War II, he probably would have suffered a similar fate as Koht—a fall from political power.

Table 11 indicates that in 1939, Belgium is the one example of a democratic state that did not act on the lessons of history in the forma-tion of its alliance policy: this reflects Belgium's decision in the late 1930s to abandon its alliance with France in favor of neutrality, in contravention to the lesson from World War I that neutrality is undesir-able. Significantly, this decision resulted from a variety of domestic political factors that undercut public and parliamentary support for the French alliance, encouraging the shift to neutrality. Although Bel-gium's decisions counter those expected (that is, Belgium is an example of a democracy not acting in accord with the lesson of the formative event), it is significant that the policy choice of breaking with France was made because of pressures from public opinion. Therefore, this case ought to be interpreted as evidence against two of the specific propositions described here (the Condorcet Jury Theorem and the Sleeping Elephant Syndrome) or perhaps a demonstration of the imprecision of the model but not as evidence against the general theoretical proposition that in a democracy foreign policy is more representative of public opinion. The Belgian decision to exit the alliance is not good evidence in favor of the Bureaucratic Learning Model, for it is not a good example of a democracy bucking the lessons of a formative event to make better policy. The Belgian return to neutrality in 1936 undercut Western efforts to resist the rising German threat, most seriously by impeding Franco-Belgian military cooperation.

But how robust is this rather strong finding? To explore this question, one can test the hypotheses on some other learning data sets. The empirical strategy here is to examine which states in these other data sets did and did not act in accordance with the lessons of history and then to see whether democracies were significantly more or less likely to do so. Two other quantitative studies of learning in international relations looked at crisis bargaining strategies and extended deterrence. Both tested learning hypotheses somewhat different from the formative events theory, tests described in greater detail below. If democracies are systematically more likely to act on the basis of the lessons of history in these other data sets which rely on these different learning models, then this would be evidence in favor of the robustness of the proposition. If such a relationship is not uncovered, then the proposition is not very robust outside of a formative events conception of learning.

Russell Leng proposed that a central characteristic of a state's crisis bargaining strategy is its degree of coerciveness, which, he argued, is driven by lessons drawn from the previous crisis.[22] He posited a number of specific learning hypotheses oriented around the basic theoretical proposition that states learn what he calls "realpolitik" lessons: a state will draw the lesson from a diplomatic failure in a crisis that not enough resolve was shown, so that a more coercive strategy is taken in the next crisis. Unlike the formative events model, then, this model proposes that lessons are drawn from the most recent crisis with the same adversary, not from the previous formative event. Sometimes this last crisis may be a formative event. The differences between the formative events learning model and Leng's learning model encourage us to

---

[22] Russell, J. Leng, "When Will They Ever Learn? Coercive Bargaining in Recurrent Crises," *Journal of Conflict Resolution* 27 (September 1983): 379–419.

Table 12. Political structure and acting in accordance with lessons about crisis-bargaining strategy

	Acted in accordance with lesson	Did not act in accordance with lesson
Democracies	Britain, Munich (1938) Britain, Polish-Danzig (1939) France, 2d Morocco (1911) France, pre–World War I (1914) U.S., Cuban Missile (1962) Israel, Suez (1956) Israel, Six Day War (1967) India, 2d Kashmir (1965)	U.S., Berlin Wall (1961) India, Bangladesh (1971)
Nondemocracies	Germany, 2d Morocco (1911) Germany, pre–World War I (1914) Germany, Munich (1938) Russia, 1st Balkan War (1912) Russia, pre–World War I (1914) USSR, Berlin Wall (1961) Egypt, Six Day War (1967) Pakistan, 2d Kashmir (1965)	Austria, 1st Balkan War (1912) Austria, pre–World War I (1914) Germany, Polish-Danzig (1939) USSR, Cuban Missile (1962) Egypt, Suez (1956)

Notes: Each table entry provides the country and crisis (plus the year of the crisis) during which the state could have adopted a crisis-bargaining strategy in line with the lesson of the previous crisis.

	Followed Lesson	Did not follow lesson	Probability of following lesson
Democracies	8	2	0.80
Nondemocracies	9	5	0.64
Total	17	7	0.71

take the empirical test of Hypotheses 5 and 6 on Leng's data with a grain of salt, as all three theoretical arguments—the Condorcet Jury Theorem, the Sleeping Elephant Syndrome, and the Bureaucratic Learning Model—presume a formative events model of learning.

His data included six pairs of traditional rivals, each of whom shared three diplomatic crises. The hypothesis is that each state draws lessons from the previous crisis, so that there were twenty-four opportunities to learn because twelve countries each had two opportunities. The prediction is that the democratic countries are more likely to act in accordance with the lessons from the previous crisis than are nondemocracies. Table 12 presents a cross tabulation of Leng's data.

Table 12 indicates that in Leng's data set, a higher percentage of democracies acted on the basis of the lessons from the previous crisis than nondemocracies. The relatively small number of cases (n = 24), however, casts doubt on the validity of the finding; a chi-square test reveals that the null hypothesis that there is no relationship cannot be

Table 13. Political structure and acting in accordance with lessons about reputation in attempts at extended deterrence

	Followed lesson	Did not follow lesson	Proportion that followed lesson
Democracies	5	5	0.50
Nondemocracies	36	12	0.75
Total	41	17	0.71

rejected at the 0.10 level (chi-square = 0.71, with 1 degree of freedom). Therefore, in this test of what we might call a quasi–formative events learning model, no statistically significant relationship was found between the political structure of the state and the likelihood that it would act on the lessons of history.

Paul Huth's study of extended deterrence tested a model of learning similar to Leng's. Huth examined a number of factors hypothesized to affect the likelihood that an attempt at extended deterrence in an international crisis would be successful, among which was the past diplomatic behavior of the defending state. He proposed that if the defending state had bullied or been bullied in the last crisis with the same challenger, then the challenger would learn the lesson that the defender is either a bully or an appeaser, which would undercut deterrence. Examining fifty-eight cases of extended deterrence between 1885 and 1985, he found empirical support for this hypothesis: extended deterrence either succeeded or failed in accordance with the predictions of the learning hypothesis in forty-one of the fifty-eight cases (71 percent). Like Leng's learning model, Huth's has some differences with the formative events model, so the empirical test of Hypothesis 5 and Hypothesis 6 on Huth's data has limited value.[23]

Is the likelihood that the challenger behaved in accordance with the learning prediction related to the political structure of the challenger? Table 13 presents Huth's data, divided by whether the challenger acted in accordance with the learning predictions, that is, whether deterrence succeeded or failed based on the learning hypothesis, and whether the challenger was democratic.

In Huth's data set, democracies were less likely to act on the basis of the lessons of history than were nondemocracies. A chi-squared test reveals that the null hypothesis that political structure is unrelated to the likelihood to act on the basis of lessons cannot be rejected at the 0.10

[23] Paul K. Huth, Extended Deterrence and the Prevention of War (New Haven: Yale University Press, 1988).

level (chi squared = 2.50, with 1 degree of freedom). Therefore, these results cannot be considered evidence in support of Hypothesis 6.

In summary, Hypothesis 5 attracted statistically significant empirical support in the area of small power alliance behavior, whereas neither hypothesis was supported in the areas of crisis bargaining or extended deterrence. The preliminary conclusion suggested by these mixed results is that the proposition that democracies are more likely to act on the lessons of formative events has some validity only for formative event learning but no demonstrated validity for other types of learning. This is in some sense not surprising, given that all three democracy-learning propositions are built around the formative events model.

A final remark about this political structure finding is in order. This chapter is an initial step toward building a broader understanding of how learning fits into the foreign policy–making process. While the main thrust of this book is to demonstrate the importance of learning in international relations, a remaining task is the placement of learning as a theory of belief formation into a broader model of foreign policy–making which would predict when learning directly guides foreign policy and when it does not. Ultimately, this theory-building process would lead to the construction of a general theory of foreign policy which could make predictions about areas of foreign policy decision outside of learning. A similar model-building process appears to be occurring in the literature analyzing the democratic peace. This democratic peace was first observed as an empirical phenomenon, after which some preliminary theoretical explanations were put forth. Now, broader models of foreign policy which explain the democratic peace as well as other phenomena are being built.[24]

---

[24] Two examples of models of foreign policy which seek to explain the democratic peace as well as other phenomena are Bruce Bueno de Mesquita and David Lalman, *War and Reason* (New Haven: Yale University Press, 1992); and James D. Fearon, "Domestic Political Audiences and the Escalation of International Disputes," *American Political Science Review* 88 (September 1994): 577–592. It is worth noting that the findings in this chapter would support the structural explanation of the democratic peace, that public opinion in a democracy serves as a check on the tendency to fight other democracies.

[9]

Conclusion

We can learn only from the past, since the past is all we have.
—Harry Hearder

I set out to accomplish two tasks in this book. The first was to develop a more ambitious theory of learning, one that is general enough to be applied to a variety of nations across time and perhaps even in different issue areas. The second was to test this theory on an area of foreign policy crucial to the practice and study of international relations—alliances. This chapter summarizes the empirical results and reviews the implications for the study of international relations.

The empirical results point to the conclusion that a small power's individual experience in a formative event, defined as the most recent world war, often determines the small power's alliance choices in the years that follow that war. In a data set of 127 observations of small power alliance choices, 87 percent were correctly predicted by the learning proposition. The dominating effects of the formative experience on alliance policy can last for two decades after the formative event. This quantitative finding supports the work of several other scholars who have used case studies to argue for the heavy impact that experience in a single, significant event can have on how decision makers understand international relations.

This finding does not imply that past experience necessarily makes for wiser choices, only that policy dilemmas are framed as repetitions of past experiences. Case studies reveal quite clearly that framing a current decision problem in terms of a past experience can be disastrous because of unrecognized changes in important political or military factors. These studies join an unfortunately wide array of other books in which scholars have pointed out how lessons have been inappropriately drawn. As Samuel Coleridge lamented: "If men could learn from history, what lessons it might teach us! But passion and party blind our eyes, and the light which experience gives is a lantern on the stern, which shines only on the waves behind us."[1]

Another interesting empirical finding is that while states draw heavily on their own individual experiences, they pay little attention to those of other states in the same formative event. This tendency to ignore the experiences of others means that from a single event, different participants are likely to draw different conclusions. If one assumes that each state's foreign policy situation is not completely idiosyncratic, which implies that the experiences of other states are at least somewhat relevant to one's own foreign policy decisions, then decision makers ignore pertinent information.

The test of learning theory was strengthened by comparing its predictions with those of a dominant realist proposition of alliance behavior—balance of threat. In contrast to the empirical performance of the individual learning proposition, the level of threat was found to have only marginal effects on the propensity of a small power to prefer alliance. Significantly, this small effect was observed for only broad threats posed to an entire regional system, as opposed to direct threats posed to a single country, and even this marginal effect was in the direction opposite to that predicted by balance of threat theory, with alliance found to be less likely as a systemic threat appeared. Further, the probability of alliance decreased as the military power of the threatener increased and as the threatened nation became more geographically exposed to the threat. Therefore, the appearance of certain kinds of international threats encourages small powers to seek neutrality rather than balance against the source of threat or bandwagon with it. The robustness of these findings was proven in a series of sensitivity tests, in which it was demonstrated that the chief findings—the dominance of individual experiences and the virtual irrelevance of the level of external threats—do not change when different coding rules are used or when the parameters of the model are changed. For example, whether one assumes that the Soviet threat to Europe was constant throughout the cold war or varied, individual experiences are the best predictor of whether a small power would prefer alliance or neutrality, whereas the effect of external threat is negligible.

---

[1] Quoted in Jack S. Levy, "Learning and Foreign Policy: Sweeping a Conceptual Minefield," *International Organization* 48 (Spring 1994): 279.

Confidence in the validity of the quantitative findings is boosted by the case studies presented in Chapter 6. Analyses of a number of cases in which the individual learning prediction was correct support the conclusion that the statistical findings presented in Chapter 5 are not spurious and that the learning theory accurately describes the decision-making process. The cases also reveal that external threat can play a role in driving alliance decisions, a relation that is not a simple, universally linear one. Rather, formative experiences are the lenses through which decision makers come to understand threat and arrive at a policy solution to the problem of threat, so that it is crucially important to know a small power's formative experiences to predict how it will cope with the problem of external threat. Further, as predicted by the learning hypotheses, the world wars were decisively formative of many decision makers' beliefs about alliance policy.

These case studies also illustrated that lessons drawn from a formative event are often more multifaceted than envisioned by the learning hypotheses that were subjected to quantitative tests. As predicted, many states drew broad lessons about the general desirabilities of alliance and neutrality. Significantly, the case studies revealed that the formative experiences often had other effects on states' postwar foreign policies. Some, such as post–World War I Belgium, became much more sensitive to external threat after having suffered an invasion. Others, such as Sweden after World War II, drew lessons about the necessary level of armed forces. The observation that some decision makers drew lessons about issues other than the alliance/neutrality choice indicates some limits to the specific hypotheses, but it also demonstrates the general strength of learning theory: decision makers address important issues of foreign policy—the nature of the external threat, the choice between alliance and neutrality, and military size—based on lessons drawn from formative experiences.

Chapter 7 contained studies of all cases in which the individual learning hypothesis made an incorrect prediction, cases that indicate some important limits to the learning theory presented here. As an example, for some of these cases, the nature of the lesson learned is often determined by the goals of the state in the formative event. This is an important point in regard to alliance behavior, because the goals that alliances are intended to advance can vary from country to country and across time for a single country. Therefore, if a nation learns from an experience that a policy best maximizes a particular goal but, later, no longer seeks to meet that goal, then the lesson is no longer applicable. Consider Turkey, which learned from World War I that it does not pay to enter an alliance to achieve territorial gains. By the late 1930s, however, its primary goal had shifted from expansion to protecting national security, so the lesson of World War I could not be applied.

A final empirical issue is the generalizability of the results. The need for context-specific hypotheses limited the data set to small powers, though some brief empirical analysis of great power alliance behavior offers preliminary evidence that the learning propositions can be applied to great powers as well. The small power analysis has direct implications for understanding the alliance choices of great powers. Even though the small power hypotheses cannot be applied directly to the behavior of great powers, we can still be confident that the basic similarities between the foreign policy–making processes of small and great powers means that the learning *theory* ought to apply to great powers. Some might argue that the decision-making processes of great and small powers differ enough that we cannot be confident that a theory tested only on small power behavior can be safely extrapolated to great power behavior. But learning theory is an explanation of how organizations staffed with people operating in an uncertain environment are likely to behave. Given that this condition describes the foreign policy apparatuses of both small and great powers, the finding that the theory strongly predicts the behavior of small powers encourages the conclusion that it ought to work for great powers as well. Chapter 5 contains a brief discussion of a few great power cases, perhaps enough to begin the argument that great powers' alliance choices are substantially determined by lessons drawn from formative events.

The findings also have implications for decision making outside of the area of alliance policy. If formative events do drive beliefs, then we would expect such events to shape beliefs in virtually all areas of foreign policy. As mentioned above, some of the case studies point in this direction, demonstrating that some states drew lessons about the nature of threat and levels of armament as well as the relative desirabilities of alliance and neutrality. The finding that formative events shape beliefs about alliances is certainly in concert with the findings in the crisis-bargaining literature that bargaining strategies are often shaped by lessons drawn from past experiences. Other foreign policy areas exist in which beliefs—and, thereby, behavior—might be shaped by formative experiences. Experiences of global depressions, for example, might form beliefs about international economic policies.[2]

This theory also has applications beyond the study of international

---

[2] Stephen D. Krasner, "State Power and the Structure of International Trade," *World Politics* 28 (April 1976): 341.

relations. The principles of the theory are based on ideas about how individuals and organizations make decisions, so the finding that formative events shape beliefs and guide behavior ought to apply to other organizations, such as businesses, organs of government aside from the foreign policy apparatus, and political parties. An interesting extension of the proposition would be to examine whether political parties tend to "campaign the last election."

CONTRIBUTIONS TO LEARNING THEORY

Much of the previous scholarship on learning in international relations suffers from important empirical and theoretical limitations. The vast majority of the empirical work had been confined to case studies, forgoing the application of quantitative methods of analysis. Though case studies are an important part of the process of assessing the validity of a theory, the inability of the procedure to analyze many cases simultaneously and rigorously limits its ability to confer validity on a theory. Additionally, some theoretical models of learning have suffered from a burdensome wealth of detail, so that the sophistication of these models of information processing prevents their application to more than a few cases.

In this book I offer advances in both areas. I perform quantitative tests of learning hypotheses, comparing them to the hypotheses of a leading alternative explanation, balance of threat. The strong empirical support for the learning hypotheses offered by the quantitative tests substantially boosts our confidence that learning is an important explanation of behavior in world politics. I also demonstrate the potential of relatively simple conceptions of the learning process. From a few basic principles of social psychology and organization theory, Chapter 2 built a small set of fundamental learning propositions: learning occurs after formative events; lessons are driven by success and failure; and successes are followed by continuation of policy, whereas failures motivate policy innovation. The simplicity of this theory permits its application to virtually any area of foreign policy, thereby facilitating progress in empirical explorations of the validity of learning theory.

Some might contend that this conception is too simple to reflect reality adequately and that learning models must represent a more sophisticated understanding of the learning process. All models are representations of reality, and no "true" model exists for any process in either the social or physical sciences. Additionally, though this model may be quite simple, there is beauty in simplicity—parsimony is itself a desirable goal of model construction. Most important, though, this simple learning hypothesis performs quite well, correctly predicting 87 percent of all alliance cases. If a more elaborate model was warranted, we would see much spottier performance. Last, the case studies reveal that decision makers do in fact learn in the relatively simple fashion laid out in the theory, which confirms its basic logic. Indeed, the simple fashion in which decision makers draw lessons from history often contributes to suboptimal policy choices.

When Robert Jervis wrote about learning in international relations in 1976, he framed learning as a process in opposition to classical rationality, proposing that decision makers used their experiences as "a useful shortcut to rationality," often ignoring important information.[3] In some ways, I also indict the view that states act in accordance with the dictates of classical rationality. The learning proposition tested here envisions superstitious, experiential learning: failures encourage policy innovation, and successes encourage policy continuation. States were hypothesized to behave like Mark Twain's cat, which, after jumping on a hot stove lid, would never jump on a hot stove again—but would never jump on a cold one, either. Nothing in the theory implied that experiences made decision makers "smarter" or that experiences necessarily improved policy performance. Indeed, the data provide a number of examples of states experiencing policy failure even after acting on the basis of the lessons of past experience. For example, following its success in World War I, Norway adhered to its policy of neutrality in the interwar years, in spite of evidence that it was becoming vulnerable and acquiring greater strategic importance for the great powers. This qualifies as nonrational action, because Norway chose badly in large part because it ignored important information. This study also found evidence disconfirming what might be considered a rational theory of behavior—realism. Realism argues that states act in their own best interests, certainly a view that is close to a rational choice view. Also, realism was first discussed as a prescriptive theory of international relations: scholars presented it in the context of making policy prescriptions, recommending what states (the United States, in particular) *ought* to do to best advance their national interests. Evidence that states do not act in the manner envisioned by realists could also be seen as attacking the traditional rational choice view of international relations.

This model and these results, however, present a more sophisticated

---

[3] Robert Jervis, *Perception and Misperception in International Politics* (Princeton: Princeton University Press, 1976).

vision than a simple indictment of classical rationality. Learning is not easily classifiable as either a rational or a nonrational process. The fundamental tenet of classical rationality is that given certain information, preferences, and choices, a decision maker will act to maximize her utility. Rationality provides no guidance in determining what information is relevant, however, just as it does not determine what an actor's preferences ought to be—both are what might be called "prerational" assumptions. Therefore, it is inappropriate to deem as rational or irrational a particular information search or belief update strategy. Of course, in hindsight we can judge some decisions as better than others, but this is not the same as judging some decisions as rational and some as irrational.

Some might propose that the learning theory of this study assumes nonrational human behavior, positing that all information other than that presented in a formative experience is ignored. First, if a small power's alliance with a great power is considered to be a policy solution to the problem of a how to cope with a world war, then the highest-quality information would be experience from a world war which illustrates the performance of an alliance policy. In some ways, the *only* reliable information regarding how to cope with systemic war is past experience in systemic wars, just as earthquakes are the best source of data for seismology and airplane accidents are the best source of data for the study of safety in air travel. Second, the "wisest" information search may not be the one that takes account of all possibly relevant information. Many of the signals and possible lessons the environment provides are irrelevant and possibly misleading. There is, then, a danger of overlearning as well as underlearning, and the decision maker's difficult task is to find an appropriate balance between the two.[4] Significantly, rationality does not provide a means for striking this balance, so that the strategy of drawing lessons only from the most recent formative event should not be judged as either "rational" or "irrational" but "prerational."

There are important issues yet to be explored in relation to learning in world politics. First, the formative events proposition is only one possible process by which decision makers can learn. If one accepts the initial theoretical assumption that international relations theory requires a way of understanding how decision makers come to have beliefs about world politics, then this leaves open the possibility for a wide array of possible hypotheses about learning, or even hypotheses

[4] A similar phenomenon of being insufficiently discriminating of incoming information has been termed *hypervigilance*. Irving L. Janis and Leon Mann, *Decision Making: A Psychological Analysis of Conflict, Choice, and Commitment* (New York: Free Press, 1977).

about belief change which do not describe a learning process. As far as the formative events proposition itself, important questions remain, the most pressing and perplexing being, What constitutes a formative event? For small power alliance choices in the twentieth century, world wars present themselves as fairly obvious formative events. In other areas, though, it is less clear exactly which events are formative. It would be very useful to provide a basic theoretical framework for understanding what kinds of events are likely to be formative beyond the rough-and-ready rule that events significant in political and human terms are more likely to be formative.[5]

There is a flip side to the question of what events are likely to be formative for a given foreign policy question. It may be that a certain class of events can confidently be classified as formative, but it may be unclear in what areas a decision maker will determine failure or success. I assumed that a small power would attribute its success or failure to its alliance policy, but the case studies revealed that in at least some instances, nations drew lessons in other areas, such as the required size of the armed forces. In these other areas, the issue from which decision makers are most likely to draw lessons may be even more difficult to predict systematically. For example, a decision maker who was involved in a diplomatic crisis that escalated to an unwanted war could draw lessons about the importance of stakes involved, crisis-bargaining strategies, and/or the balance of military forces. A general theoretical proposition predicting which areas are likely to attract the most attention for the drawing of lessons would be an important advance in understanding the learning process.

Predicting how a decision maker has learned or will learn can be quite tricky. Not all areas of foreign policy easily lend themselves to the application of learning theory. Alliance behavior for small powers is a good candidate, because it is relatively easy to determine what events are formative and to define policy success and failure. A complicating factor is raised by the problem that vividness in large part determines what is formative, and vividness can be driven by unexpected factors. For example, in Yuen Foong Khong's study of the 1965 American

---

[5] On a similar track, Scott Gartner has argued that organizations make decisions when changes occur in what he calls dominant indicators. These can be, for example, public approval ratings for a ruling administration or casualty figures for an army. The question of what is a dominant indicator might be considered to be related to the question of what is a formative event. In this study, whether a state is invaded could be considered the dominant indicator of a small power's alliance policy. For an application of the dominant indicators model, see Scott Sigmund Gartner, "Predicting the Timing of Carter's Decision to Initiate a Hostage Rescue Attempt: Modeling a Dynamic Information Environment," *International Interactions* 18 (1993): 365–386.

decisions to escalate the war in Vietnam, the Korea experience was formative of the eventual decisions mostly because it had personally affected a few of the main decision makers, particularly Lyndon Johnson. If, for example, Johnson's beliefs been formed by the French experience in Indochina (as were those of George Ball), the result might have been de-escalation of the conflict and an earlier, less bloody, and far less traumatic American exit from the Vietnam War.[6]

American policy toward famine in Africa also demonstrates the difficulty in predicting beforehand what will be vivid. In 1983, Senator John Danforth showed President Ronald Reagan a series of photos depicting the famine in Ethiopia; the president was so shocked that he reversed American policy and promised more aid. The following year, television footage of the famine encouraged more donations and an expansion of aid to the famine victims. In both cases, the serendipity of visual images made famine a vivid problem, causing policy changes. A decade later, American intervention in Somalia was probably strongly determined by media coverage. Though Somalia was certainly suffering from intense famine in the early 1990s, so was its neighbor Sudan, which raises the question of why the American government elected to intervene in Somalia rather than in Sudan. One observer has pointed to the greater television coverage of the famine in Somalia than of that in Sudan (on 1992 evening news programs in the United States, there were 468 stories on Somalia and only 6 on Sudan), arguing that this greater coverage focused attention on the Somali famine, motivating action.[7] In terms of the theoretical discussion of this study, then, TV played an important role in determining which country was vivid for the American public and for policymakers. The implication is that TV (and the news media in general) may play a large role in determining both which events are vivid and what aspects of certain events are vivid.

A third demonstration of the potential power of TV in determining vividness was the political fallout from the military defeat suffered by a small detachment of American Rangers in Mogadishu in October

[6] Yuen Foong Khong, *Analogies at War* (Princeton: Princeton University Press, 1992). The counterfactual of American de-escalation is mine, not Khong's.

[7] On Ethiopia, see Christopher J. Bosso, "Setting the Agenda: Mass Media and the Discovery of Famine in Ethiopia," in *Manipulating Public Opinion: Essays on Public Opinion as a Dependent Variable*, ed. Michael Margolis and Gary A. Mauser (Pacific Grove, Calif.: Brooks/Cole Publishing, 1989), 153–174. On Somalia, see Walter Goodman, "Re Somalia: How Much Did TV Shape Policy?" *New York Times*, 8 December 1992, B4; Walter Goodman "Silent Partner Emerging in Policy Councils: TV," *New York Times*, 6 March 1993, B10; and Walter Goodman, "The Effect of Images on Governmental Policy," *New York Times*, 7 October 1993, B3.

1993. The images of the corpse of an American soldier being dragged through a Mogadishu street after the battle highlighted the human impact of the losses in the battle, contributing to a reassessment of American policy in Somalia in favor of reducing casualty risks by accelerating withdrawal. Further, this military defeat in Mogadishu may have prompted a small, lightly armed gang of toughs in Port-au-Prince, Haiti, to threaten to create "another Somalia" if American troops landed there; some of the leaders of this Haitian group claim to have been encouraged by TV images of the Somalia defeat. This almost minuscule show of force encouraged the Clinton administration to decide against landing U.S. Marines in Haiti in 1993. The Haiti and Mogadishu events stimulated a broader reconsideration of American foreign policy, in favor of minimizing the risks of suffering casualties from American military interventions.[8] If essentially unsystematic factors such as television coverage and the personal experiences of certain key individuals determine what is vivid, then it would complicate the task of predicting accurately which events are formative and what lessons are drawn from formative experiences.

An entirely different slant to thinking about learning in international politics is to ask, What factors will make it more likely that a decision maker will draw the correct lesson from an experience? The phenomenon under examination would be the level of decision-making performance rather than just what decisions were taken. Of course, this would require making judgments ex post facto as to what the correct lessons were, ex ante, a tricky job, at best. However, the results of such a study might reveal that certain organizational structures or personality types are more likely to read history correctly, which in turn affects decisions and outcomes. To give one example, such an approach might help us understand the process of what Jonathan Shimshoni calls "military entrepreneurship." He argues that the state of military technology has no objective, independent impact on the dominance of the offense or defense on the battlefield; rather, the effect emerges from what the military commanders (acting as entrepreneurs) actually do with the technology. An important part of this process is the application of past experiences:

> As in most areas of international relations, much of the data for analysis are historical events. While leaders may normally be tempted (mistakenly) to see in previous military encounters (and especially their outcomes)

---

[8] R. W. Apple, "Policing a Global Village," *New York Times*, 13 October 1993, A1; Michael R. Gordon, "Disastrous U.S. Raid in Somalia Nearly Succeeded, Review Finds," *New York Times*, 25 October 1993, 1.

indications of where technological and overall advantage lie—an arrow pointing in the direction of desirable adaptation—the military entrepreneur would use the historical record more analytically. For him battles of the past will not be repeated—he will not expect them to, nor will he let them be; he should use their record warily, to suggest problems, opportunities, potential avenues to solutions, and routes to advantage—an arrow towards consistently rejuvenated theories of victory.[9]

Shimshoni is suggesting a learning process more complicated than the simple application of a single formative experience. This conception of learning might be too complicated to predict systematically from what past experiences lessons will be drawn. It might be possible, however, to predict what kinds of factors cause individuals and organizations to be the best entrepreneurs, from which one would predict that decision makers (whether organizations or individuals) that exhibit these factors will make the best choices.

Another interesting area for future research is how learning fits more broadly into the foreign policy–making process as a whole. I approached the question by assessing the links between political structure and the propensity of states to act on the lessons of history. The empirical analysis in Chapter 8 provided limited support for the hypothesis that democracies are more likely to act on the lessons of history than are nondemocracies. Though the model of the foreign policy–making process sketched out in Chapter 8 was quite rough, it is perhaps a first step toward building a broader model that would include learning and make predictions in many areas of foreign policy.

CONTRIBUTIONS TO RESEARCH IN ALLIANCES
AND INTERNATIONAL RELATIONS

This book sheds some light on alliance behavior in particular and international relations in general. A closer examination of a dominant theory of alliance behavior—balance of threat—revealed a few important theoretical observations. The first is that special care must be taken to structure balance of threat theory so as to make it a falsifiable theory. One must understand the conditions under which alliance or no alliance is predicted and build a set of coding rules that enable a coding decision of no alliance to be made. Balance of threat theory is particularly susceptible to being built on an unfalsifiable theoretical base, as

---

[9] Jonathan Shimshoni, "Technology, Military Advantage, and World War I," *International Security* 15 (Winter 1990/91): 199.

with wide enough definitions of alliance and threat it is possible for threat always to be coded as present and for a state always to be coded as preferring alliance. Second, it is important to distinguish different kinds of threats and their appropriate responses. Whether one faces a direct or systemic threat determines possible alliance responses.

The empirical findings in this book deal a strong blow to balance of threat theory. The behavior of nearly three dozen countries over several decades was analyzed, and the predictions of balance of threat theory provide a poor match with reality. These results can be added to a growing body of scholarship which finds that balance of threat theory does not explain alliance choices. That these findings were supported by both quantitative and case study methods of analysis further boosts our confidence in their implications: balance of threat theory is not a satisfying explanation of why states join alliances.

One area of alliance literature for which this book may provide some illumination is the arms-alliance substitution model proposed by James Morrow. This model sees states as attempting to acquire security with either arms or alliances: arms cost money, and alliances cost foreign policy autonomy. The substitution model does not, however, make any a priori propositions about the exact trade-off between alliances and autonomy or about how much security arms and alliances produce, relatively. Not trivial questions for the model, these relationships are likely to determine what choices are eventually made. One way to look at these relationships is to view them as beliefs, that states have beliefs about the relationships between alliances and autonomy and the relationship between arms and alliances and security. In turn, learning provides an answer to the question of how these beliefs are formed. For example, Sweden learned from World War II that arms alone are sufficient to purchase enough security, but Norway learned that both arms and alliances are necessary. This is a good example of how learning theory can be used as a companion to, rather than as a competitor with, a theory of rational choice; James Morrow laid out an interesting theory of rational choice for alliances and arms, and learning provides a means of predicting the beliefs that states must have *in order to* act rationally.[10]

More broadly, these findings leave intact a number of realist assumptions. The learning theory laid out in Chapter 2 assumes that states are important actors in international politics, that they seek to maximize their national interests, and that security is foremost among their concerns (the model laid out in Chapter 8 challenges the first of these

[10] James D. Morrow, "Alliances and Asymmetry: An Alternative to the Capability Aggregation Model of Alliances," *American Journal of Political Science* 35 (November 1991): 904–933.

assumptions). These findings do argue that realism is fundamentally underspecified, however, in that it does not provide any theoretical space for explaining how decision makers come to understand how international politics work. Realist principles are often insufficient to predict behavior, so actions can be fully understood only if it is assumed that states act as if they have beliefs about the dynamics of world politics. The area of alliance choices illustrates the need to assume that states act as if they have beliefs: realist logic can argue in favor of balancing behavior (the balance of power) or neutrality (free riding), so it is necessary to know a state's beliefs about the relative desirabilities of these options to predict its actions. Given the inability of realism to explain behavior in such a crucial area of foreign policy choices as alliance decisions, these findings argue for the junking of realism as traditionally conceived in favor of a theory that recognizes the importance of beliefs.

Finally, the results offer support to the proposition that small powers do have real freedom of action in world politics and are not puppets following the whims of great powers. The quantitative tests indicate that small powers' alliance choices are strongly driven by their individual historical experiences, a factor that is not systematically related to great power preferences. Additionally, the case studies offer a number of examples of small powers taking actions that are inconsistent with great power preferences. Belgium's exit from its alliance with France in 1936, for example, was strongly inconsistent with French defense planning. Romania resisted courting from both Germany and Britain in 1939 as it strove to remain neutral. The strict Dutch neutrality in 1939 and 1940 inhibited Allied preparations for the coming German assault. After the war, Sweden ignored heavy-handed American efforts to persuade it to join NATO. Similarly, Finland stood up to the Soviet Union after World War II, maintaining a mostly neutral policy against the desires of the USSR. And, of all the cases in which individual learning did not make the correct prediction, only one country (Albania) appears to have had a foreign policy strongly determined by great power wishes.

The interesting thing about the learning approach to international relations is that it is not easily classifiable as belonging exclusively to a single theory. It is not classifiable as a theory presuming rational or nonrational human behavior, answering the prerational question, How do beliefs get formed? But the theorist has the option of implementing different sets of assumptions about how information is used to update beliefs: one can make optimistic assumptions about a decision maker's ability to use new information, or one can include findings from social psychology or organization theory to predict that a decision maker learns less (or more) frequently than he "ought to" and/or that he does not learn the "right" lesson. Additionally, learning can be analyzed on various levels. Predictions about how individuals or organizations ought to learn can be derived from decision-making literature, or these findings can be combined to produce predictions for learning at the level of the state.

The learning approach presents considerable promise for increasing our understanding of international relations. It can be used to combat the limitations attendant to the overly sparse theory of realism because it permits the assumption that different decision makers can think differently about the dynamics of international relations. Most important, learning models help us understand how leaders use their most valuable tools of decision—past experiences.

Select Bibliography

This bibliography contains the sources used to code the data.

Aalders, Gerald. "The Failure of the Scandinavian Defence Union, 1948–1949." *Scandinavian Journal of History* 15 (1990): 125–153.

Abadie-Maumert, F. A. "Le Pacifisme norvégien entre 1919 et 1940 et ses conséquences." *Guerres Mondiales et Conflits Contemporains* 40 (1990): 7–37.

Abrahamsen, Samuel. *Sweden's Foreign Policy.* Washington, D.C.: Public Affairs Press, 1957.

Albrecht-Carrié, René. *A Diplomatic History of Europe since the Congress of Vienna.* Rev. ed. New York: Harper & Row, 1973.

——. *Italy from Napoleon to Mussolini.* New York: Columbia University Press, 1950.

Alexander, Yonah, and Allan Nanes, eds. *The United States and Iran: A Documentary History.* Frederick, Md.: University Publications of America, 1980.

Alting von Geusau, F. A. M. "Between Lost Illusions and Apocalyptic Fears: Benelux Views on the European Neutrality." In *The European Neutrals in International Affairs,* ed. Hanspeter Neuhold and Hans Thalberg. Boulder, Colo.: Westview, 1984.

Andrén, Nils. *Power-Balance and Non-Alignment.* Stockholm: Almqvist and Wiksell, 1967.

Aster, Sidney. *1939: The Making of the Second World War.* London: André Deutsch, 1973.

Bahcheli, Tozun. *Greek-Turkish Relations since 1955.* Boulder, Colo.: Westview, 1990.

Beck, Robert J. "Munich's Lessons Reconsidered." *International Security* 14 (Fall 1989): 161–191.

Beigbeder, Yves. "La Neutralité suisse en question: Isolement ou solidarité internationale." *Revue Belge de Droit International* 24 (1991): 27–45.

Black, C. E., and E. C. Helmreich. *Twentieth Century Europe.* New York: Alfred A. Knopf, 1952.

Bond, Brian. *Britain, France, and Belgium, 1939–1940.* London: Brassey's, 1990.

——. *Liddell Hart: A Study of His Military Thought*. New Brunswick: Rutgers University Press, 1977.

Bonjour, Edgar. *Histoire de la neutralité suisse*. Trans. Balise Briad. Neuchatel: La Baconnière, 1946.

——. *Swiss Neutrality: Its History and Meaning*. Trans. Mary Hottinger. London: George Allen & Unwin, 1946.

Bonjour, Edgar, H. S. Offler, and G. R. Potter. *A Short History of Switzerland*. Oxford: Clarendon, 1952.

Bourgeois, Daniel. *Le Troisième Reich et la Suisse, 1933–1941*. Neuchatel: La Baconnière, 1974.

Brogan, Patrick. *Eastern Europe, 1939–1989*. London: Bloomsbury, 1990.

Bulletin Périodique de la Presse Belge. Paris, 1917–1920.

Burgess, Philip M. *Elite Images and Foreign Policy Outcomes: A Study of Norway*. Columbus: Ohio State University Press, 1968.

Burgwyn, H. James. *The Legend of the Mutilated Victory: Italy, the Great War, and the Paris Peace Conference, 1915–1919*. Westport, Conn.: Greenwood, 1993.

Butterworth, Robert Lyle. *Managing Interstate Conflict, 1945–74: Data with Synopses*. Pittsburgh: University Center for International Studies, University of Pittsburgh, 1976.

Carlgren, W. M. *Swedish Foreign Policy during the Second World War*. Trans. Arthur Spencer. New York: St. Martin's, 1977.

Carr, E. H. *International Relations since the Peace Treaties*. London: Macmillan, 1937.

Carr, Raymond. *Spain, 1808–1939*. Oxford: Clarendon, 1966.

Carrère d'Encausse, Hélène. *Big Brother*. Trans. George Holoch. New York: Holmes & Meier, 1987.

Challener, Richard D. *The French Theory of the Nation in Arms*. New York: Columbia University Press, 1955.

Chanady, A., and J. Jensen. "Germany, Rumania, and the British Guarantees of March–April 1939." *Australian Journal of Politics and History* 16 (August 1970): 201–217.

Charlton, Michael. *The Eagle and the Small Birds* (London: British Broadcasting Corporation, 1984).

Chubin, Shahram, and Sepehr Zabih. *The Foreign Relations of Iran*. Berkeley: University of California Press, 1974.

Clogg, Richard. *A Short History of Modern Greece*. Cambridge: Cambridge University Press, 1979.

Cole, Wayne S. *Norway and the United States, 1905–1955: Two Democracies in Peace and War*. Ames: Iowa State University Press, 1989.

Coolsaet, Rik. *Histoire de la politique étrangère belge*. French ed. Translated from the Dutch by Jan Van Kerkhoven and Claudine Leleux. Brussels: Vie Ouvrière, 1988.

Cottam, Richard W. *Iran and the United States*. Pittsburgh: University of Pittsburgh Press, 1988.

Craig, Gordon A. *From Bismarck to Adenauer: Aspects of German Statecraft*. Baltimore: Johns Hopkins University Press, 1958.

——. *Germany, 1866–1945*. New York: Oxford University Press, 1978.

Crollen, Luc. *Portugal, the U.S., and NATO*. Leuven, Belgium: Leuven University Press, 1973.

Derry, T. K. *A History of Modern Norway, 1814–1972*. Oxford: Clarendon, 1973.

d'Hoop, Jean-Marie. "Le Maréchal Foch et la négociation de l'Accord Militaire Franco-Belge de 1920." In *Mélanges Pierre Renouvin études d'histoire des relations internationales*, 191–198. Paris: Presses Universitaires de France, 1966.

Documents diplomatiques belges, 1920–1940: La Politique de sécurité extérieure. 5 vols. Brussels: Académie Royale de Belgique, 1964–66.

Documents Diplomatiques Français, 1932–1939. 2e série, tome 3. Paris: Ministère des Affaires Étrangères, 1966.

Documents on British Foreign Policy, 1919–1939. 1st ser. London: Her Majesty's Stationery Office, 1954.

Doyle, Michael W. "Liberalism and World Politics." *American Political Science Review* 80 (December 1986): 1151–1169.

Dutoit, Bernard. *La Neutralité suisse à l'heure européene*. Paris: Librairie Générale de Droit et de Jurisprudence, 1962.

Eden, Anthony. *Full Circle: The Memoirs of Anthony Eden*. Boston: Houghton Mifflin, 1960.

Eisen, Janet. *Anglo-Dutch Relations and European Unity, 1940–1948*. Hull: University of Hull Publications, 1980.

Ekman, Stig. "La Politique de défense de la Suède durant la Seconde Guerre Mondiale." *Revue d'Histoire de la Deuxième Guerre Mondiale* 32 (January 1982).

Epstein, Leon D. *Britain—Uneasy Ally*. Chicago: University of Chicago Press, 1954.

Eyck, F. Gunther. *The Benelux Countries: An Historical Survey*. Princeton: D. Van Nostrand, 1959.

Farouk-Sluglett, Marion, and Peter Sluglett. *Iraq since 1958: From Revolution to Dictatorship*. London: KPI, 1987.

Farrell, R. Barry. *Jugoslavia and the Soviet Union, 1948–1956*. Hamden, Conn.: Shoe String Press, 1956.

Feuille Fédérale Suisse. Geneva, 1919, 1938.

Fischer-Galati, Stephen. *Twentieth Century Rumania*. 2d ed. New York: Columbia University Press, 1991.

Foreign Relations of the United States. Washington, D.C.: Government Printing Office, 1947–1955.

Fox, Annette Baker. *The Power of Small States: Diplomacy in World War II*. Chicago: University of Chicago Press, 1959.

Freymond, Jacques. "The Foreign Policy of Switzerland." In *Foreign Policies in a World of Change*, ed. Joseph E. Black and Kenneth W. Thompson. New York: Harper & Row, 1963.

———. *Pas d'Armée, pas de guerre?* Lausanne: Le Matin, 1989.

Fuchser, Larry William. *Neville Chamberlain and Appeasement*. New York: W. W. Norton, 1982.

Fuller, Graham E. *The "Center of the Universe": The Geopolitics of Iran*. Boulder, Coln.: Westview, 1991.

Gaddis, John Lewis. "The Tragedy of Cold War History." *Diplomatic History* 17 (Winter 1993): 1–16.

——. *The United States and the Origins of the Cold War, 1941–1947*. New York: Columbia University Press, 1972.

Gilbert, Martin, and Richard Gott. *The Appeasers*. Cambridge, Mass.: Riverside Press, 1963.

Gooch, Anthony. "The Foreign Relations and Foreign Policy of Spain," pt. 3: "Spain, the United States, and NATO." *Contemporary Review* 260 (May 1992): 239–243.

Goode, James F. *The United States and Iran, 1946–51: The Diplomacy of Neglect*. New York: St. Martin's, 1989.

Gurtov, Melvin. *China and Southeast Asia—The Politics of Survival*, Lexington, Mass.: Heath Lexington Books, 1971.

Haftendorn, Helga. "The NATO Crisis of 1966–67: Lessons from the Past and Perspectives for the Future." Working paper. Berlin: Center on Transatlantic Foreign and Security Studies, Free University of Berlin, 1994.

Håstad, Elis. "Sweden attitude toward the United Nations." In *Sweden and the United Nations*. New York: Manhattan Publishing, 1956.

Helmreich, Jonathan E. "Convention politique ou accord militaire? La Négociation de l'Accord Franco-Belge de 1920." *Guerres Mondiales et Conflits Contemporains*, no. 159 (1990): 21–36.

——. "The Negotiation of the Franco-Belgian Military Accord of 1920." *French Historical Studies* 3 (Spring 1964): 360–378.

Hennessy, Peter. *Never Again: Britain, 1945–51*. London: Jonathan Cape, 1992.

Hetland, Tom. "The Soviet View of the Nordic Countries and NATO, 1948–1952." *Scandinavian Journal of History* 11 (1986): 149–181.

Hochman, Jiri. *The Soviet Union and the Failure of Collective Security*. Ithaca: Cornell University Press, 1984.

Holtsmark, Sven G. "Atlantic Orientation or Regional Groupings: Elements of Norwegian Foreign Policy Discussions during the Second World War." *Scandinavian Journal of History* 14 (1989): 311–324.

——. *Between "Russophobia" and "Bridge-Building": The Norwegian Government and the Soviet Union*. Oslo: Institutt for forsvarsstudier, 1988.

Hopper, Bruce. "Sweden: A Case Study in Neutrality." *Foreign Affairs* 23 (1945): 435–449.

Howard, Michael. *The Continental Commitment: The Dilemma of British Defence Policy in the Era of the Two World Wars*. Rev. ed. London: Ashfield Press, 1989.

Hurewitz, J. C. *Diplomacy in the Near and Middle East*. 2 vols. Princeton: D. Van Nostrand, 1956.

Hymans, Paul. *Mémoires*. 2 vols. Brussels: Institut de Sociologie Solvay, 1958.

L'Independance Belge. Brussels, 1918–1920, 1947–1948.

Jaquet, L. G. M. "The Role of a Small State within Alliance Systems." In *Small States in International Relations*, ed. August Schon and Arne Olav Brundtland. New York: John Wiley & Sons, 1971.

Jelavich, Barbara. *History of the Balkans*. 2 vols. London: Cambridge University Press, 1983.

Jost, Hans-Ulrich. "Menace et Repliement, 1914–1945." In *Nouvelle histoire de la Suisse et des Suisses*. Vol. 3. Lausanne: Payot, 1983.

Kieft, David Owen. *Belgium's Return to Neutrality*. Oxford: Clarendon, 1972.

Kilic, Altemur. *Turkey and the World*. Washington, D.C.: Public Affairs Press, 1959.

Kimche, Jon. *Spying for Peace*. London: Weinfeld and Nicolson, 1961.

Kiraly, Bela. "The Aborted Soviet Military Plans against Tito's Yugoslavia." In *War and Society in East Central Europe*. Vol. 10, *At the Brink of War and Peace: The Tito-Stalin Split in a Historic Perspective*, ed. Wayne S. Vucinich, 273–288. New York: Social Science Monographs, Brooklyn College Press, 1982.

Kissinger, Henry. *Diplomacy*. New York: Simon and Schuster, 1994.

Knox, MacGregor. "Conquest, Foreign and Domestic, in Fascist Italy and Nazi Germany." *Journal of Modern History* 56 (March 1984): 1–57.

Kossmann, E. H. *The Low Countries, 1780–1940*. Oxford: Clarendon, 1978.

Lenczowski, George. *The Middle East in World Affairs*. 4th ed. Ithaca: Cornell University Press, 1980.

Le Roy, André Roussel. *L'Abrogation de la neutralité de la Belgique*. Paris: Presses Universitaires de France, 1923.

Leurdijk, J. H., ed. *The Foreign Policy of the Netherlands*. Alphen aan den Rijn: Sijthoff & Noordhoff, 1978.

La Libre Belgique. Brussels, 1918–1920, 1947–1948.

Lingelbach, William E. "Belgian Neutrality: Its Origin and Interpretation." *American Historical Review* 39 (October 1933): 48–72.

Lönnroth, Erik. "Sweden's Ambiguous Neutrality." *Scandinavian Journal of History* 2 (1977): 89–105.

Loock, Hans-Dietrich. "*Weserübung*—A Step towards the Greater Germanic Reich." *Scandinavian Journal of History* 12 1977: 67–88.

Lundestad, Geir. *America, Scandinavia, and the Cold War, 1945–1949*. New York: Columbia University Press, 1980.

——. "The Evolution of Norwegian Security Policy: Alliance with the West and Reassurance in the East." *Scandinavian Journal of History* 17 (1992): 227–256.

Lungu, Dov B. *Romania and the Great Powers, 1933–1940*. Durham: Duke University Press, 1989.

Lytle, Mark Hamilton. *The Origins of the Iranian-American Alliance, 1941–1953*. New York: Holmes & Meier, 1987.

Macartney, Maxwell H. H., and Paul Cremona. *Italy's Foreign and Colonial Policy, 1914–1937*. London: Oxford University Press, 1938.

Marks, Sally. *The Illusion of Peace: International Relations in Europe, 1918–1933*. New York: St. Martin's, 1976.

——. *Innocent Abroad*. Chapel Hill: University of North Carolina Press, 1981.

Marlowe, John. *A History of Modern Egypt and Anglo-Egyptian Relations, 1800–1956*. Hamden: Archon, 1965.

Marr, Phebe. *The Modern History of Iraq*. Boulder, Colo.: Westview, 1985.

Martin, William. *Switzerland from Roman Times to the Present*. Trans. Jocasta Innes. New York: Praeger, 1971.

Massigli, René. *Une Comedie des erreurs, 1943–1956*. Paris: Plon, 1978.

Mearsheimer, John J. *Liddell Hart and the Weight of History*. Ithaca: Cornell University Press, 1988.

Melanson, Richard A. *Writing History and Making Policy*. Lanham, Md.: University Press of America, 1983.

Middlemas, Keith. *The Strategy of Appeasement*. Chicago: Quadrangle Books, 1972.

Miller, Jane Kathryn. *Belgian Foreign Policy between Two Wars, 1919–1940*. New York: Bookman Associates, 1951.

Ministère des Affaires Étrangères. Service des Archives. Brussels, Belgium.

Modelski, George, ed. *SEATO: Six Studies*. Melbourne: F. W. Cheshire, 1962.

Muggeridge, Malcolm, ed. *Ciano's Diplomatic Papers*. London: Odhams Press, 1948.

Mujal-Leon, Eusebio. "Spain: Generational Perspectives on Foreign Policy." In *The Successor Generation: International Perspectives of Postwar Europeans*, ed. Stephen F. Szabo. London: Butterworths, 1983.

Murphy, J. Carter. *Spain and the United States*. New York: Praeger, 1984.

Murray, Williamson, MacGregor Knox, and Alvin Bernstein, eds. *The Making of Strategy: Rulers, States, and War*. Cambridge: Cambridge University Press, 1994.

Néré, Jacques. *The Foreign Policy of France from 1914 to 1945*. London: Routledge & Kegan Paul, 1975.

Newman, Simon. *March 1939: The British Guarantee to Poland*. Oxford: Clarendon, 1976.

Nicolson, Harold. *The Congress of Vienna*. London: Constable, 1946.

Nissen, Henrik S., ed. *Scandinavia during the Second World War*. Trans. Thomas Munch-Petersen. Minneapolis: University of Minnesota Press, 1983.

Nuechterlein, Donald E. *Thailand and the Struggle for Southeast Asia*. Ithaca: Cornell University Press, 1965.

"L'Organisation de l'Occident." *Chronique de Politique Étrangère* 1 (January 1948).

"L'Organisation politique de l'Europe Occidentale." *Chronique de Politique Étrangère* 1 (May 1948).

Örvik, Nils. *The Decline of Neutrality, 1914–1941*. Oslo: Johan Grundt Tanum Forlag, 1953.

——. *Trends in Norwegian Foreign Policy*. Oslo: Norwegian Institute of International Affairs, 1962.

Papacosma, S. Victor, and Mark R. Rubin, eds. *Europe's Neutral and Nonaligned States*. Wilmington, Del.: Scholarly Resources, 1989.

Petersen, Nikolaj. "Danish and Norwegian Alliance Policies, 1948–49: A Comparative Analysis." *Cooperation and Conflict* 14 (1979): 193–210.

Le Peuple. Brussels, 1918–1920, 1947–1948.

Pharo, Helge Ø. "Bridgebuilding and Reconstruction: Norway Faces the Marshall Plan." *Scandinavian Journal of History* 1 (1976): 125–153.

Pirenne, Henri. *Histoire de Belgique des origines à nos jours*. Vol. 4. Brussels: La Renaissance du Livre, 1952.

Pollack, Benny. *The Paradox of Spanish Foreign Policy: Spain's International Relations from Franco to Democracy*. London: Pinter Publishers, 1987.

Porch, Douglas. "Arms and Alliances: French Grand Strategy and Policy in 1914 and 1940." In *Grand Strategy in War and Peace*, ed. Paul Kennedy, 125–143. New Haven: Yale University Press, 1991.

Proctor, Raymond L. *Agony of a Neutral: Spanish-German Wartime Relations and the "Blue Division."* Moscow, Idaho: Idaho Research Foundation, 1974.

Puzzo, Dante A. *Spain and the Great Powers, 1936–1941.* New York: Columbia University Press, 1962.

Ralston, Jerry Wilson. *The Defense of Small States in the Nuclear Age: The Case of Sweden and Switzerland.* Neuchatel: La Baconnière, 1969.

Ramazani, R. K. *The United States and Iran.* New York: Praeger, 1982.

"Rapport de Conseil Fédéral à l'Assemblée fédérale sur les relations de la Suisse avec les Nations Unies." Geneva, 16 June 1969.

Reynaud, Paul. *In the Thick of the Fight.* Trans. James D. Lambert. London: Cassell, 1955.

Reynolds, P. A. *British Foreign Policy in the Inter-War Years.* London: Longmans, Green, 1954.

Rings, Werner. *La Suisse et la guerre, 1933–1945.* Trans. Charles Oser. Lausanne: Éditions Ex Libris, 1975.

Riste, Olav. *The Neutral Ally: Norway's Relations with Belligerent Powers in the First World War.* Oslo: Universitetsforlaget, 1965.

——. "Was 1949 a Turning Point? Norway and the Western Powers, 1947–1950." In *Western Security: The Formative Years,* ed. Riste, 128–149. New York: Columbia University Press, 1985.

Ritter, Gerhard. *The Schlieffen Plan: Critique of a Myth.* Trans. Andrew Wilson and Eva Wilson. Westport, Conn.: Greenwood, 1979.

Robinson, Richard. *Contemporary Portugal.* London: George Allen & Unwin, 1979.

Ross, John F. L. *Neutrality and International Sanctions: Sweden, Switzerland, and Collective Security.* New York: Praeger, 1989.

Rothschild, Joseph. *East Central Europe between the Two World Wars.* Seattle: University of Washington Press, 1974.

——. *Return to Diversity: A Political History of East Central Europe since World War II.* New York: Oxford University Press, 1989.

Rothstein, Robert L. *Alliances and Small Powers.* New York: Columbia University Press, 1968.

Roubatis, Yiannis P. *Tangled Webs: The U.S. in Greece, 1947–1967.* New York: Pella Publishing, 1987.

Royama, Masamichi. *Foreign Policy of Japan, 1914–1939.* Westport, Conn.: Greenwood, 1941.

Rubin, Barry. *Paved with Good Intentions.* Oxford: Oxford University Press, 1980.

Sachar, Howard M. *Europe Leaves the Middle East, 1936–1954.* London: Allen Lane, 1974.

Salmon, Patrick. "British Plans for Economic Warfare against Germany, 1937–1939: The Problem of Swedish Iron Ore." *Journal of Contemporary History* 16 (January 1981): 53–71.

——. "Churchill, the Admiralty, and the Narvik Traffic, September–November 1939." *Scandinavian Journal of History* 4 (1979): 305–326.

Schwarz, Urs. *The Eye of the Hurricane: Switzerland in World War II.* Boulder, Colo.: Westview, 1980.

Scott, William Evans. *Alliance against Hitler: The Origins of the Franco-Soviet Pact.* Durham: Duke University Press, 1962.

Selby, Sir Walford. *Diplomatic Twilight, 1930–1940.* London: John Murray, 1953.

Seton-Watson, Hugh. *Eastern Europe between the Wars, 1918–1941*. Hamden, Conn.: Archon Books, 1962.

Shneidman, J. Lee. *Spain and Franco, 1949–59*. New York: Facts on File, 1973.

Skodvin, Magne. "Norwegian Neutrality and the Question of Credibility." *Scandinavian Journal of History* 2 (1977): 123–145.

Smets, Paul-F., ed. *La Pensée européene et atlantique de Paul-Henri Spaak (1942–1972)*. 2 vols. Brussels: J. Goemere, 1980.

Smith, Steven. *Foreign Policy Adaptation*. New York: Nichols Publishing, 1981.

Le Soir. Brussels, 1947–1948.

Solsten, Eric, and Sandra W. Meditz, eds. *Finland: A Country Study*. Washington, D.C.: Government Printing Office, 1990.

Spaak, Paul-Henri. *Combats Inachevés*. 2 vols. Brussels: Fayard, 1969.

——. *The Continuing Battle: Memoirs of a European, 1936–1966*. Boston: Little, Brown, 1971.

Stengers, Jean. "L'Accord Militaire Franco-Belge de 1920 et le Luxembourg." In *Les Relations franco-luxembourgeoises de Louis XIV à Robert Schuman*, ed. Raymond Poidevin and Gilbert Trausch. Metz: Centre de Recherches Relations Internationales de l'Université de Metz, 1978.

——. "Paul-Henri Spaak et le Traité de Bruxelles de 1948." In *Histoire des débuts de la construction européenne (Mars 1948–Mai 1950)*, ed. Raymond Poidevin, 119–142. Brussels: Bruyant, 1984.

Sulzberger, C. L. *The Last of the Giants*. New York: Macmillan, 1970.

Tingsten, Herbert. *The Debate on the Foreign Policy of Sweden, 1918–1939*. Trans. Joan Bulman. London: Oxford University Press, 1949.

Toynbee, Arnold J. *Survey of International Affairs, 1920–1923*. London: Oxford University Press, 1928.

——. *Survey of International Affairs, 1924*. London: Oxford University Press, 1926.

——. *Survey of International Affairs, 1926*. London: Oxford University Press, 1928.

——. *Survey of International Affairs, 1928*. London: Oxford University Press, 1929.

——. *Survey of International Affairs, 1931*. London: Oxford University Press, 1932.

——. *Survey of International Affairs, 1933*. London: Oxford University Press, 1934.

——. *Survey of International Affairs, 1936*. London: Oxford University Press, 1937.

Toynbee, Arnold, and Frank T. Ashton-Gwatkin, eds. *Survey of International Affairs, 1939–1946: The World in March 1939*. London: Oxford University Press, 1952.

Toynbee, Arnold, and Veronica M. Toynbee, eds. *Survey of International Affairs 1939–1946: The War and the Neutrals*. London: Oxford University Press, 1956.

——. *Survey of International Affairs: The Eve of War, 1939*. London: Oxford University Press, 1958.

Tuchman, Barbara W. *The Guns of August*. New York: Bantam, 1962.

Udgaard, Nils Morten. *Great Power Politics and Norwegian Foreign Policy*. Oslo: Universitetsforlaget, 1973.

Værnø, Grethe. "The United States, Norway, and the Atlantic Pact, 1948–1949." *Scandinavian Studies* 50 (Spring 1978): 150–176.

Váli, Ferenc A. *Bridge across the Bosporus.* Baltimore: Johns Hopkins University Press, 1971.

Van Campen, S. I: P. *The Quest for Security.* The Hague: Martinus Nijhoff, 1958.

Vandenbosch, Amry. *Dutch Foreign Policy since 1815.* The Hague: Martinus Nijhoff, 1959.

Van Langenhove, Fernand. *La Securité de la Belgique: Contribution à l'histoire de la période, 1940–1950.* Brussels: Éditions de l'Universitaire de Bruxelles, 1971.

Viault, Birdsall S. "La Belgique et la Hollande à la recherche d'une paix négociée (1939–1940)." *Revue d'Histoire de la Deuxième Guerre Mondiale* 32 (April 1982): 37–46.

Viñas, Angel. "Spain and NATO: Internal Debate and External Challenges." In *NATO's Southern Allies: Internal and External Challenges,* ed. John Chipman. London: Routledge, 1988.

Wandycz, Piotr S. *France and Her Eastern Allies, 1919–1925.* Minneapolis: University of Minnesota Press, 1962.

Weber, Frank G. *The Evasive Neutral.* Columbia: University of Missouri Press, 1979.

Weinberg, Gerhard L. *The Foreign Policy of Hitler's Germany: Diplomatic Revolution in Europe, 1933–36.* Chicago: University of Chicago Press, 1970.

Wels, Cornelius Boudewijn. *Aloofness and Neutrality.* Utrecht, Netherlands: HES Publishers, 1982.

Whitaker, Arthur P. *Spain and Defense of the West.* New York: Harper & Brothers, 1961.

Wolfers, Arnold. *Britain and France between Two Wars.* New York: Harcourt, Brace, 1940.

Wood, F. L. W., and Roderic Alley. "New Zealand Foreign Policy." In *Australia, New Zealand, and the Pacific Islands since the First World War,* ed. William S. Livingston and Wm. Roger Louis, 62–81. Austin: University of Texas Press, 1979.

Woodhouse, C. M. *Modern Greece: A Short History.* London: Faber and Faber, 1968.

Wullus-Rudiger, J. A. *La Défense de la Belgique en 1940.* Villeneuve sur Lot: Alfred Bador, 1940.

Zhivkova, Ludmila. *Anglo-Turkish Relations, 1933–1939.* London: Secker & Warburg, 1976.

Index

Numbers followed by *t* indicate pages with tables.

CORNELL STUDIES IN SECURITY AFFAIRS

edited by Robert J. Art, Robert Jervis,
and Stephen M. Walt

The Warsaw Pact: Alliance in Transition? edited by David Holloway and
   Jane M. O. Sharp
The Illogic of American Nuclear Strategy, by Robert Jervis
The Meaning of the Nuclear Revolution, by Robert Jervis
The Vulnerability of Empire, by Charles A. Kupchan
Nuclear Crisis Management: A Dangerous Illusion, by Richard Ned Lebow
Cooperation under Fire: Anglo-German Restraint during World War II,
   by Jeffrey W. Legro
The Search for Security in Space, edited by Kenneth N. Luongo and
   W. Thomas Wander
The Nuclear Future, by Michael Mandelbaum
Conventional Deterrence, by John J. Mearsheimer
Liddell Hart and the Weight of History, by John J. Mearsheimer
Reputation and International Politics, by Jonathan Mercer
The Sacred Cause: Civil-Military Conflict over Soviet National Security, 1917–1992,
   by Thomas M. Nichols
Bombing to Win: Air Power and Coercion in War, by Robert A. Pape
Inadvertent Escalation: Conventional War and Nuclear Risks, by Barry R. Posen
*The Sources of Military Doctrine: France, Britain, and Germany between the World
   Wars,* by Barry R. Posen
Dilemmas of Appeasement: British Deterrence and Defense, 1934–1937,
   by Gaines Post, Jr.
Crucible of Beliefs: Learning, Alliances, and World Wars, by Dan Reiter
Eisenhower and the Missile Gap, by Peter J. Roman
The Domestic Bases of Grand Strategy, edited by Richard Rosecrance and
   Arthur A. Stein
Winning the Next War: Innovation and the Modern Military,
   by Stephen Peter Rosen
Israel and Conventional Deterrence: Border Warfare from 1953 to 1970,
   by Jonathan Shimshoni
*Fighting to a Finish: The Politics of War Termination in the United States and Japan,
   1945,* by Leon V. Sigal
The Ideology of the Offensive: Military Decision Making and the Disasters of 1914,
   by Jack Snyder
Myths of Empire: Domestic Politics and International Ambition, by Jack Snyder
The Militarization of Space: U.S. Policy, 1945–1984, by Paul B. Stares
The Nixon Administration and the Making of U.S. Nuclear Strategy,
   by Terry Terriff
Making the Alliance Work: The United States and Western Europe,
   by Gregory F. Treverton
The Origins of Alliances, by Stephen M. Walt
Revolution and War, by Stephen M. Walt
The Ultimate Enemy: British Intelligence and Nazi Germany, 1933–1939,
   by Wesley K. Wark
The Tet Offensive: Intelligence Failure in War, by James J. Wirtz
The Elusive Balance: Power and Perceptions during the Cold War,
   by William Curti Wohlforth
Deterrence and Strategic Culture: Chinese-American Confrontations, 1949–1958,
   by Shu Guang Zhang